BOATS IN A STORM

BOATS IN A STORM

Law, Migration, and Decolonization in South and Southeast Asia, 1942–1962

KALYANI RAMNATH

STANFORD UNIVERSITY PRESS

STANFORD, CALIFORNIA

Stanford University Press
Stanford, California

Printed in the United States of America on acid-free, archival-quality paper

ISBN 9781503632981 (cloth)
ISBN 9781503636095 (paper)
ISBN 9781503636101 (ebook)

Library of Congress Control Number 2022051126

CIP data available upon request.

Cover design and collage: Lindy Kasler
Cover art: Shutterstock and historical documents
Typeset by Elliott Beard in Adobe Caslon Pro 10.5/15

CONTENTS

ILLUSTRATIONS

PREFACE

Many families in South India today narrate stories to willing listeners about traveling to countries elsewhere in South or Southeast Asia, reminiscing about attending university in Sri Lanka or going on a shopping expedition to Singapore. They proudly show off their artifacts made of "Burma teak" or cook meals that feature spices or condiments used in Southeast Asian cooking. The names of Penang, Singapore, Colombo, and Rangoon appear on names of streets, houses, and markets—Burma Bazaar, Singapore House, Malaya Cottage, Colombo Tailors. In South India, where I spent my childhood and undergraduate years, remnants of travel and migration between South and Southeast Asia were everywhere I looked.

Many families will also tell listeners that at some point the connections formed by these travels began to unravel, although they are often unclear on when and why. They might, for example, remember the dark days in 1962 when a military coup forced families to leave Burma. But fewer are likely to remember how they struggled to retain the rhythms and patterns of migrant life following the wartime occupation of Southeast Asia in 1942, when hundreds of thousands of them fled and had to negotiate their return with the new governments that emerged in the aftermath of the Second World War. In this book, I narrate how these negotiations with new states took place through law. In demonstrating how states and people negotiated legal claims and counterclaims with each other, *Boats in a Storm* provides an account of the postwar period in South and Southeast Asia in which decolonization is not strictly political, partitions are not only territorial, and postwar reconstruction is not solely economic. Personal and familial histories narrated before the law disrupt and reframe the understanding of these events.

The chapters that follow also reflect how I traveled between South and Southeast Asia, from Calicut and Chennai to Colombo, Singapore, and Yangon, and from New Delhi to London, following the intertwined itineraries of law that connected these places in an age of disconnection, as the political processes of decolonization unfolded in Asia and beyond. In doing so, I bring together my professional training as a lawyer and as a historian to bear on my interest in writing histories of (dis)connected places, peoples, and things, and of the legacies, afterlives, and remnants of legal struggles.

A note on usages, references, and translations: place-names in the text follow official name changes (for example, "Ceylon" before 1972, "Sri Lanka" thereafter; "the Straits Settlements" before 1946, "Malaya" for British Malaya and the Federation of Malaya between 1946 and up until 1957, and "Malaysia" thereafter). "India" before 1947 is British India; after 1947, it refers to the government of independent India. Any references to countries are to their governments, unless specifically noted that reference is being made to the geographical unit. "Postwar" is a reference to the time period following the official end of World War II in 1945. I use "Bay of Bengal" and "eastern Indian Ocean" synonymously. "South Asia" and "Southeast Asia" are designations invented during and used after the war to shape academic fields of inquiry and are therefore not inappropriate for the themes explored in this book. However, this is not a comprehensive or comparative study of every country in South and Southeast Asia. Instead, my use of the contemporary regional labels together is meant to indicate that a history of post-1945 South Asia is incomplete without a reference to Southeast Asian history, and vice versa. For readability, in transliterating non-English words I have avoided the use of diacritics. Unless otherwise noted, translations from Tamil and Malayalam are my own.

Finally, a word about the title of the book. The Tamil novelist P. Singaram wrote two novels about the war and its aftermath in South and Southeast Asia from the perspective of migrants—*Puyalile Oru Doni* (Boat in a storm), which inspired the title of this book, and *Kadalakku Appal* (Beyond the seas). Singaram's novels about longing and belonging across the Bay of Bengal, connecting Madras, Medan, and Malaya, capture in fiction what *Boats in a Storm* traces in the archives of law. Although the protagonists in these chapters followed routes different from those of Singaram's characters, the chapters that follow are equally about migrant worlds in tumult in South and Southeast Asia, as the effects of the war and decolonization rippled through it. People had once traveled across and around the Bay of Bengal as imperial citizens, but new legal regimes created swells and storms that migrants' worlds could scarcely withstand. Beginning in 1942, this book charts the progress of these storms and the detritus left in their wake. I am grateful for the opportunity to rechart and retell these histories.

ACKNOWLEDGMENTS

I thank the archivists, record room workers, and librarians in Chennai, Colombo, Yangon, Singapore, Princeton, Cambridge, and London who made this book possible; it would not exist without their labor. I thank the registrar-general of the Madras High Court, T. Kalaiyarasan, for permission to work with the records at Madras High Court that form the heart of this book, and Justice Prabha Sridevan, Justice Chandru, N. L. Rajah and N. G. R. Prasad for engaging conversations about the court's institutional history. At the Department of History at Princeton University, Gyan Prakash, Hendrik Hartog, Bhavani Raman, and Mitra Sharafi (as external examiner) offered exceptional mentorship. The best elements of this book are owed to them. I also thank Margot Canaday, Beth Lew-Williams, Jeremy Adelman, Elisabeth Davis, Kim Scheppele, and Max Weiss for expertly navigating questions of law, labor, and empire as part of graduate school coursework. At Harvard, Emma Rothschild and Sunil Amrith gave me the unparalleled gifts of time and resources to think about the key ideas in the book, to rework the arguments, and to put the book back together. The support and enthusiasm for this book from colleagues at the Department of History, the School of Law, and the Willson Center at the University of Georgia carried me through the important final phase of writing and editing. Many longtime mentors have stuck with me—and this book—over its many iterations, including Rohit De, Renisa Mawani, Durba Mitra, Mitra Sharafi, Kalyanakrishnan Sivaramakrishnan, Julie Stephens, and Nurfadzilah Yahaya. Manu Goswami and Mrinalini Sinha encouraged my thinking on political imaginaries in the early phases of research; Lauren Benton, Bianca Premo, Yanna Yannakakis, Debjani Bhattacharya, Sanne Ravensbergen, and Laurie Wood helped sharpen my ideas about law and geography. Yael Berda, Sarah Carson, Katlyn Carter, Rohit De, Joppan George, Rotem Geva, Nabaparna Ghosh, Maeve Glass, Sadaf

Jaffer, Manav Kapur, Emily Kern, Radha Kumar, Dana Lee, Jane Manners, Nikhil Menon, Maribel Morey, Emily Prifogle, Amna Qayyum, Deborah Schlein, Katharina Schmidt, Devika Shankar, Dan Sheffield, Lindsey Stephenson, Tara Suri, Paula Vedoveli, and Niharika Yadav were exemplary colleagues at Princeton. At the Center for History and Economics, Aditya Balasubramanian, Fahad Bishara, Shane Bobrycki, Catherine Evans, Franziska Exeler, Diana Kim, Ian Kumekawa, Mike O'Sullivan, Padraic Scanlan, Melissa Teixeira, and Fei-Hsien Wang helped reorient a dissertation into a book. A seminar series on Barriers and Borders cohosted with Franziska Exeler, Ira Katznelson, and Gareth Steedman Jones in 2021–'22 helped place this book alongside kindred scholarly projects. Sana Aiyar, Ren Chao, Emma Meyer, and Gitanjali Surendran discussed the place of Burma in South Asian history over the course of a semester-long works-in-progress group. Bérénice Guyot-Réchard and Elisabeth Leake built a vibrant collaborative academic space with New International Histories of South Asia during the years of a global pandemic when in-person academic gatherings were impossible. Swati Chawla, Jessica Namakkal, and Lydia Walker were key to rethinking the ideas of Indian citizenship. Sahana Ghosh, Ketaki Pant, and Nethra Samarawickrema offered valuable insights into borders, diasporas, and trade as they worked on their own important projects. John Rogers, Tamara Fernando, Mythri Jegathesan, Sujit Sivasundaram, Sharika Thiranagama, Mahendran Thiruvaragan, Ramla Wahab-Salman, and Nira Wickramasinghe welcomed me into the community of scholars working on Sri Lanka. Isabel Alonso, Andrew Amstutz, Pamela Ballinger, Sanjib Baruah, Daniel Bass, Binyamin Blum, Neilesh Bose, Divya Cherian, Lynette Chua, Michelle Foster, Mark Frost, Durba Ghosh, Swargajyoti Gohain, Paul Halliday, Usha Iyer, Anil Kalhan, Tarunabh Khaitan, Elizabeth Lhost, Noora Lori, David Ludden, Karuna Mantena, Alastair McClure, Jaclyn Neo, Vasuki Nesiah, Ninad Pandit, Pooja Parmar, Lalita du Perron, Jothie Rajah, Surabhi Ranganathan, Mahesh Rangarajan, Gautham Rao, Gabriel Rocha, Nadeera Rupesinghe, Jayita Sarkar, Andi Schubert, Mira Siegelberg, Christoph Sperfeldt, Mytheli Sreenivas, Ravindran Sriramachandran, Carolien Stolte, A. R. Venkatachalapathy, Suchitra Vijayan, Natasha Wheatley, and Anand Yang have, in their capacities as interlocutors, panel organizers, discussants, editors, and reviewers, greatly clarified the ideas in this book. Miriam Alphonsus, Brigitte MacFarland, Anant Sangal, and Praggya Surana offered crucial research assistance. I am grateful to the American Historical Association, the Princeton Institute for International and Regional Studies, the Center for History and Economics, the Hart Fellowship for Tamil Studies at the University of California, Berkeley, and the American Institute for Lankan Studies, which funded parts of the research. Reul Schiller and the Fellows of the Wallace Johnson First Book Program (2019–20) and Mitra Sharafi and the Fellows of the Hurst Institute for Legal History (2017–18), both organized by the American Society for Legal History (ASLH), had a transformative effect on the book manuscript. The annual conferences for the ASLH, the Law and Society Association, and the Association for Asian Studies, and the Annual Conference on South Asia at University of Wisconsin-Madison, functioned as venues to receive thoughtful, constructive, and rigorous feedback. Kristy Novak, Jaclyn Wasneski, Rachel Golden, Jayne Bialkowski at Princeton, Jennifer Nickerson, Emily Gauthier, and Kimberly O'Hagan at Harvard, Inga Huld Markan, Amy Price and Mary-Rose Cheadle at Cambridge, and Laurie Kane and Cilla Cartwright at University of Georgia eased the way for administrative engagements within and beyond those universities. Finally, Thomas Blom Hansen, Sunna Juhn, Kapani Kirkland, Marcela Maxfield, Tiffany Mok, Cat Pavel, Sarah Rodriguez, and Dylan Kyung-lim White at Stanford University Press have been steadfast supporters of this book. I am grateful for the careful reading of the manuscript by the two anonymous reviewers for the book, Elizabeth Magnus, and Rachel Lyon and for Lindy Kasler's cover design, which so accurately captures the soul of the book. I could not have asked for a more wonderful team to work with.

As a graduate student and postdoctoral fellow, I was supported by the childcare centers at Princeton and Harvard, and during research trips in India, Sri Lanka, and Myanmar, by loving and dedicated childcare workers. Their work made my work possible. Sudha Ramalingam, Akila Ramalingam, Poongkhulali Balasubramanian, Thriyambak J. Kannan, and Sampoorna made Chennai a home away from home. Meenakshi, Sachin and Ishani make my days in my other adopted home in the United States meaningful, and a large circle of family and friends in Trivandrum, Kochi, Bengaluru, Princeton, Cambridge, and London, particularly my in-laws Sreekrishnan and Jyothi, who have shown unconditional love and pride in seeing me pursue an academic career make it all worthwhile. I am beyond grateful to my partner Anish and daughters Avani and Katyayani, who remind me of the pleasures of everyday life and have weathered every storm with patience and good humor. My parents Ambili and Ramnath nurtured a love for learning and travel and modeled how to live gently, humbly, and fully. My grandmother Anandam told me the very first stories about family members who had fled Burma during the war and sang me a ditty about escaping from Japanese bombs that sparked many of the ideas in this book. This book is for all of them.

TIMELINE

1935 Burma separated from India

1942 Japanese forces occupy Burma, Malaya, and Singapore

1945 World War II ends

1946 Malayan Union is proposed

1947 India and Pakistan win independence from Britain; the Partition of India

1948 Burma becomes an independent Union of States

Ceylon becomes a Dominion within the British Commonwealth

Ceylon Citizenship Act comes into force

Union Citizenship Act comes into force in Burma

The Malayan "Emergency" is declared

1950 Indian Constitution comes into force

1954 Nehru-Kotelawala Pact is signed

1955 Indian Citizenship Act comes into force

1957 Malaysia secures independence

1962 Military coup led by General Ne Win in Burma

1964 Sirimavo-Shastri Pact is signed

1965 Singapore separates from Malaysia

BOATS IN A STORM

BOATS IN A STORM

BOATS IN A STORM is a history of citizenship and decolonization set in South and Southeast Asia, narrated through seemingly banal encounters with law. When Japanese forces occupied Burma and Malaya in 1942 during the Second World War, hundreds of thousands of people—many of whom had migrated from India—had to flee their adopted homes and places of work. After the war, as they attempted to return, they became entangled in legal disputes. In the years following the end of imperial rule, they could not have known how new nation-states, eager to perform their newly won sovereignty, would judge wartime displacements. The implicit questions that government officials posed in these legal disputes were: Where were you in 1942? Did you abandon your adopted home or place of work? If so, why should we admit you to citizenship? *Boats in a Storm* explores responses to these questions, given in courts of law and before commissions and recounted through personal and familial histories that crisscrossed India, Burma/Myanmar, Ceylon/Sri Lanka, and Malaya/ Malaysia and Singapore, while they tried to preserve what I will call the rhythms and patterns of migrant life around the Bay of Bengal / eastern Indian Ocean.

The seemingly unimportant legal disputes featured in *Boats in a Storm* have rarely been included in the postwar history of South and Southeast Asia, which is usually narrated from the perspective of those involved in political and diplomatic negotiations over the administrative aspects of decolonization. In contrast, it was in these seemingly inconsequential encounters—collecting on unpaid debts, paying income tax, remitting money to relatives, writing up a will—that people experienced the aftereffects of the war and witnessed decolonization. Migrant laborers who fled from Rangoon to South India during the Japanese occupation struggled to return to work when magistrates could not issue the right travel permits. Sayed Abdul Cader, a shopkeeper and trader in Colombo who had remitted a large sum of money to his family in India before fleeing across the Palk Strait, found himself the subject of a tax investigation in both countries. A similar assessment from income tax authorities sent Veerappa Chettiar, a partner in a moneylending firm that operated between Rangoon and Madras, into paroxysms of anxiety, convinced that he would lose all his carefully acquired wealth. Laborers like Kandaswamy Muthiah who worked on Ceylon's tea plantations found that although they had stayed on the plantation and even contributed to wartime relief funds, their applications for naturalization in Ceylon were regarded with suspicion. Ramiah, a dockworker at Singapore Harbor whose parents had been indentured laborers on plantations in Malaya, regretted his decision to join a trade union strike for higher wages after the war when he was deported to India, a home he had never known. All of them narrated—or were compelled to narrate—personal and familial histories before the law as they struggled to explain lives lived around and across an ocean. These are individual accounts, but they are representative and offer glimpses into postwar South and Southeast Asia, (dis)connected in the age of decolonization. These postwar encounters with the law took place within a set of political discourses that framed wartime displacements as disloyalty. The contrast here is stark: on the one hand, new networks of solidarities were being forged between former colonies after the war. During the time period covered in this book, representatives of governments across Asia convened at the Asian Relations Conference in 1947 in New Delhi to consider the consequences of the war; leaders of governments across South and Southeast Asia gathered at Bandung for the Asia-Africa Conference in 1955; and many Afro-Asian states eventually joined the Non-Aligned Movement as an alternative way of navigating the rising tensions of the Cold War.[1] On the other hand, beyond these highly visible events that took place on an international stage, the small, mundane, seemingly unimportant legal encounters between governments and migrants recharted the once-intertwined histories of South and Southeast Asia.

These wartime displacements and their aftermath also stand in contrast to the comparatively better-known events that marked decolonization and the beginning of the end of empires in South and Southeast Asia. Take, for example, the violence and displacement that accompanied the territorial partition of India into the new states of India and Pakistan in 1947 ("the Partition") or the "resettlement" following counterinsurgency operations that accompanied the creation of the Federation of Malaya in 1948 ("the Emergency"). In India and Pakistan, between twelve and twenty million people suffered and were killed in Partition-related violence as they attempted to cross borders that had been capriciously drawn by a departing British administration in the provinces of Punjab, Bengal, Assam, and Kashmir and elsewhere on the subcontinent. Across the Bay of Bengal, British imperial forces in Malaya sought to purge those with communist sympathies, conducting counterinsurgency operations and "resettling" more than four hundred thousand people, many of them Indian and Chinese migrants. But the laborers, traders, moneylenders, and dockworkers whose postwar lives are chronicled in *Boats in a Storm*, often categorized in government records as "evacuees," "repatriates," or "migrants" rather than as "refugees" or "displaced people," often sink beneath the surface of the histories of this time, their submerged presence in the archival records reflecting the comparatively minimal interest that they received from national governments or international institutions following their wartime displacements. Indeed, these "migrants"—the double quotes are used to indicate that by the time of the war this term was used to describe many long-term residents or second- or third-generation immigrants in Burma, Ceylon, and Malaya as well as more recently arrived immigrants—were painted in monochrome as either villains or victims as new nation-states in South and Southeast Asia emerged from the collapse of imperial rule.

Boats in a Storm is set against the historical backdrop of imperial labor, capital, and trade networks and the nearly twenty-eight million journeys that were charted between India, Burma, Ceylon, and the Straits Settlements between the mid-nineteenth and mid-twentieth centuries.[2] During the global economic depression of the 1930s, these journeys, often back and forth across the eastern Indian Ocean, which had been established for over 150 years, were slowed and even stilled: there were fewer circular migrations, and more people settled in their adopted homes and places of work. During the Second World War, as Japanese imperial forces overpowered British, American, and Dutch colonies in Southeast Asia and as territorial borders between colonies hardened, these migratory circuits of labor, capital, trade, and finance appear to have been severed.

Historical accounts of networks and connections between South and Southeast Asia often end with the Japanese occupation and accounts of the "long march" out of Burma. From these accounts, it might seem that the war ended any hopes people had of retaining the connections that had linked the two regions. But this interpretation, based on historical data on migration patterns, privileges the perspectives of the British and Dutch imperial forces that returned to former colonies at the end of the war. Following the end of the war, administrative decolonization proceeded along separate and divergent paths, took on different constitutional forms within the former British Empire, and had different timelines. India first acquired a Dominion status within the British Empire, then became a constitutional republic in 1950; Burma, a former British Indian province, became a Union of States in 1948; Ceylon, a former Crown colony separate from India, became a British Dominion and a constitutional republic in 1972; and what had been the Straits Settlements of Penang, Malacca, and Singapore formed a federation that included sultanates ruled by Malay rulers, known first as Malaya and after 1957 as Malaysia.[3] In these places, new constitutions and citizenship legislation struggled to cope with the rising tides of postwar insurgencies, ethnic conflict, and civil wars—wars often forgotten, as historians Christopher Bayly and Tim Harper have shown—in the shimmering promise of postwar national sovereignty.[4] To capture this unraveling along multiple and overlapping temporalities, *Boats in a Storm* invokes historian Sujit Sivasundaram's discussion of "partitioning" as an ongoing process of separation through creating distinct forms of knowledge—here, that of law—alongside the violence of territorial partitions that took place at this time.[5] So the book begins not only with the redrawing of land and river boundaries during the 1947 Partition but also with the unraveling of networks of labor, credit, capital, and trade in law and the creation of two separate regional identities of South and Southeast Asia, which I refer to as the "other partitions" of this time. To borrow the literary metaphor in the book's title, the storms in the lives of migrants did not end with the end of wartime hostilities. On the contrary, they were only just beginning.

After the war ended, temporary displacements threatened to become permanent. As many discovered during legal disputes that followed, borders were as much jurisdictional as geopolitical, existing not only at checkpoints and quarantine camps but everywhere—a dense, complex, and ever-tightening net of laws that caught within it every aspect of postwar life.[6] Legal definitions of "refugee" or "displaced person" in international legal conventions initially restricted the category to the immediate displacements following the war in Europe; they did not extend to wartime displacements in Asia.[7] In Asia, categories of "refugee" and "displaced person" acquired their own meanings and gained traction during the partition of India into the new nation-states of India and Pakistan, but by then these categories were already an uneasy fit for those displaced by the war from Southeast Asia.[8] As with the aftermath of the Partition, these wartime displacements began to have legal consequences in India, Burma, Ceylon, and Malaya, as ethnonationalist movements seized the opportunity of unraveling networks and ambiguous legal provisions to rid new nation-states of "foreigners" and "outsiders." Moneylenders like Veerappa Chettiar faced the prospect of lost debts due to demonetized currency and the nationalization of landholdings in Burma, and traders like Sayed Abdul Cader faced unresolved double-taxation cases not only because of conflicting rules about tax residence but because of a growing distrust of Muslims in Sri Lanka. Plantation laborers struggled to explain to judges adjudicating an application for citizenship why their plans to visit relatives in their ancestral village were not at odds with their plans to settle in Ceylon permanently, or why signing off as a "temporary resident" on a foreign exchange remittance form did not indicate that they were only sojourners on the island. The decisions in ordinary exchanges involving states and officials—how migrants paid tax, changed immigration status, avoided deportation, got married, and willed away property—began to have profound consequences for lives that had once been lived across South and Southeast Asia.

LAW AS ARCHIVE

At first glance, it might seem that questions of political belonging after the formal end of empires could be resolved through nationality and citizenship regimes that offered the possibility of a fixed legal status. But these regimes developed on varying timelines across South and Southeast Asia. In India, Burma, Ceylon, and Malaya, legislative frameworks for nationality and citizenship were brought into force at different times during decolonization—in Burma and Ceylon as early as 1948, soon after the end of imperial rule, but in India as late as 1955, more than eight years after it gained political independence, and in Malaya in 1957, after independence. *Boats in a Storm* shows that nationality and citizenship regimes did not resolve questions of political belonging; instead, debates over political belonging were initiated in ordinary legal disputes about the relationship between new nation-states and their sovereign right to shape their body politic, in cases about unfulfilled debt or a contested will, before citizenship became a possible resolution. As legal scholar Renisa Mawani writes, the promise and peril of (il)legalities traveled across the oceans. Former migrants—now putative minorities within new constitutional frameworks—quickly realized that nationality and citizenship regimes made it more difficult to recover the rhythms and patterns of migrant life that had existed before the war unraveled them.

Law—understood not only as doctrine or principle but as practice—is a rich archive from which one can reconstruct histories of decolonization in South and Southeast Asia, an archive sometimes characterized by accidental accretion rather than intentional organization.[9] Migrant journeys across oceans intersected with law and legalities at multiple points, from procurement of travel documents to restrictions on the amount of money or personal belongings one could carry.[10] But these lives were also lived in the shadow of the law—awaiting judges in small courtrooms over petty cases, scrambling for a stamp or a signature from officials on a remittance form or a renewal of permissions for work, staving off the possibility of deportation for overstaying a residence permit, or searching for ways to negotiate around the rigor of these documentary requirements.[11] Within the archives of law, personal and familial histories provide glimpses of lives that cannot be captured in statistical tables of emigration and return. The archives built up from legal practice retain documentation of these encounters of migrants with law, for they are created not only as a record of constitutional reforms and legislative changes by national governments but also through the minutiae of legal disputes over taxation, immigration, and detention across new international borders. All of these underwent profound changes in the wake of wartime displacements. A peopled history, written from the archives of law, thus helps us understand decolonization in South and Southeast Asia in ways not captured by military, diplomatic, or administrative histories of this time, which often assume the fixity of territorial borders, instead of recognizing the fluidity of jurisdictional claims.[12]

These jurisdictional claims are central to the histories in this book. Here both migrants and governments make claims to jurisdiction, reflecting legal scholar Sundhya Pahuja's formulation of jurisdiction as an encounter in international law.[13] Typically, claims to jurisdiction are either an invocation of or a submission to legal authority; in international law, these claims assert that somebody or something is within a particular state's territory, or alternatively within its legal purview, and determines who has the authority to say where and when disputes can be adjudicated. Historically, claims to jurisdiction were bound up with territorial conquest in settler colonies and European imperial hegemony over its Asian colonies; they were often used to erase or eclipse plural legal traditions, to demarcate communities from each other, and to separate insider from outsider.[14] Historians of South and Southeast Asia have used the legal concept of jurisdiction to highlight the agency that indigenous peoples had in crafting their own legal identities within the structures of colonial law. In postwar South and Southeast Asia, these distinctions through multiple jurisdictions continued to be reinscribed, but circular migrations across oceans also occasioned a different set of jurisdictional claims because of new nationality and citizenship regimes. Consider, for example, how a trader like Mohammed Ibrahim Saibo explained to the judges at the Madras High Court why he remitted money from Ceylon to India during the war but still intended to make Ceylon his permanent home or "domicile" (see chapter 5), or how the proprietors of the Shanmugham Rubber Estate in Malaya who lived in Madras argued that income from the plantation lay outside the ambit of Indian income tax law (see chapter 3). In claims and counterclaims about nationality and territory, people demonstrated their understanding of new geopolitical realities, but they also sketched out how these had unexpectedly drifted away from the prewar labor, capital, and trade assemblages and the circuits of mobility, to their detriment.

These claims and counterclaims made in the context of cross-border legal disputes show that jurisdiction was not only territorial but also temporal. As this book will show, nationality and citizenship regimes often invoked the wartime displacements in 1942 as a marker, tying definitions of residence and settlement to that year; they effectively designated those who fled as "migrants," limiting their access to full citizenship upon their return. Jurisdictional claims were a chronotope, as in legal scholar Mariana Valverde's framing; these claims underscore law's power to shape space and time, the scenes and rhythms of everyday life.[15] As claiming jurisdiction became a means of situating oneself in both space and time, migrants from present-day India in present-day Southeast Asia—especially those displaced by the war—became vulnerable to charges of disloyalty, which in turn threatened their acquiring citizenship in those places. Jurisdictional claims thus show that the legal status of citizenship in adopted homes and places of work was not accessible to all former "migrants," not only because of where they were born or where they lived, but also because of where they were at the height of the war in 1942 in South and Southeast Asia.

While lawyers and legal professionals often think of law in terms of areas of practice, such as family law or criminal law, the legal histories in this book span a range of areas of practice; in surveying cross-border legal encounters and in accordance with the time period covered in the book, the book blurs lawyerly distinctions between public and private law and between national and international law. The cases examined range from direct taxation (chapters 3 and 5), to contracts and remedies (chapter 2), to immigration (chapter 4), to property and inheritance (chapter 5), to constitutional law and criminal procedure (chapter 6). This range reflects how migrants encountered "the law," a capacious understanding that often, but not always, conflated law with the state. Their experiences were markedly different from those of lawyers or judges of the time, who might have classified these disputes differently—in terms of cases and materials on constitutional, administrative, or international law.[16] International law is key here, although these cross-border disputes take place in the shift from imperial to national rule during which the notion of "international" was itself being worked out. Where migrants and their lawyers themselves explicitly used the language of "international law"— as in the case of the All Malaya Nattukottai Chettiars' Association in chapter 2—this language gestured to the fact that they recognized that in a postwar world, legal claims had to reckon with multiple emergent national regimes rather than appealing to an imperial law across a fast-dissolving British Empire.[17] Taking these gestures seriously, I follow the migrants at the center of these cases across the jurisdictions where they lived, worked, and made their legal claims, from Rangoon to Devakkottai, from Madras to Malaya, or from Colombo to London and back again, for this circulation not only was a central feature of the social and economic life of migrants in the region before the war but intertwined with how "law" was practiced at the time.[18] In *Boats in a Storm*, I read both along and against the grain of these archives of law.

To track the travels of law as jurisdictional claims and counterclaims, *Boats in a Storm* begins with and returns to disputes at the Madras High Court, the highest court of appeal in the province of Madras in British India. Madras, which included parts of the present-day Indian states of Tamil Nadu, Kerala, and Andhra, had several important ports, including those in the city of Madras itself (Chennai), Vizagapatam (Visakhapatanam), and Tuticorin (Thoothukudi). Madras was thus a key point of departure for emigrants in the colonial period, and during and after the war it was an important locus of transit and return. For a study of law and migration, the focus on provinces—rather than the central government—is important because until 1954, provincial governments like the one in Madras, as opposed to the central government, issued permits and passports, administered quarantine measures, and set up relief and rehabilitation measures for evacuees and refugees; they also policed the coasts to prevent "illicit" immigration. Madras was also an important node in colonial legal networks: as law circulated—in the form of doctrine and precedent; as paperwork in the hands of traders, laborers, and lawyers; as invocation in speeches of political leaders, activists, and intellectuals—we can see Madras receding and reappearing on the horizon. The legal disputes woven through the chapters that follow reflect how law travels. These travels are nonlinear, not necessarily flowing up and down from one level of judicial hierarchy to another—from trial courts to appellate courts—but more like the migrant journeys across the oceans, moving back and forth, sometimes disappearing from official law reports and lawyers' memoirs only to surface in family papers or personal recollections. Law's travels are visible in the pronouncements of judges, in the assertions of legal representatives, in the carefully assembled pieces of evidence and proof clutched in the arms of a nervous litigant.[19] "Law" is thus valuable beyond its role as judicial precedent, especially because we have only scanty official and unofficial statistics on those displaced during the war in Asia; law leaves stories of migration and return in its wake. The book is also organized not by groups of claimants such as traders or laborers but by type of legal regime—taxation, immigration, detention, and so forth, and within it, by legal issues to emphasize jurisdictional claims themselves. The narrative thus shifts between different groups—from traders to laborers to professionals—not only because they were connected to each other within assemblages of labor, capital, credit, and trade, but also because of how they were made visible in legal records (for example, Chettiar litigants are prominent in taxation disputes and are thus the focus of the chapters on the taxation regimes, but they were by no means the only ones who were affected by those regimes). Finally, not all forums discussed in *Boats in a Storm*—including the Advisory Council under the Madras Maintenance of Public Order Act of 1949 (chapter 6) and the Commission for the Registration of Indian and Pakistani Residents (chapter 4)—kept comprehensive statistics of cases admitted, dismissed, or adjudicated. Nor was every dismissed or decided case formally reported in a legal magazine or a law reporter. In the context of migrations, this makes the emphasis on the travels of law, rather than principles laid down in an individual judicial ruling or a quantitative analysis of cases adjudicated, even more important.

Boats in a Storm reconstructs personal and familial histories from a historian's treasure trove of legal and administrative records, previously unexplored and scattered across multiple repositories in what are now multiple countries (India, Sri Lanka, Myanmar, and Singapore). These include disputed income tax assessments, unfulfilled promissory notes, discarded foreign exchange remittance forms, and dismissed immigration appeals that crisscrossed new national regimes. Some—such as the archives of the Madras High Court in India (see figure o.1 for the Writ Appeal Record Room where I worked) and the Commission for the Registration of Indian and Pakistani Residents in Sri Lanka—were at the time unassembled and uncatalogued, but I worked with and across these documents to frame the arguments in this book. I tracked down law offices in Chennai in India and consular offices in Kandy in Sri Lanka, to which people turned in a time of crisis. I used memoirs, community histories, and oral history transcripts in English, Tamil, and Malayalam to supplement official records. I traveled to ports of emigration along the coast of present-day Tamil Nadu and Kerala in India. Piecing together documentary fragments and exploring the present-day remnants of this legal past are crucial for research into postwar legal and geopolitical changes, for government archives were often destroyed or disappeared during the war. Law is thus a dispersed archive of decolonization rather than an orderly accounting in terms of doctrine or principles of nationality and citizenship in newly created nation-states.

RETHINKING CITIZENSHIP AND DECOLONIZATION

Boats in a Storm shows that citizenship as a legal status did not resolve question of political belonging. People put forward their own claims in the minutiae of legal disputes over taxes, inheritance, remittances, and wages. Indeed, in shifting attention from legal status to legal practice, from citizenship claims to jurisdictional claims, and from the territorial to the temporal dimensions of citizenship, *Boats in a Storm* shows that people who lived and worked in more than one place did not see themselves as limited to opposing legal categories of citizenship or statelessness. Political belonging in postwar South and Southeast Asia was, as it continues to be today, a spectrum, on which citizenship and statelessness

FIGURE 0.1: *Madras High Court Record Room. Photograph by author.*

were but two points.[20] In a world that demanded proof of political loyalty, those whose stories figure in these chapters—Seethalakshmi Achi, Kandaswamy Muthiah, Umbichi Haji and Katheesa Bi, Ramiah and many others—negotiated and navigated this spectrum, attempting to revive the rhythms and patterns of prewar migrant life.

There is a growing community of scholars who study the twentieth-century struggle for citizenship rights of global and diasporic South Asians in settler colonies in Europe and the Americas.[21] These scholars trace how, in the early twentieth century, the descendants of Indian indentured laborers and others who had been transported to settler colonies and penal settlements in Asia, Africa, and Caribbean demanded their rights, as literary scholar Sukanya Banerjee notes, not only as British subjects, but indeed as imperial citizens.[22] Others who formed part of the many trading diasporas from West and South India, from present-day states of Gujarat and Tamil Nadu, also fought to secure political rights in new homes.[23] More often than not, the focus is on the role of political leaders, diplomats, or envoys from India who traveled there.[24] In relation to this body of scholarship, historian Alison Bashford identifies decolonization in Asia and Africa as the "missing political moment," one that slips through the cracks between, on the one hand, this vibrant scholarship on colonial-era immigration histories of exclusion in settler colonies that comes to an end with the Second World War and, on the other, scholarship that details the contemporary exclusion of formerly colonized peoples.[25]

Historians of South Asia have addressed this "missing" moment in multiple ways, linking it to South Asia's many partitions. Charting the shift from imperial to national citizenship in South Asia, scholars of citizenship have shown how it was shaped by the violence and displacement following the establishment of nation-states in India and Pakistan. Niraja Gopal Jayal and Anupama Roy show that the displacements following the Partition and the ensuing debates over political belonging were central to how citizenship was wrought. Jayal traces how a *jus soli* conception of citizenship—one that was grounded in territory and enmeshed in the politics of the Partition—gave way to a *jus sanguinis* model in contemporary India, one in which bloodlines and familial descent determine access.[26] Tracing these shifts through amendments to citizenship legislation in India, Roy shows that exceptions were created first for Assam during the Partition; later, following the liberation of Bangladesh in 1971, to address the demographic shifts that had resulted in large numbers of migrants and refugees in India's "Northeast"; and finally, in 2003, to establish a deterritorialized notion of citizenship through the creation of a new status, "overseas citizen of India," that encompassed India's far-flung diasporas.[27] Historians of the 1947 Partition and of liberation of Bangladesh in 1971 have also traced how any understanding of the category of citizenship is thus incomplete without exploring how refugees displaced by newly drawn territorial borders in the subcontinent were incorporated into the developmentalist logic of new nation-states.[28] Beyond the context of the Partition involving India, Pakistan, and later, Bangladesh, Valli Kanapathipillai shows how the disenfranchisement of laborers on plantations in Sri Lanka—the *malayaika thamilar* recruited during British rule from India—was central to the making of the categories of citizenship and statelessness in Sri Lanka.[29] Complementing this rich body of work on migration, displacement, and partitions but shifting the scope and scale of these explorations to adopt the perspective of unraveling circular migrations within Asia and across the oceans following the war helps us rethink citizenship and decolonization.

The co-constitution of migration and citizenship during decolonization is also often explored from the perspective of metropolitan Britain itself, not from the perspective of those who attempted to retain the rhythms and patterns of migrant life between its former colonies in South and Southeast Asia.[30] Although postwar amendments to the Nationality and Status of Aliens Act in 1948 did offer former British subjects a legal means of emigrating to Britain, they were not expected to result in a huge wave of migration. Defying these expectations, nearly five hundred thousand former British subjects emigrated between 1948 and 1971.[31] More significantly, in the immediate years following political independence, former British colonies were expected to work out their own principles of national legal citizenship. For people who traveled between South and Southeast Asia, many of whom were now recast as minorities under the national citizenship schemes in their adopted homes and places of work, access to the rights and privileges of citizenship involved navigating legal encounters within new national regimes, where national loyalties were measured out by one's presence or absence from the new country at specific moments, such as during the war, or for specific lengths of time that often overlapped with wartime displacement. The legal encounters I describe here—those of migrants who once traveled between South and Southeast Asia—reveal that decolonization as a process was not only a negotiation between imperial metropoles and colonies: these disputes also unfolded between and among the national legal regimes of India, Sri Lanka, Myanmar, Malaysia, and Singapore. In other words, decolonization was also intercolonial: national geographies were constructed not only from the debris of shipwrecked empires and the residues of imperial collapse but also from competing nationalisms between colonies. Even as national myths were being created against colonial constructions of origins and beginnings, community legends, myths, and imaginations that cut across emergent boundaries jostled for space.[32]

A comparison might be drawn here with the alternative political possibilities to the nation-state and national citizenship imagined by anticolonial leaders in French West Africa between 1945 and 1960 that historian Frederick Cooper describes.[33] This transregional perspective on legal citizenship has been explored in the scholarship on other geographic regions; outside of South Asia, partitions and minority citizenship are discussed using global, transnational, and comparative methods. Scholars have documented how, in interwar Europe and the Middle East, national legal regimes surrounding citizenship transformed migrants into minorities and, simultaneously, minorities into perpetual migrants—the same "array of legal tactics" designed to effect partitions and population transfers that would be implemented in South and Southeast Asia during decolonization. In interwar Europe, as Mark Mazower has written, the League of Nations and its Minorities Treaties used the terms *minority* and *minority protection* in the context of the creation of nation-states that emerged from the collapse of the Russian, Ottoman, and Habsburg Empires.[34] As Mira Siegelberg shows in her intellectual history of the legal category of "statelessness," minorities were made dependent on nation-states for their legal status, which they were stripped of during the Second World War; this historic background is what would lead philosopher Hannah Arendt to describe postwar citizenship as "the right to have rights."[35] The other side of minority protection was forced deportations in the British and French mandates set up by the League.[36] Laura Robson has described a similar situation in the interwar Middle East, where population transfers between Greece and Turkey took place in the context of partition of territories in Cyprus and Palestine.[37] The translation of ethnic identities into and through legal identities that, according to Robson, characterized the interwar period in Europe was a feature of colonial rule in South Asia from its very first days. For example, it is reflected in the ways that what is known as "personal law" (different laws for different groups, such as "Islamic law" and "Hindu law") legally set different groups apart from each other in South and Southeast Asia. Indeed, the legal practices employed by emergent nation-states in South and Southeast Asia appear to be a continuation of, and coterminous with, colonial legal regimes that were already in place. They are similar to the legal tactics that Robson describes as employed by the League of Nations in British and French mandates in the interwar period, but they have longer, murkier histories. Postimperial sovereignty in South Asia was firmly yoked to the political form of the nation-state, not least because of the demands of international law, as legal scholars Luis Eslava and Sundhya Pahuja note. So in this book, the alternative political possibilities that decenter the territorial limits of the nation-state, and which we might envision in migrant histories, are linked to jurisdictional claims.[38] If these projects of "worldmaking," to use scholar Adom Getachew's phrase, that consider the transition from empire to nation-states often focus on how anticolonial political leaders reimagined a postwar world order, *Boats in a Storm* reimagines what worldmaking might have looked like from the perspective of ordinary migrants, attempting to recreate prewar circuits of mobility across the eastern Indian Ocean.[39] By following legal struggles between South and Southeast Asia—between former colonies, as an intercolonial process, rather than between the metropole in London and colonies in Asia—this book offers a lesser-known perspective of how migrants sought to reimagine their worlds in the aftermath of war, partitions, and displacement.

Boats in a Storm is therefore not an account of the political or diplomatic events following the end of the war. Decolonization, seen from migrant perspectives, is not only the triumphant final chapter in the history of revolutionary struggles or anticolonial activism. Scholarship on India's international relations that has emphasized political and diplomatic negotiations, particularly in the 1960s and 1970s, and has discussed India, Burma, and Malaya within the same frame has also emphasized the role of migration, particularly labor migration.[40] Historians of the Indian Ocean have also shown that migrant lives were caught up in, and often shaped, transnational political currents.[41] But even as prominent political leaders— for example, Jawaharlal Nehru, Aung San, Subhash Chandra Bose, or U Nu and the ideals that they espoused—certainly figured in people's imaginations, the aspirations of political leaders receded into the background in the harsh light of migrants' immediate attempts to navigate a world of new nation-states through taxation, immigration, and detention regimes after the war ended. Most of the migrants in the chapters that follow proposed no political or constitutional alternative to nation-states in the legal claims that they put forward; they were not revolutionaries or radicals who sought, in the aftermath of and because of the war, to craft a new political solution to the rapidly unraveling of the ties that had once connected South and Southeast Asia. Instead, they told their stories, which show how their lives were once lived within a connected world of land, labor, capital, and credit across South and Southeast Asia. In the postwar period, these stories were also narrated by journalists and writers who traveled with their work across new national borders. In the years leading up to and immediately following independence, many invoked the language of "greater" diasporas and their homelands—as in the case of Greater India, which projected a shared "Indian" civilizational influence over present-day Southeast Asia from ancient times.[42] Scholars of international law and international affairs keen on reviving India's place on a new world stage put forth revised versions of this "history" as well.[43] But there were other less grand narratives being spun as well across the oceans; as historian Lakshmi Subramanian shows, through a reading of Chettiar-sponsored Tamil periodicals in India, Malaya, and Burma, there was also a growth of newspapers, magazines, and pamphlets characterized by narrow concerns about thriving materially in adopted homes rather than forging a shared political future between India, Burma, and Malaya.[44] Political organizing did take place around a shared linguistic identity, slipping uneasily into a conflation of linguistic and racial identities and suggesting that claims to being "authentic" citizens could be established because of the language that one spoke.[45] So while migrants from South India to the Straits Settlements did organize around and leverage a Tamil identity that was often used to describe them in colonial-era government documents, Tamil-speaking migrants in Malaya existed in an uneasy relationship with political movements in India; as Darinee Alagirisamy shows, Tamil nationalisms in India and Malaya were linked but took on different forms.[46] Simultaneously, on the other shore of the Bay of Bengal, in the first decade following independence, the demands for reorganizing the provinces of independent India, including the present-day state of Kerala, on the basis of majority language spoken in each district—the linguistic reorganization of states—was built on a shared diasporic identity of being Malayali but was articulated differently in Singapore than in India.[47] Reflecting these possibilities, what follows is not an attempt to explore these vernaculars of political belonging, as reflected in literary, religious, or political texts; rather, it seeks to show how language—when pressed into service as a political and juridical marker—helped disrupt the teleological narrative of anticolonial struggles that ended with decolonization. In other words, it offers an account of how migrant futures were marked by imaginaries of a shared linguistic identity and how this found expression in legal disputes.[48] These imaginaries and their materializations in legal documents circulated both within and beyond migrant networks, and were often marginalized within political and diplomatic circles. These legal struggles, many still ongoing, are the unfinished business of the end of empires in South and Southeast Asia.

While a straight line cannot—and arguably, should not—be drawn from 1942 to the present, these insights in *Boats in a Storm* inform debates on migration, citizenship, refugeedom and statelessness today. India alone, leaving aside the other countries in South Asia, has the world's largest diaspora at 17.9 million people as of 2020, and Indian migrants remit $89 billion as of 2021, making up a significant component of the global South Asian diaspora.[49] At the same time, however, about 78 percent of the global South Asian and nearly 66 percent of the Southeast

Asian diaspora are located within South and Southeast Asia respectively, not in Europe or the Americas.[50] However, the "long shadow" of the end of empire continues to cast a pall over those who wish to reside or seek the citizenship of a country other than that of their origin. In 2019, India's citizenship legislation was amended to provide a quicker path to citizenship by naturalization for non-Muslims from Afghanistan, Pakistan, or Bangladesh who entered India before December 31, 2014; these amendments were strongly condemned as discriminatory in nationwide protests and continue to be challenged in courts.[51] Although it was widely touted as a replacement for a refugee law, Lankan Tamils who sought refuge in India following the outbreak of the Sri Lankan civil war in 1983 and the Tibetan refugees who fled to India in 1959 found no mention in the act and continue to face challenges in naturalizing as Indian citizens.[52] About 40 percent of the world's 4.2 million stateless persons live in Southeast Asia, many because of borders arbitrarily drawn and mobilities ignored during decolonization.[53] News cycles highlight "crises" such as the forced expulsion of ethnic and religious minorities from Myanmar and the creation of citizens' registers in South Asian borderlands that demand documentary proof of citizenship.[54] *Boats in a Storm* reveals parallels and continuities in global conversations about displacement, dispossession, belonging, loyalty, and citizenship that cut across national borders: how the phantasmic fear of the "illegal" immigrant fuels ethnonationalisms, how the violence of bureaucratic procedures that determine citizenship results in lost lives, and how the stamp of authenticity is accorded only to those with personal histories that align with state-sanctioned political histories.

CHAPTER OUTLINE

In 1942, following military occupation by Japanese forces in Burma and Malaya and fearing attacks on the Indian subcontinent, people abandoned coastal towns and cities around the Bay of Bengal or the eastern Indian Ocean for the relative safety of villages in the hinterland. The affluent bought tickets to board ships, steamers, and trains; those who were unable to do so trekked hundreds of miles across mountains and jungles on the India-Burma borderlands. They arrived at ports, railway stations, and rehabilitation camps that dotted India's eastern coastline and waited for the war to end. Ongoing negotiations on immigration control between India, Burma, Ceylon, and Malaya had been abandoned because of the war. When the war officially ended in 1945, there were no agreements in place, only a patchwork of rules for movement, travel, and residence between colonies. Taking advantage of this uncertainty, political leaders in Burma, Ceylon, and Malaya, many of whom had long portrayed migrants as outsiders stealing jobs, market shares, and land from locals, argued that migrant laborers, traders, and financiers who had fled during the war should not be allowed to return. These governments imposed jurisdictional borders in the form of remittance limits, double taxation, and rapid land nationalization that reinscribed new territorial borders between nation-states. Chapter 1 recounts this story through oral histories, memoirs, and newspaper reports, describing wartime displacements and the migrants' thwarted plans for postwar return.

In chapter 2, I trace what happened as these migrants struggled to return to war-devastated economies; the wartime displacements of these migrants formed the context and presumption for the legal encounters that they were being forced to navigate after the war. Struggling to recover from galloping inflation during the war, postwar economies in South and Southeast Asia teetered on the brink of collapse. Business communities in Burma and Malaya, notably the politically prominent Nattukottai Chettiars, who lent money and owned mills, mines, and plantations, claimed that any repayments of debts in "banana money"—currency circulated by the Japanese occupation government—were invalid, affecting debt recoveries, property transactions, and land ownership. This roused the suspicion and resentment of governments that were already skeptical about the place of foreign-owned business in postwar national economies: these businesses' claims of wartime loss and collapse did not ring true. Even as ordinary people, laborers, small shopkeepers, and plantation workers, whose meager earnings or small plots of land might have been pledged as collateral to these moneylenders, governments claimed that wartime profits were being siphoned out of the country through the flight of "refugee capital." This chapter offers an alternative view of postwar economic reconstruction: through legislative debates, petitions, and pamphlets from India, Burma, and Malaya, it shows how businessmen, traders, and financiers battled to remain part of the postwar economy, fighting not only restrictive foreign exchange regulations and land nationalization but also nativist stereotypes that portrayed them as having profited disproportionately off the land and labor of their adopted homes.

As chapter 3 shows, the allegations of the flight of "refugee capital" were not wholly untrue. In the years leading up to their displacement from Burma, moneylenders and financiers—including the Nattukottai Chettiars, who had lived in Burma and Malaya for over a century and a half but had retained ties to their ancestral villages in India—remitted nearly $1.3 billion from Burma. This chapter shows how the Chettiars' money was fought over by emerging nations with competing claims to their wealth. The legal battles over these fortunes give us a glimpse of how the Chettiars' business practices (including circular migration, family and kinship structures, and customary business practices) were disrupted by the growing separations within emerging nation-states. After many Chettiar firms ended operations in Burma during the war, restrictions on travel and land ownership made it difficult for them to return to claim the rest of their fortunes. At the same time, India redesigned its income tax regimes and definitions of tax residence to claim that their remittances to India from Burma were subject to Indian income tax. Using tax advisory opinions written by judges of the Madras High Court, chapter 3 shows how Chettiar financiers responded to these jurisdictional claims. Although the income had indeed been earned outside India in Southeast Asia, customary Chettiar familial and commercial practices had kept their transactions tied to India, and they argued that these customary ties did not mean that the money should be subject to Indian taxation. At the same time, the Chettiar communities were fighting on another front: just as they were being treated by India as Indian businesses and made to pay income tax on income from Burma, they were also lobbying to persuade Burmese and Malayan governments that they were integral to postwar economies and should be allowed to return. Their wartime displacements were held against them, and in the end many were judged to be foreigners and noncitizens: their landholdings were nationalized, in some places their fortunes were confiscated or taxed heavily, and their businesses were closed or interrupted. The Chettiars were left holding worthless paper—

title deeds, contracts, remittance forms—that had once represented their fortunes in Burma and Ceylon.

The Chettiars' property deeds and documents are but one example of how bits of paper possessed by migrants could become suddenly worthless—or suddenly valuable. Chapter 4 focuses on the fluctuations in the nature and value of paperwork for migrants, particularly the application forms for the permits, passes, certificates, and passports that would enable migrants to continue traveling between India, Sri Lanka, Myanmar, and Singapore after the war ended, and the documentation that would prove their presence in (or absence from) their adopted homes. Postwar governments wielded paperwork as a threat, with citizenship held out as the prize for compliance with documentation regimes. The demand for paperwork to establish ties to adopted homes was an enormous burden, particularly on plantation laborers. In chapter 4, I examine naturalization applications made by laborers who worked on tea plantations in Sri Lanka to show how remittance forms, property deeds, letters to loved ones, and travel tickets were used as adverse evidence in legal claims about political belonging. While political leaders in Ceylon claimed that these plantation laborers had never intended to permanently settle there, those in India claimed that their long absence implied they had abandoned any claims to Indian citizenship: as these pieces of paper crossed the border between India and Ceylon, their value changed, posing different types of threats in the two new nation-states of India and Ceylon. These fragile pieces of paper, seemingly unimportant, would separate families who had once lived across India and Ceylon.

In chapter 5, bringing strands of the argument in the previous chapters together, I focus on intertwined cases of immigration and taxation between India and Ceylon, where familial attachments were translated into political attachments. In 1942, many migrant traders fled from Ceylon to their hometowns in South India, fearing Japanese air attacks on the island. After the end of the war, they found themselves having to answer the question "Where were you in 1942?," some in the context of income tax assessments, others in the context of a citizenship application. They were asked to show why the fact that their wives and children lived in India should not be construed as loyalty to that country. These encounters took place in a political climate that conflated race, religion, and ethnicity with territory. In the courts, migrant traders sought to prove that these sojourns were customary, but their now cross-national familial, marital, and kinship ties were used to exclude those who lived and worked in both India and Ceylon. The chapter ends with the story of Katheesa Bi and Umbichi Haji, which upturns ideas of "women who wait, while men migrate," as well as the themes of family, loyalty, and migration that undergird notions of national citizenship.

These ordinary encounters went largely unnoticed, even as new nation-states in South and Southeast Asia began to forge postcolonial solidarities along political and diplomatic lines. In chapter 6, I show that in India, Burma, Ceylon, and Malaya, major political parties leading movements for independence saw no place for labor migrants in the country's postwar future and sought to use the postwar circumstances—including charges of communist sympathies in certain groups—to push them out. They found common cause with ethnonationalist movements that demanded that homelands be reserved for "original" inhabitants and sought to exclude newer settlers. In response, I show how left-wing trade unionists, writers, and journalists with leftist sympathies became advocates for migrant rights—both for those on plantations and for those waiting in port cities to return to their adopted homes. These advocates included prominent labor leaders and lawyers such as S. P. Amarasingam and S. Nadesan in Ceylon and journalists and writers including G. Sarangapany and R. Ramanathan in Malaya. As I show here, postwar nation-states mobilized legal regimes of banishment and deportation against migrants by labeling them communists and insurgents, setting a precedent for similar actions in a rapidly escalating Cold War in Asia. This chapter follows the legal encounters of six dockworkers banished from Singapore and detained on arrival in India. These descendants of Indian indentured laborers had been born in Malaya and sent back to a "home" that they had never seen or been to. The chapter draws on habeas corpus applications that these workers filed in the Madras High Court as well as letters that they wrote to their families and leaders of various political parties to show how they navigated being at the risk of statelessness caused by deportation, justified by the suspicions surrounding their political affiliations.

The final chapter, chapter 7, returns to Burma in 1962, twenty years after the Japanese occupation. In 1962, General Ne Win took over the civilian government in Burma with the help of military forces under his command and implemented measures that resulted in a second wave of displacement. These legislative measures were adopted to restrict migrant remittances, raise rates of income tax, and subject "foreigners" to increased surveillance and documentary requirements. From this vantage point, the chapter surveys the twenty years that had elapsed after wartime displacements in 1942 and the outcomes of disputes involving taxation, immigration, and detention regimes, noting how the invocations of wartime displacement in ongoing legal disputes mirrored the rhythms and patterns of circular migration and return, and illustrating how legal temporalities reshaped the official chronology of postwar events that moved linearly from the end of the war to the Partition to independence and economic reconstruction. Following the military coup in Burma, the execution of repatriation schemes for plantation laborers from Ceylon to India following diplomatic negotiations between India and Ceylon, the dwindling number of legal migration schemes that were not predicated on citizenship choices, and the growing number of opportunities to migrate to the Middle East, Europe, and the United States, legal claims attempting to revive the rhythms and patterns of migrant life seemed increasingly unviable. The unraveling of labor, trade, capital, and credit networks appeared to be complete, and claims to jurisdiction that crisscrossed borders were swept aside by claims to citizenships. With the choice of citizenship recognized as the primary marker of political belonging, the government in India sought to incorporate refugees and repatriates into nation-building projects that focused on development and the potential for economic contributions.

In the Conclusion, I recall how 1942 became a juridical marker in nationality, immigration, and citizenship regimes in South and Southeast Asia and how the territorial and temporal dimensions of jurisdictional claims and counterclaims reshape our understanding of the first two decades of decolonization. In legal disputes around debt recovery, income tax, immigration, and detention that took place across new national borders, wartime displacements loomed large and were reframed in political discourse as disloyalty. In response to these disputes that followed the unraveling of migrant trade, capital, and labor networks, people attempted to narrate personal and familial histories that showed why these charges were unfounded, but in a postwar world where choices around citizenship were framed as political attachments, these narrations were rendered insignificant. Here decolonization unfolded not only as a political or diplomatic process but as a legal process that continually invoked wartime displacements in people's everyday lives. These processes generated legal temporalities that altered how decolonization was experienced in, and continues to mark, the lives of former migrants.

PART I

ONE

1942

ON MARCH 7, 1942, Japanese troops marched into Rangoon, the capital of British Burma. This moment had been some months in the making: air raids had unleashed chaos and destruction in the city since December 1941. Now Burma lay in ruins. Its world-famous oil fields were on fire, expanses of paddy crushed into the mud. Roads, bridges, and railways had been demolished. Burn marks from incendiary bombs were etched into the walls and roofs of buildings on Rangoon's waterfront. Fuselage from stricken aircraft lay smoking in the fields. Boats in Rangoon Harbor lay battered, splintered, debris half-floating on the water. Rangoon—city of migrants—was destroyed, plundered, and emptied out.

The Japanese occupations during the war and the displacements that followed had far-reaching consequences for the lives of Indian migrants in Southeast Asia—ordinary laborers, traders, shopkeepers, and moneylenders—whose lives crisscrossed the eastern Indian Ocean. Beginning in the mid-nineteenth century, both Indian and Chinese migrations had created labor, credit, and capital networks within and around the British and Dutch empires in Southeast Asia. These networks appeared to have been severed as people fled occupied cities, attempted to escape forced labor or military service or salvage their businesses, and struggled

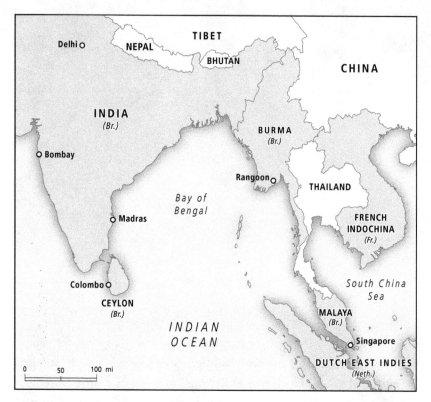

MAP 1: *Empires in South and Southeast Asia on the eve of World War II. Source: The CShapes 2.0 Dataset.*

to return to their adopted homes and places of work after the war ended. The story of these migrant networks in South and Southeast Asia is often cut off at this point. This chapter—and this book—instead begins there.

In 1942, people abandoned coastal towns and cities around the eastern Indian Ocean, fleeing military occupation or the threat of air raids and heading for the relative safety of villages and towns in the hinterland.[1] Historian Indivar Kamtekar terms this "a shiver," a feeling of fear and dread that rippled through towns and cities in India as they braced for potential attacks.[2] In Burma, where this threat had materialized, many bought tickets to board steamers from its largest ports, Akyab and Rangoon, and then boarded trains from Calcutta onwards to Madras. Others waited for a seat or a berth on a steamer or a train to become available. Most decided not to wait but to walk, trekking hundreds of miles from Burma's cities and towns. Nearly five hundred thousand people—equivalent to the population of the entire city of Rangoon in 1941—trekked through the jungles and swamps that separated the two British colonies of India and Burma. In the initial reports, only over twelve thousand deaths were officially recorded. Many tens of thousands more perished.[3] Those who made it out alive arrived at ports, railway stations, and rehabilitation camps that dotted India's eastern coastline in Chittagong, Calcutta, Vizagapatam, and Madras. From Singapore and Colombo, from battlefields across Southeast Asia and as far away as Hong Kong, people made their way to India. Many saw this as only a temporary return, not a permanent abandonment of their longtime homes and places of work. For Indian migrants to Southeast Asia, although they did not know it then, these wartime displacements would alter their everyday lives, reorient ideas of national citizenship, and reshape the trajectory of decolonization in South and Southeast Asia.

THE JAPANESE OCCUPATIONS

On the eve of the Japanese occupation, worlds collided in Rangoon. With its occupation of Burma, Japan was on the verge of being able to cut off India's supplies to China, with whom it had been engaged in heightened wartime hostilities since 1937, and gain valuable access to oil fields in Syriam and Yenanyaung. Christopher Bayly and Tim Harper describe this maneuvering as part of the "forgotten wars" of the years between 1942 and 1945, critical to the making of modern South and Southeast Asia.[4] Allied forces comprising Indian, Chinese, West African, Australian, British, and American soldiers had fought Japanese imperial forces in battlefields on land and at sea. Japanese imperial forces were joined by revolutionary armies—the Burmese Independence Army, led by Aung San, and the Azad Hind Fauj, led by Subash Chandra Bose—who believed that a Japanese victory would further the cause of Burmese and Indian independence from Britain. And these new and old political forces coincided with a challenge to the American Empire: the attack on Pearl Harbor took the US Navy by surprise in December 1941. Shortly after, the great colonial port cities in Asia—including Hong Kong, Manila, Batavia, and Singapore—fell in quick succession.

But Rangoon was more than a place where wartime worlds met, and it was different from these other Asian cities that fell to Japanese forces, for it brought the war to India's doorstep. As Sir Akbar Hydari, a member of the Indian viceroy Lord Linlithgow's Executive Council and a representative of the Nizam of the princely state of Hyderabad, observed, if Burma had not been partitioned from India in 1937, India itself—the British Empire's most valuable possession in Asia—would have been under attack.[5] But the threat to the subcontinent never materialized, although villages on the still-porous border of India and Burma, in Assam, Manipur, and Nagaland, eventually saw most of the active hostilities in the war.[6] Many fled the densely populated cities of Rangoon, Colombo, and Singapore to the relative safety of India's villages and the "hill stations" in South India and Ceylon, including Kandy (which would eventually become the headquarters of the Southeast Asia Command), Kodaikanal, and Yercaud.

The occupation of Rangoon during the world war also posed another dilemma for migrants from India: to stay on in the city and wait until the war clouds passed over, or to go to India, leaving their lives and livelihoods behind. When the Japanese forces began their incursions into Burma in late 1941, moving troops by land into the Tenasserim and proceeding north from Thailand and Malaya, Aung San and Subash Chandra Bose had already made a case for the Japanese as liberators for Burma and India from British colonial rule. Bose's speeches, urging Indians to rally behind the cause of Azad Hind—independent India—were broadcast over radio across South and Southeast Asia. Many rushed to donate their labor and wealth to its cause. The Indian National Army had already received a warm reception in Malaya, Thailand, and Singapore, gaining volunteers in each place.[7] As historian John Solomon notes, migrants from India performed a version of "Indianness" that went beyond their regional identities—Tamil or Malayalee, for example—as a result of Bose and the presence of the Indian National Army.[8] Indian migrant families in Pegu and Tharrawady in Lower Burma helped them move further northward.[9] In each place, migrant families might have hoped these affiliations would help them survive, or they might have acted out of cautious optimism about a political future after the end of British rule.

Take the case of the Nattukottai Chettiars, who figure in chapters 2 and 3. Like members of other caste-based trading diasporas from British India who ventured beyond its borders, the Chettiars were migrant traders, moneylenders, and financiers who had set up offices in Burma, Malaya, and across Southeast Asia beginning in the nineteenth century. Their businesses and political fortunes alike were at risk during wartime; unlike traders and moneylenders who emigrated from British India to Uganda, Tanganyika, and Kenya, who remained prominent economic actors but marginal political figures there until independence, the Chettiars had acquired both significant economic and political capital in Burma, Ceylon, and Malaya from the beginning of the twentieth century.[10] During the war, they supported Bose's Indian National Army and its political wing, the Indian Independence League, contributing to the newly established Azad Hind Bank, which would fill the coffers and supply the financial needs of Bose's revolutionary army.[11] Indeed, the tale went around that, not least owing to their monetary support, the Japanese military administration had appointed a Chettiar as "High Commissioner" in Malaya; so widespread was this belief that *Kumaran*, a Tamil periodical with a large readership among the Chettiars, took notice and implored its readers not to believe these rumors.[12] In Burma, the Chettiars' collective wealth, which amounted to millions of rupees, was at risk under Japanese occupation, and they (and many other Indian migrant families in Burma and Malaya) sought the protection that membership in the Japanese-allied Indian Independence League offered.[13] However, as these troops made their way northwards to Mandalay, hopes for a postimperial Burmese future dissolved in the turbulence of political infighting, disorganized troops, and lack of a map for the future of postwar South and Southeast Asia. Like other migrant communities, many Chettiar firms—or so goes the popular understanding—closed shop and fled to India.

A RETREAT FROM RANGOON

On the eve of the Japanese occupation of Rangoon, the British governor-general of Burma, Reginald Dorman-Smith, boarded one of the last airplanes to fly out of the Myitkyina airport in northern Burma. The Government of Burma that he headed had already gone into exile in Shimla. When Dorman-Smith left, wealthy Rangoon families had already been evacuating on steamships via Chittagong, Calcutta, and Madras for weeks, ever since the first air attacks on Rangoon in December 1941. Most of Burma's migrant laborers and traders were forced to flee on foot, unaided and with little relief along the treacherous way (figure 1.1).[14]

The "long march" out of Burma has been the subject of academic and popular histories, military memoirs, and autobiographies.[15] People walked through the Bengal–Burma borderlands in the Arakan Valley to Chittagong, a port city and Allied military base in East Bengal, and to other places of relative safety in present-day Assam and Manipur in northeastern India. Official relief was not available until they had crossed over to India from Burma, beyond the reach of the Japanese troops and airplanes on the Burmese side of the border. There was a widespread shortage of food and clean water, and malaria, cholera, and dysentery raged through the swelling masses wearily making their way over the Kachin Mountains through the Pangsau Pass. In a fictional rendering of the long march, the Assamese novelist Debendra Nath Acharya captures this spectacle of death and disease, describing the bloated bodies of those who perished lying unattended, now-worthless valuables strewn about the road in what

FIGURE 1.1: *Refugees flee along Prome Road. Imperial War Museum Collections.*

his translator Amit Baishya describes as a necropolis.[16] Those who survived the long march arrived in South India, where many of Rangoon's
migrant laborers had homes, drenched by the monsoons, emaciated, and
sickened.

In contrast to Acharya's rendering, most contemporary accounts—
recollections, memoirs, and oral histories of the long march and the flight
from the Japanese occupation were written by military personnel (British,
Indian, and American troops forced to retreat to British India) or by mis-
sionaries and middle-class families that lived in Burma when it was still
part of British India.[17] Each offers only a partial glimpse at the scale of
devastation. For instance, official accounts written up in the beginning
of wartime evacuations failed to capture the magnitude of death and destruction. According to an early report from R. H. Hutchings, the agent
of the Government of India in Rangoon, the evacuation from Burma was
"quiet" and "orderly," and only seven of those who attempted to reach India
by the land route died.[18] A short few years later, as with Acharya's fictional
rendering of the long march, a wildly different picture emerged: a cha-
otic, disastrous, and disorderly exit from Burma that left cities and towns
behind desolate and smoking, people's lives in shreds, and armed forces
battling for control on the northernmost shores of the Bay of Bengal. This
latter version is reflected in the memoir of one S. Devas, a longtime civil
servant in Burma who returned to Madras on foot. Devas filled his text
with vivid descriptions about the horrors of the "long march," removing
any illusions people about the deadly challenges that people had to face in
the Arakan Valley: "the home of malarial mosquitoes more deadly than
most, the haunt of leeches so fantastically innumerable as to have become
a legend, the stamping ground of typhus ticks, and the place of sneaking
winds which strike down the unwary with pneumonia."[19] People had left
almost everything behind—properties were looted, families separated,
children given up for dead.

Like Hutchings's report and unlike Devas's narrative, evacuation registers retained in the archives of colonial governments give only a fleeting glimpse of the laborers who fled Burma during the war. The registers
noted their occupations—coolie, sweeper, porter, scavenger, typist, tele-
phone operator.[20] Newspapers that managed to keep publishing during the

war contained scattered references to those whose livelihoods had suffered during the air attacks: Raman, who worked in a hotel on Fraser Street in Rangoon, whose workplace had been struck by an incendiary bomb; Suryanarayana Rao, who abandoned his efforts to hold on to his dyeing factory in Rangoon as business declined after the Japanese air attacks.[21] We have no further details of either Raman or Suryanarayana in the official archive. In March 1942, when the immediate threat of air raids had passed, Indian laborers who had fled Rangoon to villages and towns in Upper Burma or Assam cautiously returned to the city. The prospect of banditry, looting, theft, and breaking and entering loomed large, and rumors of the extreme cruelty of Japanese soldiers flew thick and fast, taking on a larger-than-life horror in the minds not only of the returnees but of those who had remained in Burma—and those who anxiously waited in India for news of family there.

In the same report that inaccurately described an orderly and quiet exit from Rangoon in February 1942, Hutchings noted that most of the work done in Rangoon was being done by Indian laborers.[22] Many migrant laborers were labeled "essential workers" and kept Rangoon functioning amid wartime devastation. Their employers housed the workers outside the city in camps during the night and ferried them across the river into the city for work during the daytime. It was their labor, as the Government of Burma observed from its exile in Shimla in British India, that kept trains, trams, and telegraphs functioning as usual, even during the worst of the air attacks on Rangoon in early 1942. But these differences between "migrants" who stayed and those who left would map uneasily onto perceptions of loyalty and disloyalty as questions of citizenship and political belonging were debated in the first years of Indian and Burmese independence.

With the destruction of Rangoon, as people embarked on the long march, two distinct colonial-era trading and travel routes—the first overland from Calcutta and Chittagong and the second by way of the sea from Madras and Vizagapatam—merged. The former route had been used for trading primarily by Marwari, Bengali, Afghani, and Multani migrants from North India and the latter by Tamil-, Telugu-, and Malayalam-speaking migrants from South India. With the destruction of Rangoon

Harbor closing off sea routes to the port of Chittagong in India, these two routes of travel and trade merged into one route for escape, carrying a silent, sickened stream of weary humanity northwards toward Mandalay and across the border to India, struggling to make it to relative safety.

AN ESCAPE THROUGH COLOMBO

When Burma and Malaya were occupied by the Japanese, India and Ceylon became places for transit and refuge for those fleeing the occupation. By February 1942, the wives and children of European civil servants in Hong Kong, Malaya, and Singapore, wearing gas masks and helmets, began to arrive in rescue ships in Colombo.[23] These arrivals, fleeing war and devastation, although not widely publicized, ended up making the front pages of the newspapers in Ceylon and added to the miasma of fearful anticipation that already hung in the air. As whispers of an impending attack on Ceylon began to circulate, many Indian migrants living there prepared to leave the island until the threat of war passed. Ceylon was considered a significant military asset, prized by both the Allied forces and the Japanese. From Japan's point of view, Ceylon—although not officially part of the imagined Greater Asia Co-Prosperity Sphere—an imagined community of Asian nations, ruled by Asian emperors, that stretched from Sakhalin to Bengal, covering Burma, Thailand, and the Straits Settlements—could help supply other Axis powers, particularly German allies in northern Africa and the Middle East. From the Allies' point of view, the island both supplied the bulk of their wartime rubber needs and was a critical strategic position, especially after the fall of Singapore and Allied possessions east of it. The island hosted military troops critical to the defense in the Indian Ocean. British war propaganda compared Colombo Harbor on the Indian Ocean with Pearl Harbor on the Pacific Ocean, confidently proclaiming that "the battle of the Indian Ocean" would be fought and won from Colombo.[24] They were not wrong about Ceylon's importance: no sooner did the Allied forces create the Ceylon War Council in March 1942 than Japanese forces attacked Colombo and Trincomalee from the air.[25] Although nearly fifty people died from the air raids, the Ceylon government claimed a victory, saying that the Japanese airplanes had been roundly defeated.[26] Owing to the heavy censorship of newspapers during the war, little detail was available; the *Civil and Military Gazette* simply noted that Colombo City was "completely unperturbed."[27] Yet after the attack, many people in Ceylon—both newly arrived evacuees from Hong Kong, Singapore, and Malaya and merchants, traders, and shopkeepers living in Colombo, who already frequently traveled across the Palk Strait to acquire goods or visit family—fled to India until the danger passed.

These wartime movements across the Palk Strait—a shallow body of water that separated the two colonies of India and Ceylon, a mere twenty-two miles at its narrowest point—were not facilitated by the British Indian government and were intended to be a temporary return to homes in coastal villages and towns along India's southeastern coast in Madras.[28] Over a tense few days in April 1942, the rail and ferry service from Talaimannar in northern Ceylon to Dhanushkodi in South India—the only rail link between the island and the mainland—had all but stopped, but people still rushed to the railway stations, hoping to get away to India (figure 1.2).[29] By April 1942, 33,408 evacuees from Ceylon had made their way to India,[30] with nearly 27,000 of them arriving in the ten days following the Colombo raid.[31] While they planned to return once the fear of air raids had passed, the *Times of Ceylon*, a Colombo-based newspaper, labeled them "runaway Indians" and claimed that they had refused service to their adopted homes in their hour of need.[32] As we will see in chapter 5, these early murmurs of discontent would culminate in calls to deny the citizenship of Ceylon to anyone of Indian origin that lived on the island.

On the other hand, laborers who were once recruited from South India to work on the tea, rubber, and coconut plantations in Ceylon and who had been settled on the island for decades did not—and could not—exercise this option of escaping across the Strait. Even before the war, many were deeply in debt to foremen, overseers, or managers on the plantations and could not afford to travel or risk being unemployed upon their return.[33] During the war, they feared that they would be unable to return to Ceylon if they left. These laborers—on the plantations but also beyond it—not only stayed, keeping Ceylon working during the war, but also contributed to the welfare funds for the troops—presumably hoping that it would be a sign of their loyalty to the British Empire.[34] Their demonstrations of

FIGURE 1.2: *Boarding the Dhanushkodi-Talaimannar ferry. Author's collection.*

loyalty too would go unnoticed in the context of postwar immigration and citizenship regimes.

The two British colonies of India and Ceylon were also places of transit for those fleeing wartime occupations in multiple places east of the island: Malaya, Singapore, Hong Kong, and the Dutch Indies and the Philippines. But according to estimates from the Government of India's Department of Indians Overseas, created in 1942 and headed by the lawyer-politician M. S. Aney, only 8,000 Indians had evacuated from Malaya and Singapore, with nearly 750,000 staying behind.[35] Commercial steamer and airplane services were halted during the war. Many of those who stayed behind in Malaya were forced to labor to construct and maintain the Burma-Siam railway—often referred to as the death railway—in service of Japanese imperial ambitions.[36] It was estimated that anywhere between 180,000 to 270,000 Asians—Indians, Chinese, Malays, Javanese, Burmese, and Thai—labored on the railway alongside Allied European prisoners of war.[37] For other Indians who remained in Malaya or Thailand during the war, their lives were marked in one way or the other by the successes and failures of the Azad Hind Fauj; as chapter 6 will show, for some these wartime affiliations would shape whether their lives would be lived out as loyal citizens or in exile in homes that they had never known.[38]

Because India and Ceylon were also places of transit, there is little evidence beyond these scattered figures, anecdotes, and recollections from Burma, Malaya, and Ceylon that would allow us to comprehensively estimate return Indian migration during the war. For example, there were no official estimates of the number of Indian migrants evacuated from the British colony of Hong Kong; they were likely recorded as being in transit through Ceylon. By 1942, only a small number of Indian migrants were living beyond the British Empire, in French Indochina or the Dutch East Indies; most had moved away during the years of economic depression in the 1930s.[39] Many of those who remained moved away from the occupied cities to smaller towns in the same colonies. A comprehensive account of wartime displacements or transits to India from present-day Southeast Asia is thus not feasible. To further complicate quantitative assessments of this kind, many migrants from India in Southeast Asia rushed to acquire proof of Indian nationality—such as passports, certificates, or permits—at the local high commissions so that they could be repatriated, and their numbers were likely submerged in the sea of others passing through the ports of Singapore or Colombo on their flight to Bombay, Karachi, or Madras. It is thus to Madras in 1942 and the unforeseen legal consequences of wartime displacement that the rest of the book now turns.

AN ARRIVAL IN MADRAS

In the first wave of the exodus in late 1941 following the first air raids in Rangoon, the Madras government reckoned that 15,808 out of an estimated 17,281 evacuees were from Burma. This was likely a severe underestimate.[40] Over time, the figure grew as it incorporated those fleeing Malaya and Ceylon, but Burma evacuees continued to make up a very high percentage of returning Indian migrants. As we saw, these evacuees first traveled through Chittagong and Calcutta. Reception committees and medical assistance for the evacuees were set up in Calcutta and Madras, funded and organized by local politicians and notables, including tea planters' associations in Assam. Many eventually arrived in South India—in Madras—

where they were taken to transit camps in Vizagapatam, which held mostly evacuees from Burma, or Malabar on Madras's opposite coast, which held evacuees from both Ceylon and Burma.[41]

Political leaders in India braced themselves to receive returning Indian migrants fleeing wartime occupation, but they had already expressed ambivalence about being dragged into another expensive imperial war. Some saw the war as likely to further India's agitation for independence: C. Rajagopalachari, the former premier of Madras, suggested that the war was "a blessing in disguise," an opportunity for Indians to rally together as one behind the cause of freedom.[42] In a memoir of the events of 1939 and 1940, Major Akbar Khan of the Royal Indian Army Supply Corps pointed to the war as an opportunity for Indian citizens to develop solidarity and a sense of strong national pride: "If we are determined, as the people of London were determined in 1940, that nothing would make us leave our homes short of military necessity, our cities will be saved as London was saved."[43] But as the wartime displacements took place, optimism appeared to have been misplaced. Instead, pessimism and anger were dominant moods. In a press statement released after his tour of Assam, which he undertook to examine evacuation routes, Jawaharlal Nehru, the leader of the Indian National Congress at the time and soon to be the first prime minister of independent India, savaged the response of the colonial government to the crisis: "Officials have not covered themselves in glory in this work of evacuation. They have shown inefficiency and partiality, and the sooner they realize that others can function better, the nearer shall we be to a solution to this problem."[44] The political mood in India thus ranged from optimism at the beginning of the war to despair as wartime displacements steadily escalated.

The Government of India issued administrative orders designating those who had fled Burma as "evacuees"—a category that qualified them for relief and rehabilitation efforts. An "evacuee" was defined as someone who arrived in India after December 8, 1941, either having left territory to the east of India "in consequence of military operations" or having been interrupted in transit to any territory east of India because of ongoing military operations.[45] Evacuees had to register their arrival at the nearest magistrate, police station, or political office and were fined a hundred rupees if they did not do so. At the time of registration, evacuees also had to fill out a questionnaire that asked for details about the nature of their employment in Burma, Malaya, Sumatra, Hong Kong, or elsewhere, the quantum of wealth that they had amassed, and whether they were in a "fit" state to return to the employment that they had had. This information was critical because it would determine who would receive relief and rehabilitation. Aney and the Department of Indians Overseas tasked provincial governments like Madras with being at the forefront of carrying out relief and rehabilitation efforts for evacuees. A Central Refugee Employment Bureau was set up in four zones across India—including over twenty-five registration offices opened in Madras alone, more than in any other Indian province—to deal with employment for evacuees from Burma and Malaya.[46] "Able-bodied Burma evacuees" were sent to work in labor camps in Orissa and Vizagapatam, rebuilding new ports and airfields on the Andhra coast, which had been hit by the Japanese air raids.[47] The Government of Madras also periodically disbursed funds to applicants. Some applied for funds to set up vegetable shops, others for sewing machines; in the archival files of the Madras government from this time period, the list of wants and needs submitted is long and varied.[48] But these initiatives did not have the intended effect. It was difficult for evacuees to navigate district-level bureaucracy for relatively low sums, compared with what they had received as wages in Burma.[49] This dissuaded many from making the effort for so little return.[50] Nevertheless, these relief and rehabilitation efforts allowed most evacuees to eke out a living while they waited for the war to end, allowing them to return to their homes and places of work across the Indian Ocean.

For the Burma "evacuees" in India, it would have appeared to be a long wait, one during which it would have been unclear whether they would ever be able to return home. Allied military efforts to recapture Burma began in 1943, and the Allies were eventually able to recapture Rangoon after Japanese forces withdrew to Thailand and Malaya. British airplanes cautiously scanned the ground below for signs of the enemy, and the prisoners of war left behind in Rangoon by retreating Japanese forces frantically gestured to the reconnaissance pilots that all was well; the city was free from Japanese occupation. It was the beginning of a new chapter in Burma's history.[51] Following the horrific atomic bombing of Hiroshima and Nagasaki by American forces, Japanese forces surrendered to Allied forces, signaling the formal end of the war. The headlines of the *Straits Times*, a progovernment newspaper in Singapore, on September 7, 1945, screamed: "Singapore is British again!" and these waves of excitement rippled through other British colonies in Asia. But there would be no return to the imperial past, and things would not go back to how they were.

ABANDONED AGREEMENTS

The jubilation that marked the end of the war quickly dissipated, both for those who had fled Burma, Ceylon, Malaya, and elsewhere in Southeast Asia and for those who had stayed. In the aftermath of the war, new borders—not only geographic but also juridical—emerged. While the idea of juridical borders was not new, it gained traction and became further entrenched in people's lives.

In the years leading up to the war, resentment against foreigners in Burma and Ceylon had already been rising. In 1938, shops and businesses in the Sooratee Baazar in Rangoon were destroyed in a wave of violence that rippled out from Rangoon to the surrounding districts. The violence that ensued echoed that of the Hsaya San rebellion in Burma in 1930—both sets of riots sought to enforce a sharp distinction between residents of Indian origin or ancestry and indigenous Burmans.[52] Viewed as a test case for the new constitution of Burma, set up soon after its separation from India in 1935, the response to this violence in 1938 had distressing political implications for the long-term peace of the new colony. The British government in Burma set up the Riot Inquiry Commission, made up of lawyers and headed by Justice H. B. L. Braund. The Braund Commission recommended that India and Burma sign an agreement laying out the terms on which immigration should take place between the two colonies—a recommendation that seemed to implicitly endorse the idea that migration was at the center of law-and-order problems in Burma.

Indeed, just before the war, the Governments of Burma and Ceylon set up commissions to inquire into the impact of Indian immigration on their economies. The Jackson Commission had been set up in October 1936 to look into immigration to Ceylon from India, exploring whether migrants from India would cause "economic injury" to the island's "permanent" population;[53] the Baxter Commission in Burma, appointed in July 1939, inquired into whether Indian immigration to Burma had displaced Burmans from gainful employment.[54] Although both commissions concluded that Indian immigration was no threat to the economy in either Burma or Ceylon (a finding that helpfully aligned with the motives of business and commercial interests in both places), public sentiment had by then already turned decisively against "outsiders." The conflict over the economic impact of Indian labor, which had deepened after the constitutional separation of India and Burma in 1937, set the stage for juridical borders to be put in place. These borders began to firm up in 1940, when both India and Burma passed Registration of Foreigners Acts. These acts revived older methods of regulating travel and residence for colonial subjects, mandating that foreigners register with the local police station upon arrival. Although India and Burma exempted each other's nationals from registering in this manner, the threat of paperwork barriers hung over the relationship. On the eve of the war, in 1939, the immigration negotiations that the Braund Commission had recommended collapsed.

At the height of the tensions of the war in 1941 and 1942, the Government of India again attempted to negotiate immigration agreements with Burma and Ceylon. An India-Burma agreement was signed in 1941 by diplomat and civil servant Girija Shankar Bajpai on behalf of India and by the prime minister U Saw for Burma. Bajpai was no stranger to diplomatic negotiations involving migrant Indians, for he had served as secretary to the seasoned diplomat V. S. Srinivasa Sastri, who led the campaign for the rights of Indians in South Africa.[55] U Saw too was a senior politician and the leader of the Myochit Party, who had become prime minister of Burma after overthrowing the flamboyant Ba Maw, the Burmese premier during the years of wartime occupation.[56] The agreement was heavily criticized, particularly in Indian business circles, for conceding their interests. A similar immigration agreement was being considered by Ceylon and India when the war broke out and put a stop to negotiations. While the representatives of governments in India and Ceylon recognized the need for relative mobility around the eastern Indian Ocean, proposing a common identity certificate (something like a nationality certificate) for people traveling between places on the coasts of the eastern Indian Ocean, both agreements also crucially added an expanded set of administrative barriers to migration and circulation: they added different classes of permits for stays of different proposed lengths, as well as certificates, examinations, and stamps, as we will explore further in chapters 4 and 5.[57]

With the Japanese attacks, both these agreements—one signed, the other proposed—were all but abandoned. After the war ended, they were revived, but any discussion on immigration was complicated by the scale of wartime displacements across South and Southeast Asia and the many administrative categories fashioned to capture the wartime experiences of former migrants. For example, prior to the war, although it was part of the British Empire, Burma attempted, in the wake of the constitutional separation from India in 1935, to disaggregate its economy from India's. However, the two countries still shared a land border of over a thousand miles, and many borderland dwellers—between Chittagong and Arakan, for example—engaged in cross-border trade. The question of cross-border mobility was thus uppermost in people's minds, and the use of the term *immigration* to include long-standing cross-border mobility was ubiquitous: for example, by 1946, a tract by B. R. Pearn, professor of history at Rangoon University, began with the sentence "Immigration from India to Burma is by no means a recent phenomenon." With the equation of mobilities in South and Southeast Asia with "immigration," the terms of the debate had been set. By May 1946, only about 140,000 and 246,000 Indians displaced by wartime occupation had returned to Burma, less than one-fifth of the Indian population of Rangoon before the war.[58] Eventually, the government in Burma revoked the exemption from foreigners' registration, and those of Indian and Chinese ancestry rushed to register themselves as "foreigners," because only residents so designated could send remittances back to their countries of origin, where their families often remained. After independence, when the question of citizenship occupied political centerstage, this prompted deportations and a slew of cases before the law courts in Rangoon.

POSTWAR RETURNS

In the first five years after the war ended, political configurations and federations that did not fit the typical model of modern nation-states and
that had once seemed a possibility in South and Southeast Asia began to
fade away. There was no Greater East Asia Co-Prosperity Sphere headed
by an Asian imperial power, as Japan had once proposed.[59] K. M. Panikkar, the Indian diplomat, historian, and lawyer, proposed a "triune Commonwealth" of India, Pakistan, and Burma, but this appeared to be well
beyond the realm of possibility as tensions escalated between India and
Pakistan over the Partition.[60]

Instead, as colonial governments that had gone into exile during the
war returned to power, they confronted the demand for independence
from national movements. During the provincial elections in India in
1946, the partition of the subcontinent into India and Pakistan was already
part of the political discourse; it came to fruition in the space of a few short
months in 1947. By the time the interim Indian government was formed
in 1947 with Jawaharlal Nehru as prime minister, twelve million people
had died in the bloody violence that accompanied the territorial partition
of India and Pakistan, and twenty million more had been displaced from
their homes in the Punjab, Bengal, and Assam—the only homes they had
ever known. On August 14, 1947, Pakistan, led by Mohammed Ali Jinnah,
officially celebrated its independence; the day after—August 15—was India's Independence Day. Burma and Ceylon too won independence in
1948; they too held elections for new national governments, with U Nu becoming the leader of the Anti-Fascist People's Freedom League (AFPFL)
and the prime minister, following the brutal assassination of Aung San,
and D. S. Senanayake of the United National Party becoming the first
prime minister of Ceylon.[61] Across the Bay of Bengal, in the former Straits
Settlements (including Malaya and Singapore) and the Netherlands East
Indies, British military administrations took over from the Japanese,
promising a return to imperial order and relative peace. However, as historians Chris Bayly and Tim Harper show, this peace was fragile, and
the years that followed the end of the Second World War would feature a
string of broken promises, ethnic conflict, and civil war.[62]

During this period of decolonization, the question of citizenship was left to the former colonies themselves. This period in 1947–48 saw intense and rapid legislative activity, as the newly created countries (India, Pakistan, Burma, and Ceylon) elected new governments and laid down requirements for national citizenship. Constituent assemblies were elected in India and Pakistan to draft and debate new constitutions; in Ceylon, the Soulbury Commission discussed the terms on which the Dominion would be established; the Union of Burma's constitution was ratified amid the tensions of a civil war between the majority Burman and minority Karen and Shan States. None of the interim constitutional provisions recognized dual nationality, and migration and mobility across these borders were rendered suspect because of war and partition. Even in other British colonies in Southeast Asia that did not face the question of national citizenship just yet—in Malaya, for example, which would not gain independence (as Malaysia) until 1957—the question of citizenship and form of government was fraught because of tensions between indigenous Malays and those who were of Indian and Chinese ancestry, considered to be "alien." The question of citizenship as legal status was caught in the crosswinds of constitutional protections, ethnic and religious affiliations, and the politics of indigeneity, which would trace back, in unexpected ways, as this book will show, to wartime displacements.

After the end of the war, the Burma Indian Congress, which represented Indian interests, reintroduced the intertwined questions of migration and citizenship. The official response was often not encouraging. Soon after S. A. S. Tyabji took on the role of adviser on Indian affairs, the Immigration (Temporary Provisions) Act of 1946 was enacted in Burma. The act seemingly accommodated for wartime displacements; it redefined the "immigrant" category to include "evacuees" and "refugees," but it placed longtime residents of Indian ancestry in Burma at the risk of being ineligible for Burmese citizenship. Tyabji was caustic in his response memo to the act. He noted that the overhaul of the immigration regime in Burma creating multiple routes to enter and exit the country was sweeping and asked, "Why not directly amend the [Burma] Passport Act?" Tyabji's response, which centered on changes to passport regimes, belied an uneasy slippage of travel documents into identity documents. But most migrants, awaiting a resolution on the citizenship question in India, did not register as citizens in either place. For these noncitizens ineligible for passports, a two-track system of residence permits was reintroduced: an "A" permit for long-term stays and a "B" permit authorizing the holder for a temporary stay. As we will see in chapter 5, similar provisions appeared in legislation around citizenship by registration in Ceylon.

Far from the heated political and diplomatic negotiations in Delhi, Rangoon, or London, laborers who had evacuated from Rangoon during the war lined up before the offices of tahsildars or magistrates, waiting for certificates allowing them to return to Burma.[63] To accommodate the demand, special magistrates were appointed in the districts of Vizagapatam, East Godavari, Ganjam, Chittagong, Ramnad, and Malabar—districts that many of these laborers migrated from.[64] By 1947, Madras alone had housed more than sixty-seven thousand evacuees, about forty-seven thousand in Vizagapatanam and around twenty thousand in Ramnad.[65] The process of getting the certificates of return was based on labor needs: when Burma needed more labor, it would notify the Government of India, and the requisite numbers of laborers would be issued embarkation notices, leaving camps in Madras City and Vizagapatam to board ships back to Burma. All of the evacuees chosen for these certificates of return were to have an economic reason to return; the government memo detailing these requirements noted that "carpetbaggers" with no "genuine roots" in Burma were to be refused entry at all costs.[66] During this period, Burma sought to reduce its need for migrant laborers from India, bringing agricultural land under state control, nationalizing inland water transport services, and drastically reducing the number of rickshaw puller licenses, industries that had relied on Indian labor in the prewar period. The certificates of return and identity cards were intended to be based on the results of a 1943 evacuee census—recall that the definition of an "evacuee" was shaped by wartime exigencies and the questionnaires that returnees filled out—but the results of this census were in fact unavailable to many magistrates to cross-check against applications.

If this appears to be labyrinthine and haphazard, it is because it was. The complexity of the system that governed the return of Indian laborers shocked U Tun Nyoe, the controller of immigration for the Government of Burma, who in June 1946 had toured the various ports of embarkation

in India—Madras, Vizagapatam, Calcutta, and Chittagong, the gateways
to the sea route back to Burma—and filed a blistering report with the
Government of Burma. He found that in the absence of immigration legislation, a complicated system of immigration controls had sprung up—a
system that he claimed was unfair and unsatisfactory. Despite the Government of India's assurance that evacuee identity certificates would be
acceptable documentation for repatriation, the reality in Vizagapatam was
completely different. Indian "evacuees" were to be given priority for repatriation, but several recruiting agents for public bodies like the Rangoon
Corporation freely recruited labor from "nonevacuees" for the types of
manual work—sweeping and scavenging—usually performed by migrant
laborers from South India in Burma. A plethora of passes, identity certificates, and permits were issued without any coordination. While U Tun
Nyoe's report was being filed to the Government of Burma, N. G. Ranga,
member of the Indian Legislative Assembly and chairman of the Andhra
Provincial Congress Committee, where Vizagapatam was located, also
criticized the government for allowing Indians to return to Burma and
Malaya with no assurance of adequate wages and living conditions.[67]

This system of border controls and paper barriers had implications for
cross-border mobility across land borders too. The Partition had divided
the eastern Indian province of Bengal, which bordered Burma. Traders
in Burma who wanted to return to India were stranded when routes to
India closed. They petitioned the Government of Burma for permission
to return. For example, Mulki Ram, a rice mill owner, wanted to return
to India to get spare parts that he had been unable to get during wartime,
and Gulam Hosari Shvazee in Bhamo, a busy trading town on the border
with China's Yunnan province, wrote to the deputy commissioner that he
had to return to buy goods for his cloth shop. According to Shvazee, he
had been a prisoner for two years and had lost goods worth 16,000 rupees,
and now that the war was over, he wanted to restock his shop. In 1946,
when these letters were written, it was not clear what documents or permissions were required to go back and forth between India and Burma—
note the passports and permits system on the one hand, and the petitions
that borderland dwellers requested.[68] When Ahmadullah, the headman of
a village in Sagaing who had hosted over a thousand evacuees on his land

in 1942, wrote for permission to take his wife and elderly family members to India for medical treatment, he asked for a "permit" to return to Burma, and traders like Mulki Ram and Gulam Hosari Shvazee were issued certificates (or sometimes "identity passes," the authority of which was unclear at best) instead of official passports. It reveals the scale of interruptions, not only geographic but also juridical borders, brought about by war, military occupation, partition, and postwar reconstruction in the daily lives of ordinary people.

These postwar return migrations—from Burma to India, from India to Burma—continued into the twilight days of formal British rule in 1948, and the uncertainty and chaos surrounding mobility regimes elicited the sympathy of even the intelligence officers stationed at the Rangoon port. Noting how refugees left for India with their meager possessions and "rolling tears," one of the officers noted that the laborers' inability to read made these regulations even more opaque, and a difficult journey even worse. Authorities seized gold ornaments from passengers boarding steamships for Calcutta and Madras, and in the absence of certificates and permits from the collector of Customs or the controller of foreign Affairs, gold rings, chains, and bangles were seized from women, who were simply handed a paper receipt in exchange, as if it were an official transaction. Officials were able to identify the problem: men of means were aware of the (nascent) restrictions on personal possessions, and "illiterate" laborers were not. The proposed solution—to publish notices in vernacular newspapers—was thus no solution at all, for it would not have helped them understand their rights.[69]

As these myriad postwar schemes for migration and citizenship indicate, the category of "migrant" in mid-twentieth-century South and Southeast Asia was in flux, caught up in multiple national and regional political projects, and could be deployed not only to indicate mobility but also to restrict travel, movement, and residence. The category of "migrant" slipped uneasily into the constitutional frameworks that included "minorities," which migrant communities from India potentially were. It is also likely that many people who crossed borders on land and across oceans did not describe themselves as "migrants." However, as war, partition, and reconstruction revived political interest in the place of migrant labor and capital, it became clear to ordinary people that rebuilding their lives was contingent on describing oneself in terms of these administrative categories, as an "immigrant," an "evacuee," or a "refugee."

Nor was the category of "returnee" or "repatriate" free of judgment; the taint of wartime collaboration marked those who returned to India. This question of collaboration was dominant as war crimes trials began to unfold; in Delhi, the trials of the Indian National Army officers Shah Nawaz Khan, Prem Kumar Sahgal, and Gurbaksh Singh Dhillon on charges of treason against the Government of India before a British military court commanded national attention.[70] Public sentiment in India, backed by the Indian National Congress, was not in favor of the trials, and Prime Minister Nehru and John Thivy, the agent of the Government of India in Malaya, had worked behind the scenes to ensure that a suitable defense was ready. With India on the eve of independence, anticolonial insurrections repeatedly flaring up, and Indian Army troops landing in Southeast Asia to quell the increasing unrest, the question of loyalty seemed particularly important.[71] Indian civilians returning from Burma and Malaya faced a further obstacle. They were marked as "gray" or "black," depending on whether intelligence agencies believed that they had come under the influence of or "collaborated" with the Japanese occupation—a charge that was also levied against those who had supported Bose's Indian National Army, such as Khan, Sehgal, and Dhillon. Even as the very public treason trial unfolded in Delhi, thousands of Indians were being repatriated from Malaya and subjected to extensive surveillance.[72]

This period's complexities around nationalities and loyalties are clear in the story of G. V. Panicker, a journalist who worked for *The Indian*, the official newspaper of the Central Indian Association of Malaya, which preceded the Malayan Indian Congress as the major representative of Indian interests. Ahead of Panicker's return to India, the British Military Administration's Malayan Security Service sent intelligence about him to his hometown in Travancore, noting that he had worked for the Japanese Domei and for the newspaper services of the Provisional Government of Free India that Bose had inaugurated in Singapore in 1943; this intelligence put the police on notice about potential conflicts of loyalty.[73] Like Panicker, other repatriating Indian citizens were interrogated upon arrival in India from Burma and Malaya and were restricted to their villages or towns for two months to comply with India's 1944 Restriction and Detention Ordinance, an ordinance or temporary legislative measure promulgated by the governor to allow persons suspected to be acting prejudicially toward the interests of India to be detained without trial.[74] The detention of returnees like Panicker under the 1944 Ordinance was a prelude to preventive detention laws in the guise of "public safety" or "public order" laws that were passed in India following independence. Like Panicker, postwar returnees could suddenly find themselves detained upon arrival in India on the grounds of suspicion alone, continuing the legacy of wartime emergency laws. Although in 1946 most prosecutions relating to the former Indian National Army members were dropped, membership in the Indian Independence League, the Indian National Army, or any allied organization gave rise, in the initial years of independence, to the presumption of guilt by association. On the opposite shores of the Bay, these affiliations also caused anxieties for those who wished to stay on in Malaya after the war ended but were perceived to have divided loyalties.

These postwar migrations and returns around the Bay of Bengal took place in the shadow of—and because of—new borders, catalyzed by wartime exigencies. Some might have had access to the citizenship of the Federation of Malaya, first proposed in 1948, if they had been born to immigrant parents from India within the territory of the former Straits Settlements.[75] Since Malaya was still under British rule in 1948, others might have embarked on the journey from India, hoping to eventually naturalize as British citizens. But by 1949, Indian passport-issuing authorities received word that Malaya would strictly enforce the 1919 Sea Passengers Ordinance, which allowed those landing without an "assured income" to be turned away. These paperwork barriers, under new and revived immigration regimes, proliferated. In 1950, Burma too enacted new passport regulations. Tyabji's irritated comment on the immigration agreement between India and Burma appeared to come to fruition. Beginning in 1951, the older immigration permits and evacuee identity certificates became invalid, and foreigners, including Indians, required a valid passport and visa to enter Burma. Reviving the distinction between citizens and foreigners that had marked prewar negotiations on immigration, those staying more than ten days had to register at the Foreigners' Registration Office in Rangoon, and exit permits had to be secured from the local police station; the permits had to be surrendered when leaving Burma.[76]

Political leaders in Burma, Ceylon, and Malaya took advantage of the postwar chaos and uncertainty to revive the question of migration from India. These groups had long portrayed migrant laborers, traders, and financiers as outsiders stealing jobs, market shares, and land, charges that the British-led governments in Ceylon and Malaya had sought to address through the Baxter and Jackson Commissions. As negotiations over immigration failed and wartime occupations displaced hundreds of thousands of migrants, these politicians campaigned to make permanent the temporary return migrations occasioned by the Japanese occupation with the help of juridical borders. These juridical borders did not only take the form of citizenship as legal status, as political and diplomatic negotiations tend to indicate. Instead, as the chapters that follow will show, governments used an array of tactics—rigid control of remittances, harsh taxation regimes, rapid nationalization of agricultural land, unclear standards of proof for identity papers—to make migration, citizenship, and decolonization irrevocably bound up with each other. Nationality and citizenship regimes already shaped by differing timelines for decolonization in South and Southeast Asia offered no clear answers to the dilemmas faced by migrants who went back and forth between the two regions. These ambiguities forced former migrants to navigate taxation, immigration, and detention regimes, charting new courses within meandering bureaucracies and confronting paperwork barriers, setting in motion legal processes that would last for decades. In these disputes, officials frequently questioned why migrants fled and where they sought refuge in 1942; as we will see, wartime displacement was regarded with suspicion, reframed as disloyalty and abandonment of their adopted homes and places of work. In response, before courts and commissions, people narrated personal and family histories in the shape of claims to jurisdiction. It is to this vast, relatively unexplored sea of legal papers—afloat and adrift from Madras—that this book now turns.

TWO

BANANA MONEY

IN 1945, AFTER THE war ended, Seethalakshmi Achi, the widow of a
Nattukottai Chettiar moneylender whose firm had operations in Madras
and Burma, filed a debt recovery case before the district court in Devakkottai in Madras.[1] The substance of the case was this: Seethalakshmi's
husband, Meyappan Chettiar, had borrowed from another Rangoon-based
firm, owned by Veerappa Chettiar. When Burma was under Japanese occupation in 1944, Meyappan Chettiar's agent who transacted on his behalf
had reportedly made several repayments toward the loan to Veerappa
Chettiar's agent. However, a year later, Veerappa Chettiar successfully
sued Meyappan Chettiar in Madras, alleging that these payments were
never made. Seethalakshmi Achi, Meyappan Chettiar's legal representative, appealed the decision before the Madras High Court. The litigation
dragged on for six years, from 1945 to 1951. It brought up questions about
the validity of the Japanese wartime currency in which Veerappa Chettiar had repaid the debt, as well as the broader legal issue of the status of
the contracts between Chettiar firms in India and their agents in Burma.
These agents and their principals were pushed to opposing sides in the war,
putting the validity of the contract of agency between them into question.
In international law, these legal issues were framed as being about the

54

nature of wartime occupation and the implications of the legal status of "enemy alien" for Indians who remained in Burma during the war.[2] This seemingly unimportant debt recovery case gestured to the difficulties that Indian migrants faced in reviving capital, credit, and money circulations in the wake of the postwar economic collapse in South and Southeast Asia.

Traders, financiers, and businessmen were eager to return to Burma from India at the end of the war. But as the British military administration and later the elected Burmese government formulated plans for postwar reconstruction, they encountered a swift backlash of nationalist sentiment directed at returning "foreign" capital. As noted in chapter 1, these sentiments had been on the rise since the 1930s. Those in debt to Chettiar moneylenders, who had borrowed money and extended land as collateral, found themselves dispossessed when they defaulted on payments. Alongside the rising resentment against Chettiar moneylenders, the dominance of migrant laborers from India in Rangoon's industries—from the harbor to the timber mills—was also a cause for concern. It was therefore not surprising that public sentiment went against the return of foreigners to Burma after the war. As chapter 1 showed, governments imposed rigid requirements on people attempting to access citizenship in Burma and on the associated rights of travel, movement, and residence across new national borders. But these claims to citizenship began, not with declarations of political loyalties, but with jurisdictional claims in cases like Seethalakshmi Achi's. This chapter begins with debt recovery cases and the legal issues around "banana money" and then looks at how the situation was further complicated by restrictions on migrant remittances and property transfer by "foreigners." These measures solidified jurisdictional borders between India and Burma. This latter set of financial restrictions began to have a profound and immediate impact on the daily lives of traders, financiers, and moneylenders like the Nattukottai Chettiars, for whom the first years of decolonization and political independence were marked by litigation over them. In response, moneylenders approached courts in Madras, not Rangoon. The outcome of their legal cases had rippling effects on the life of other migrant communities in Burma as well.

(IL)LEGAL TENDER

Wartime displacements complicated an already fraught financial relationship between India and Burma; Burma's separation from India and its constitution as a separate Crown colony between 1935 and 1937 had made the circulation of credit and capital between the two colonies more expensive than previously. On the eve of the war, under the Upper Burma Land and Revenue Regulations, the Nattukottai Chettiars' Association in Rangoon was also engaged in negotiations with the British Burma government over resumption of nearly four hundred acres of *ayadaw* (Crown) lands that had come into their possession as a result of foreclosed mortgages, one of many different ways in which their capital had become tied up in land instead of freely circulating.[3] Faced with these already dwindling circulations, many left Burma with their wealth or savings during the war. This was portrayed in newspapers in Burma as the flight of "refugee capital" and, after the war ended, was leveled as a charge of political disloyalty against displaced traders, financiers, and moneylenders in the context of legal cases. In response, they claimed that their wealth had been destroyed by the changes in currency in circulation, giving rise to a set of legal issues around what came to be known as "banana money."

"Banana money" was a moniker for the currency or military scrip circulated by the occupation government in Malaya. Currency notes were stamped with the image of banana plants to evoke the country's tropical landscape—hence, "banana money" (figure 2.1); similarly, in Burma, such notes featured images of pagodas. When the war ended, business communities like the Chettiars in Burma and Malaya realized, as Seethalakshmi Achi did, that because of the galloping inflation during the war, "banana money" was worthless and that debts repaid to them in "banana money" were invalid. This set legal disputes in motion, affecting a world of commercial transactions beyond debt recoveries, including property transactions, land ownership, and migrant remittances, and threatening the stability of postwar economies.

In May 1942, the occupation-backed government in Burma, headed by lawyer-politician Ba Maw, issued the Burma Monetary Arrangements Ordinance, which replaced the British Burmese rupee with the Burmese kyat, equal to a hundred cents—on par with other currencies in the pro-

FIGURE 2.1: *Japanese occupation currency in Malaya. CC BY 2.0.*

posed Greater East Asia Co-Prosperity Sphere. Initially, both the rupee and the kyat were in circulation. But those using the British-issued rupee instead of the occupation's military scrip were suspected of being spies and faced the possibility of retribution; the rupee gradually dropped out of circulation.[4] By 1943, almost all transactions in Burma were carried out in occupation currency rather than in the old British Burmese rupee.[5] Between 1940 and 1943, nearly 310 million occupation rupees had been printed and circulated, compared to a circulation of 335 million British Burmese rupees before the war began.[6] It would become one of the most consequential decisions made by the occupation government in Burma.

This wartime decision transformed everyday economic transactions. The occupation governments pumped money into the economy.[7] Indeed, the noted scholar and diplomat Maung Maung wrote of this time that laborers were paid in currency notes that were freshly printed on portable presses, the paper still wet with ink. These changes to the legal tender took place within an economy that was rapidly collapsing: in the face of imminent enemy occupation, the retreating British forces had adopted a "scorched earth" policy, destroying bridges, boats, and timber mills. Transport and communications systems broke down almost entirely. Without railway networks, rice could not be transported from Lower to Upper Burma. At the same time, the devastation of Rangoon Harbor meant that no exports were made to Ceylon, India, or Europe. Burma and its biggest export markets were arraigned on opposite sides of the war. Paddy fields grew into jungles as prices for rice on the world market crashed. Traders, financiers, and moneylenders—many of whom owned or were invested in mines, timber mills, or plantations—faced seemingly unsurmountable challenges.

Similar events were under way in Malaya under Japanese occupation. Rubber plantations and tin mines stopped yielding much-needed tax revenue. As Maung Maung noted in the case of Burma, migrant laborers, both Indian and Chinese, who stayed on the plantations in Malaya were also paid in "banana money"; they likely accepted these notes because, by contrast, those forced to toil to build the "death railway" from Bangkok to Moulmein were not paid at all and faced the risk of certain death.[8] Prices for everyday goods soared: a loaf of bread cost eight dollars, a single banana was forty cents.[9] Hoarding, profiteering, and black-marketing thrived. As the occupation economy showed ominous signs of decline and collapse, the value of its currency—banana money—dropped like a stone in the sea.

To add to the confusion, three of the four currencies in circulation during the war in Burma were identical in appearance to the Indian rupee, making it impossible to detect or demonetize during the war.[10] Neither the Burmese government in exile in India nor the Colonial Office in London seemed to know how much circulating British currency remained, for in the chaos of an impending military occupation, many officials had not signed off on certificates attesting to the destruction of currency.[11] By comparison and to give a rough estimate of the economic impact, according to historian Paul Kratoska, the records of the Selangor administration in Malaya that survived from the war indicate that nearly $104 million worth of stock was destroyed and almost $4 million worth of valuables went to Australia for safekeeping.[12] From Singapore, stock was also destroyed, and nearly $39 million was shipped to India.[13] In Burma, this confusion over currency gave rise to propaganda-fueled rumors that "refugees" fleeing to India from the Japanese invasion were not really refugees but speculators planning to cash in their "Burma notes."[14] Currency speculation was also a specter for the Burma government-in-exile in India, who feared that the Japanese occupiers would leverage it to reduce the economy's reliance on Chinese and Indian capital and replace them with Japanese commercial interests.[15] In the face of these dire economic prospects, the caricature of people fleeing across borders with enemy-issued money was a useful distraction from the chaos and confusion.

These multiple circulating currencies and galloping inflation deeply worried Chettiar firms with long-standing financial interests in both Burma and Malaya. According to Marilyn Longmuir, who studied the Burmese currencies in circulation between 1937 and 1947, Chettiar firms were especially "heavy users" of banknotes.[16] Partially because of Depression-era foreclosures in the 1930s, Chettiar firms owned paddy fields and timber mills in Burma and rubber plantations and tin mines in the Straits Settlements. The circulation of the Chettiars' credit and capital had already been hampered by legislative restrictions on moneylending in the aftermath of the global economic depression and forced foreclosures. It was now dealt a significant blow by wartime inflation and worthless currency.

These fears were transmitted back to Madras. Pamphlets in Tamil intended to circulate in Madras noted that during the war, migrants from South India in Burma were subjected to all manner of horrors and were forced to flee to India or hide out in the countryside, away from the plundering and looting in Rangoon, where many of the Chettiar firms were located. Although many fled Rangoon during the air raids, the pamphleteer observed that the retreat of the Chettiar agents was singled out in public discourse as *mudalali durokam* (treachery by proprietors). Chettiar agents who stayed were forced to transact in military scrip—recall the wartime transactions between Meyappan and Veerappa and their agents in Burma—and in response many firms converted their funds into gold to preserve value.[17] The Japanese occupation was thus believed to have obliterated the Chettiars' economic presence in Burma. Scholars also note that Chettiar firms in Malaya were forced to make voluntary contributions for the welfare of Japanese troops. Reportedly, the Nattukottai Chettiars' Association in Singapore alone donated as much as $100,000. Other Chettiar firms contributed to the cause of the Azad Hind Fauj and to the Azad Hind Bank, to the tune of nearly 20 million rupees;[18] Indeed, Umadevi Suppiah estimates that almost 17.5 percent of Chettiar revenue in Malaya during this time went into Indian National Army coffers;[19] overall, nearly 215 million rupees were contributed to the Azad Hind Bank, largely through the contributions of Indians in Southeast Asia in "banana money." More generally, as land and business owners, the Chettiar firms were forced to continue to pay property and real estate taxes, according to Kratoska, but were left with only Japanese currency to meet these expenses.[20] Across present-day Southeast Asia, the Japanese invasion froze the circulation of credit and capital that kept caste-based trade, capital, and credit networks like those of the Chettiars afloat.

In 1945, nearly 3 billion rupees in "banana money" was in circulation. These currency notes, now worthless, were often burnt in the streets. At the end of the war, wartime currencies were demonetized, and "banana money" was no longer legal tender.[21] The legality of transactions carried out and of debts repaid or incurred in "banana money"—as in Seethal-akshmi Achi and Veerappa Chettiar's case—was rendered suspect. Simul-taneously, restrictions on remittances and landholdings were put in place when U Nu's government came to power in Burma, through the Import Control Act and the Land Nationalization Act in 1947–48, bringing to fruition long-standing political interests. Although the 1948 Constitution of the Union of Burma invested the ownership of all property in the state, the details of a compensation scheme for former landowners were hazy.[22] New laws—along the lines of those enacted for Ceylon and Malaya in the 1930s—regulated moneylending and interest rates and added recourse for debtors against creditors in case they had defaulted on loans during the war. The possibility of defaulting on loans—the primary reason why land had passed into Chettiar hands in the first place—was almost eliminated through legislation. A network of state-controlled agricultural credit was proposed in order to eliminate Burma's dependence on Indian and Chi-nese capital, including the rural credit that the Chettiars had once ad-vanced. With the introduction of these measures, those who had hoarded "banana money" were left facing almost total ruin; those who fled to India, as we saw in the previous chapter, did not know when it would be possi-ble to return to reclaim any remaining wealth. But these restrictions did not go unchallenged. Against the collapsing postwar economy, leveraging their social and political capital, the Chettiars resorted, as they had in the prewar era, to every available legal remedy to secure their financial inter-ests in Burma and Malaya.

The legality of wartime transactions in "banana money" was so widely disputed that the British military administrations of Burma and Malaya considered creating special tribunals to deal with these disputes. In the end, however, the cases were rerouted to ordinary law courts.[23] It was in these ordinary district-level courts that cases like the one between Seethalakshmi Achi and Veerappa Chettiar, mentioned in the introduction to this chapter, took place. The demonetization of wartime currency in Burma, which had so profoundly affected cases like Seethalakshmi Achi's, itself had several twists and turns. In Rangoon, the High Court of Burma ruled in one of the earliest judicial discussions around this issue that Japanese occupation currency was not—and, crucially, never had been—legal tender. The judges ruled that it was only a medium of exchange, like a token. But given the extensive debtor-creditor relationships in Burma that had been conducted in occupation currency, this position was quickly recognized as unsustainable. In 1947, Burma's interim government enacted the Japanese Currency (Evaluation) Act, which specified the Burmese rupee equivalent value of the Japanese currency notes that had been legal tender between 1942 and 1945. This legislation stated that any debt that had been partly paid during the occupation, irrespective of whether the debt was incurred before or during the war, was to be repaid in accordance with a schedule that calculated equivalent value for wartime currency. It also decreed that no interest accrued during wartime, when there was likely to have been no communication between creditor and debtor.[24] This appeared to have resolved cases like that between Seethalakshmi Achi and Veerappa Chettiar.

Legislation like the Japanese Currency (Evaluation) Act of 1947 in Burma was enacted to blunt the effects of postwar demonetization. It created a sliding scale, noting the equivalent value of "banana money," which could be used for repaying debts. However, it was but a poor stop-gap measure, for in the absence of a clear sense of how specific contracts were concluded during the war, a scale for repayment was not useful.[25] U Tun Wai, an economist from Rangoon and a graduate student at Yale University at the time (who would go on to work with the United Nations Economic Commission for Asia and the Far East), carried out an audit of the banking and currency facilities in postwar Burma and published a contemporary account. He noted that the schedule appended to the Burma legislation did not reflect the actual levels of inflation during the war and that there was too much money in circulation and only a crumbling remnant of an administrative structure in place to regulate and enforce the bill's provisions.[26] The rates of litigation around these laws soared as people approached courts to try and recover their prewar wealth. The legislative measures thus did not address the problems they were written to address; indeed, they created new ones. Since the Chettiars in Burma were "heavy users" of "banana money," it appeared that their wealth was all but wiped out.

CREDIT AND CITIZENSHIP

The legislative measures to decide the fate of "banana money" were one of many weak efforts at postwar economic reconstruction that spluttered and went under in the stormy seas of postwar Burma, prompting litigation like Seethalakshmi Achi's before the Madras High Court. In 1947, on the eve of Burmese independence, the Anti-Fascist People's Freedom League (AFPFL), led by Aung San, the Socialists, and the Burma Communist Party, once a coalition and now splintered, was battling to take over from the British. Soon after the votes in the first elections to the Constituent Assembly were counted and it was announced that the AFPFL had acquired 171 out of 182 seats, Aung San and four of his ministers were brutally gunned down in Rangoon. In the same year, on the India-Burma borderlands, government forces clashed with Karenni militia who were unhappy with their integration into a state dominated by the majority Bamar.[27] Even after these storms appeared to blow over, Burma found itself confronting an uneasy, fragile peace—a peace that, for the first years of Burmese independence under U Nu, was regularly interrupted by counterinsurgency operations against communists, who had previously allied with the AFPFL. Steadying the postwar economy, now wrecked by inflation, appeared to be futile.

Even as successive administrations attempted to place the economy on a stable footing, the place of migrant business communities in postwar Burma was unstable at best. In a newly independent Burma battling schisms between its minority "nationalities," the argument against economic imperialism by British, Indian, and Chinese capital was particularly powerful. Migrant traders and financiers were widely perceived to have profited from the war; for many, the migrants' claims of wartime losses and collapse owing to the demonetization of "banana money" did not ring true. As a result, the Government of Burma tightened regulations controlling the amount and frequency of remittances, foreign exchange, and the transfer of savings certificates. They also implemented a series of land reforms nationalizing land ownership—measures shaped by the AFPFL's own approach to democratic socialism, buttressed in no small measure by stereotypes of migrant businessmen, traders, and moneylenders as having profited disproportionately off the land and labor of their adopted homes.[28]

In the context of this first wave of administrative reforms in Burma, the situation for migrant moneylenders and financiers like the Chettiars was complex. Prominent Chettiar families were part of the urban elite in Moulmein and Rangoon and were members of the legislative bodies, and they were able to gain significant concessions during the negotiations for the constitutional separation of Burma from India in 1935. These concessions were wrangled on the basis that Chettiars were not just moneylenders and financiers but long-term residents invested in the country's success, integral to the future of Burma's economy. While Chettiars were owners of paddy fields, timber, and sawmills, and rice merchants and proprietors of export houses, these investments were also made possible on the backs of an indebted peasantry, in many instances, by the terms of defaulted loans and foreclosed mortgages. According to one estimate, based on data provided by the secretary of the Nattukkottai Chettiars' Association in Rangoon, there were nearly 1,883 offices for Chettiar firms in Burma, with about 1,400 of these being in the "districts," outside of Rangoon, mostly in Pegu, Arakan, and Tennaserim.[29] After 1935, nearly 60 percent of the advances made were through mortgages by deposit of title deeds.[30] With nearly nineteen million acres under cultivation in Lower Burma in which these systems of credit were intertwined, the fears surrounding the flight of "refugee capital" from Burma that gained political traction were not without basis. Images of wealthy migrant families in Rangoon, Moulmein, and other towns fleeing during the war were widely circulated, and it was easy to assume that refugees from wartime Burma had taken all their wealth with them and did not intend to return.

In the wake of the wartime collapse of its rice and timber export facilities, Burma struggled to regain its prewar role as the granary for most of the world, despite the temporary respite owing to the demands of the Korean War in 1950 to 1953. Despite the public perceptions of migrants as wealthy, many migrant businesses struggled to stay afloat amid losses in land ownership, strict control on capital and credit flows, and limited access to permanent residence and citizenship rights. The collapse of Chettiar networks not only affected them but also seeped into other migrant lives, for Chettiar credit was regularly extended to much of Rangoon's urban poor and working classes, both Burman and Indian. For example, dockworkers from India at the Rangoon port and rickshaw pullers in the city were both within the circle of indebtedness, and Chettiars came to finance and control much of these networks. When limits on remittances and land ownership were put in place, the consequences rippled out across these networks of poor laborers, the bulk of Rangoon's population, reverberating far beyond the Chettiars' own circuits of credit and capital between South and Southeast Asia.[31] Ordinary migrants—laborers, small shopkeepers, and plantation workers—whose meager earnings or small plots of land might have been pledged as collateral to moneylenders—bore the brunt of these measures.

Amid this widespread impact of postwar legislative measures, Chettiars became the paradigmatic Indian migrants whose return to Burma was put in question, although in numerical terms migrant laborers from South India to Rangoon had far exceeded those associated with Chettiar firms. Consider, for example, that according to the Baxter Commission Report, there were 164,374 "unskilled" laborers—dockyard laborers, harbor workers, rice mill workers, rickshaw pullers, and conservancy workers—out of whom 67,845 were "Telugus" or laborers from South India.[32] Postwar, these trends had been reversed, with the Burmans making up the bulk of laborers. In their place, ire against foreigners was directed against the Chettiars. As Chettiars attempted to return to Burma from India after the war, they presented networks of credit and capital between the two places not as a siphoning of capital but as evidence of deep roots and investment in the communities in Burma. Prominent Chettiars with access to national and international audiences claimed that they provided the capital that kept

Burma going. While they were certainly important financial intermediaries between European banks and lending institutions and locals without access to credit, this was an inflated claim, for British firms controlled most of Burma's exports and imports. The Chettiars sought to stretch the claim even further: although Lower Burma had come under the plow by the Mons of the Pegu kingdom even before parts of it were conquered by the British and labeled Lower Burma, Chettiar leaders presented the region as having been developed because of their financial prowess. Considering these claims, postwar Burma, particularly the returning British military administration, struggled to reconcile its dependence on Chettiar credit with its desire for economic self-sufficiency.

PROFITS AND PARTITION

The postwar debate on the place of migrant-owned businesses, and specifically the place of Chettiar capital, invoked long-standing arguments that dated from well before Burma's partition from India. Going back to the years before the economic depression, in 1932, Raja Annamalai Chettiar (figure 2.2), a member of the Madras Provincial Banking Enquiry Committee and of the Burma India Chamber of Commerce and a Nattukottai Chettiar himself, noted that the Burmese economy depended on Indian capital and labor and that the Burmese were therefore "bound in honor" to secure the rights of Indians resident there.[33] In 1935, on the eve of new constitutional reforms for India and Burma, the Raja led the Burma India delegation to London to advocate for the rights of Indians in Burma. He returned with the triumphant claim that Indians' right of free trade and occupation had been secured and that British Burma had dropped its plans to restrict selling or mortgaging land to agriculturists.[34] As evidence of the power of the Chettiars in Burma, a seat in the newly expanded Burmese legislature was allotted to a Nattukottai Chettiars' Association representative.[35] In 1936, the Raja moved even closer to the centers of political power when he became a member of the Indian Legislative Assembly in New Delhi, but (despite the best efforts of migrant business communities, who wished to retain the profitable connection between the two countries) Burma was constitutionally separated from India in 1937. The first fractures in the circulation of commodities, credit, and capital had appeared.

FIGURE 2.2: *Raja Sir Annamalai Chettiar. Studio Portrait Negatives Box 1 [1950–2002], British Library, EAP737/4/4/1, https://eap.bl.uk/archive-file/EAP737 -4-4-1.*

On the eve of the war, in 1939, as a member of the Indian Legislative Assembly and of the Viceroy's Executive Council, Raja Annamalai Chettiar also voiced his reservations about India's Finance Bill for the year, which contained specific rates of income tax for different categories of potential taxpayers or assesses. Speaking to the widening tax net, he noted that Chettiar financial interests in Burma and Malaya were at stake and extended his analysis to implications for British subjects more broadly to show that it was not only Chettiars who ought to be concerned. In his speech demanding that taxes not be collected on incomes from Malaya and Burma, he cartoonishly characterized the figure of the income tax officer as an ignorant fool who was blithely unaware of the destruction he was wreaking: "He goes on, in his usual way, as if nothing has happened, issuing notices, carrying on assessment proceedings, levying and collecting tax and imposing penalties for default."[36] But even as Chettiar banking firms were protesting against the separation of Burma from British India because of the financial implications, given the proposed changes to the income tax legislation, many also made preemptive moves to ensure that their interests would be protected in case of a partition.[37] Some firms had moved operations back to India, where they invested in Madras's and India's nascent efforts at industrialization. The Indian Overseas Bank, for example, one of the most prominent banking ventures in Burma funded by Chettiar monies, also began to open operations in Madras; other examples included the Bank of Chettinad and the Chettinad Corporation. Following their initial successes in the textile and transport industries in the late nineteenth century, these new sectors also benefited from returning Chettiar capital.[38]

Others sought to discourage the separation of Burma from India by emphasizing the long history of connections between the two places. On the eve of the separation, new narratives emerged about the connections between Burma and South India, claiming that ties between the countries went back two thousand years and had only grown closer in the last three hundred years, since the medieval Chola kings had expanded in the sixteenth century from the southeastern coast of India to Burma and indeed to what would become the Straits Settlements and beyond.[39] The Chettiars invoked this history of trading connections between the two countries as they claimed a place in Burma's postwar economy. The dominant narrative about the Chettiars was that they were onetime salt and grain traders who had, to quote historian Raman Mahadevan, "followed the British flag" overseas in the mid-nineteenth century to engage in trading and moneylending activities; British officials (including the secretary of state for India and Burma at the time, Leo Amery) even went so far as to concede during postwar reconstruction discussions that the Chettiar presence in Burma predated the British. These claims, first invoked in the case of the separation of India and Burma, were voiced with renewed vigor after war and independence to establish the Chettiars' continued presence and access to citizenship rights in postwar Burma.

These concerted attempts by powerful Chettiar firms to claim a share of Burma's postwar economy created political resentment. Many longtime Indian residents in Burma felt that the extension of citizenship rights to migrant traders, businesses, and financing firms like the Chettiars would compromise their own claims to citizenship. Devas, the civil servant whose harrowing account of the "long march" from Burma featured in the previous chapter, corresponded with the Indian government over the plight of Burma Indians. In his account of his own experiences of the war, he argued that Burma was not equipped to deal with the aftereffects of the Japanese invasion and that the future of Burma depended on alliances with India. But he made a notable exception: he specifically noted that the "Chettyar," who had probably earned back his investment in Burma many times over since his arrival, had no place in its future and would have to be excluded.[40] The All Burma Indian Congress—the primary association tasked with representing Indian interests to the Government of Burma—was also wracked by dissents within the leadership.[41] The opinion of Indians in Burma on the place of Chettiar financiers in Burma was thus not a unified one. However, these murmurs of dissent from within migrant Indian communities were usually ignored in the general public discourse, which lumped together all Indian migrants as rapacious Chettiar moneylenders.[42] Their loss of wealth because of the demonetization of "banana money" was not one that elicited sympathy.

RESTRICTED REMITTANCES

Raja Annamalai Chettiar's caricature of a bumbling income tax officer as posing a challenge to Indian and Burmese economies connected through Chettiar capital and credit networks was not accidental; migrant remittances were intrinsically bound up with the question of income tax. In 1933, income tax legislation was reworked to accommodate commercial practice and bring many businesses under the tax net: Section 4(2) of the Income Tax Act of 1922 in India was amended to tax foreign profits if they were "brought into" or "received in British India" within three years of their accrual.[43] Until this amendment, Chettiars had been able to keep their profits abroad in Ceylon, Malaya, or French Cochinchina and not pay tax on them in British India. This also explains why, when the constitutional separation of India and Burma was proposed, the Chettiars were deeply worried about the tax implications of having a business across two separate colonies; after the separation, Burma would also be a "foreign" country. They were right to be worried, for on the eve of the India-Burma partition, in 1935–36, an Income Tax Enquiry Committee set up by the British Indian government began to look into the difficulties associated with defining "residence" for tax purposes, primarily in order to widen their tax base: the legislative reforms enacted were designed to raise the number of putative assessments outside of British India, extending them to Burma, Malaya, and beyond. By the time the war began, changes to income tax legislation in India had already dealt a serious blow to migrant businesses in Burma—particularly to highly profitable ones like those of the Chettiars.

These legal struggles were not new; the governments had been struggling to tax across the borders with other British colonies since before the war. When asked in 1922 about the question of remittances from Chettiar businesses abroad, the commissioner of income tax in Madras admitted, "We are absolutely groping in the dark."[44] Taxing these businesses was contingent on them being "resident" in British India, but as we will see in the next chapter, owing to the complex legal structures of Chettiar businesses, there was no easy solution. One proposed solution was that legislators would define "residence," not in territorial or geographic terms, as it had traditionally been defined, but in temporal terms—a change that more closely reflected the rhythms and patterns of how money moved between India, Burma, Malaya, and Ceylon. As a result of this proposal, one could be "resident" in British India in one year and not resident in another. During the periods in which one was a "resident," any income accruing, arising, or received in British India could be taxed. A separate category of "resident but not ordinarily resident" was introduced; if one fell within this category, like many wealthy Indian migrants abroad, tax would be levied on any income accruing, arising, or received in British India as well as any income earned abroad that was brought into British India. These new categories of tax residence were intended to include more people under the rubric of a taxable population.

Thus the 1933 tax amendment had already begun to raise problems for remittances from Burma to India. Typically, money moved between Burma and Madras using telegraphic transfers, either through the Imperial Bank of India set up by the British government, through the Office of the Accountant General, or through the exchange banks in Bombay or Calcutta. These newer methods of moving money existed alongside customary forms, including the *hundi* and demand drafts used by Chettiar firms in Madras. After Burma and India separated, it became more expensive to send remittances, for postage and telegraph rates to India were doubled. A letter that had cost one anna and three pies to send from Burma to India before the war now cost two annas and six pies after the war ended. This was compounded by restriction of shipping and travel during and after the war, as steamer services on which agents and employees of Chettiar firms traveled between South India and Burma were greatly reduced. As people sensed impending changes to immigration regimes and as war loomed on the horizon, they reportedly remitted 32.5 million rupees out of Burma to India—"the largest amount in Indo-Burman history and more than twice the sum sent to India from any other country."[45] Before 1948 anyone could remit up to 275 rupees per month, but as a result of this large-scale movement of money it became necessary shortly after independence to secure permissions from the controller of foreign exchange in Rangoon before money could be sent through money orders.[46] This lent credence to rumors about capital flight and currency speculation, which turned public opinion in Burma against the return of Indian migrants after the war.

"BANANAS ARE RIPE!"

In the former Straits Settlements, the British Military Administration that took over from the occupation government faced a backlash on the question of "banana money" similar to the one in Burma, even as it tried to create a blueprint for the constitutional future of British Malaya. These discussions took place, as they did in Burma, alongside negotiations about the nature and scope of constitutional protections for minorities, indigenous peoples, and migrants who had long made Malaya their home, an issue that proved to be a challenge in fashioning a postwar society. The proposals for an initial Malayan Union, put forward by the returning British administration, did not offer any special protection for Malays, who responded by demanding political representation as the indigenous race and original inhabitants of Malaya, in contrast to communities of Indians and Chinese, whom they portrayed as later arrivals. This distinction had not been made under the terms of "common citizenship" for the Malayan Union (1946–48), under which all those born and permanently resident in Malaya were to become citizens by operation of law, and "aliens" would have to apply for citizenship through a process of registration. This proposal was rejected by Malay nationalists, led by the United Malays National Organization. In 1948, the Federation of Malaya was formed within the British Commonwealth (Penang, Malacca, and the Federated Malay States) with special guarantees for Malay rights, including protections in land ownership, business ownership, and preference in government employment. These constitutional negotiations unfolded against the British Military Administration's counterinsurgency operations against "communists" in Malaya that heavily targeted Indians and Chinese communities who were believed to be members of the Malayan Communist Party and the Malayan People's Anti-Japanese Army, or trade unions supported by the former ("the Emergency"). The question of minority rights in Malaysia would not be settled for years: unlike India, Burma, and Ceylon, which charted a course to political independence in 1947–48, Malaya and Singapore took a much more meandering route, and these countries did not gain their political independence until 1957 and 1965, respectively.[47] These schisms had been exposed by the end of the occupation, not only in debates over citizenship, but initially, in confronting the wartime collapse of the economy. As in Burma, a revival of prewar economic fortunes, particularly curbs on galloping inflation fueled in no small measure by banana money, would become important to the resolution of the question of citizenship.

In Malaya, as in Burma, Chettiar firms were an important part of the colonial economy and had been affected by the Japanese occupation. Chettiars supplied loans to plantations, tin mines, shipowners, and traders in Malaya, as well as extending credit across social classes, from peasants to sultans. Much less of their wealth was tied up in land in Malaya than it was in Burma, in part because of legislation introduced in the interwar period that restricted ownership of land by "aliens"; two examples of this kind of legislation were the Malay Reservations Act, first introduced in 1913 but amended in 1933, and the Small Landholdings Act of 1931, both of which sought to reduce the risk to debtors of landlessness.[48] Simultaneously, Chettiars' moneylending activities in Malaya, as in Ceylon, were regulated following the recommendations of banking inquiry commissions in the interwar period.[49] Even given these restrictions, on the eve of the war Chettiars owned, according to historian Sinnappah Arasaratnam, the greater part of the 87,795 acres under cultivation in the Federated Malay States like Perak, Selangor, and Negri Sembilan.[50] On the eve of the war, Kratoska estimates that fully half of Chettiar investments in Malaya, valued at $120 million, was tied up in land.[51] During the Japanese occupation, many Chettiar firms moved employees and capital back to India as a temporary measure; others likely lost contact with their agents stationed in their offices across the Bay. The end of the war gave rise to situations like the one that Seethalakshmi Achi faced with her agent in Burma. In Malaya, Chettiar firms equally attempted to collect money due to them under mortgages and promissory notes and challenged the legality of "banana money" and of contractual obligations during the war.

Just as Seethalakshmi Achi and her agent in Rangoon were situated on either side of a juridical line of war, so were other traders and businessmen who went back and forth between Madras and Malaya, the latter under military occupation, the former not. Litigation around these issues began even when Malaya and Singapore was still under occupation. For example, in a prominent case that came up before the Madras High Court around the same time as the *Seethalakshmi Achi* appeal, two parties in an ordinary breach-of-contract case sparred over the legal issues of trading with an "enemy alien." One of the parties involved was Gemini Studios, a prominent movie production house in Madras.[52] In 1942, Gemini Studios produced *Bhakta Naradar*, a Hindu mythological film in Tamil directed by S. Soundarrajan. The film was to be widely circulated, including in the Federated Malay States, Penang, and Singapore. The exhibition rights for Malaya and Singapore were held by the Manasseh Film Company, associated with the wealthy Baghdadi Jewish family of Sir Mannasseh Meyer in Singapore. Manasseh had contracted with Gemini Studios to receive prints of the movies. Owing to the war, this contract between Gemini and Manasseh could not be fulfilled, and the prints could not be delivered. The lawyer for Gemini Studios, V. C. Gopalratnam, contended that the partners of Manasseh Film, A. Thiruvengada Mudaliar and his son Soundarrajan, were "enemy aliens" disentitled to sue in British Indian courts because the company was formed in the Straits Settlements. Moreover, Gopalratnam contended, an unnamed Singaporean national held the power of attorney to act on behalf of the company when its partners left Singapore for India in October 1941. This case dragged on for two years, from 1942 to 1944, even as the possibility of an Allied victory in Southeast Asia looked increasingly likely. Justice Chandrasekhara Ayyar, the lone judge deciding whether Gemini Studios would have to return a sum of 5,000 rupees paid as advance for exhibition rights, perused the Defence of India Rules—wartime emergency regulations—for definitions of "enemy" and "enemy territory." He ruled that the partners of Manasseh Film were British subjects, not "foreigners," and that the occupation of Singapore by Japanese military forces did not lend Singapore the character of "enemy territory," contrary to the definition of "enemy territory" under the Defence of India Rules. Alongside *Seethalakshmi Achi*, this became an important precedent for cases across Southeast Asia on the validity of wartime contracts.

The Chettiar litigation around "banana money" was more complex. Responding to this situation after the war ended and sensing that a formal resolution was necessary, the government in Malaya sought to pass legislation rectifying transactions and contracts likely affected by the occupation. Like Burma, Malaya introduced legislative measures to deal with the demonetization of wartime currency, escalating remittances, and forfeited contractual arrangements.[53] In 1948, Malaya introduced a Debtor and Creditor (Occupation) Ordinance.[54] This essentially legitimized banana money as legal currency during the occupation and offered a method to revalue prewar and occupation-era currency and stop interest from accruing during the occupation period, which brought on a spate of attempts to exchange banana money for current legal tender.[55] "Bananas are 'ripe,'" proclaimed the *Singapore Free Press* tongue-in-cheek, in an August 1948 story about businessmen exchanging Japanese occupation-era currency for current British money.[56] Thus "banana money" began to exit the economy: British subjects in Malaya wrote asking the British government to pay their investments in post office savings bonds in British currency, and government servants received their "back pay" in British currency.[57] A similar law was passed to address the problem of wartime contracts, which had a much more profound impact on Chettiar business practices. The Agents and Trustees (Occupation) Ordinance enacted in 1949 established that contracts of agency subsisted throughout the occupation period in Malaya, solving the central issue in cases like *Seethalakshmi Achi* by means of legislation. It made partners in Chettiar firms responsible for the acts of their agents, including agents' voluntary acceptance of debt repayments in "banana money" during the war. Finally, the Moneylenders' Ordinance in 1951 placed even more restrictions, requiring loans to be registered and attested to by a judicial magistrate. So widespread was the problem of litigation around "banana money" in relation to wartime contracts that it became the subject of everyday conversation; "a lawyer" writing a regular legal advice column in the *Straits Times* noted how all debts had to be settled in line with the sliding scale provided in the ordinance and offered advice on how to interpret the complicated legal provisions.[58] The anonymous lawyer writing the column predicted, accurately, that it would be lawyers, not litigants, that would reap a "rich harvest" from the uncertainties created by the settlement of debts in occupation-era currency. As a result of these legislative changes, many Chettiar firms wound up and repatriated their capital to Madras. However, ongoing litigation still circled back to wartime displacements in 1942: between 1952 and Malaya's independence from British rule in 1957, many Chettiars still sought to salvage what was left of their wealth in Malaya, bringing debt recovery cases at the Federal Court of Malaya.[59]

Indeed, because Chettiars' capital was not restricted to Malaya alone and instead circulated between South and Southeast Asia, they had to approach multiple venues for resolution, particularly relating to the question of debts repaid in "banana money" to agents. In 1946, concerned about the effect this legislation would have on their business interests, the All Malaya Nattukottai Chettiars' Association approached the Government of India and the secretary of state for colonies in London. With solicitors in London at the ready, armed with a "mass of legal opinion," the association went into legal battles to recover their landed wealth.[60] It was represented by the lawyers Robert Braddell and R. Ramani, both of whom were well known and respected and often traveled between Madras, Malaya, and London. Braddell had appeared in high-profile "test cases" under the Moneylenders' Ordinance for the Chettiars and was familiar with their business practices.[61] It was also not a mere coincidence that Ramani was involved in debates over Malayan Union citizenship, where he claimed that making a declaration of loyalty to a singular nation-state was unnecessary and that, in effect, dual citizenship of India and Malaya should be permitted for those Indians who had resided in Malaya for a long time.[62] In its petitions to the agent of the Government of India in Malaya, John Thivy, the association claimed that wartime debts and contracts were invalidated, whether or not the monies due had been paid to their legal agents in Malaya; they argued that it was Chettiar custom to terminate any relationships with their agents during periods of war.[63] Note that this argument is identical to the one raised in the *Seethalakshmi Achi* appeal that I introduced at the beginning of this chapter—an indication that there was some measure of coordination between the lawyers who represented Chettiar clients at the Madras High Court and those who traveled from there to Malaya and London. In response to the association's petitions, John Thivy, himself a lawyer and son of the prominent Perak-based politician Louis Thivy, retorted that commercial customs could not be an excuse to terminate contractual relationships in common law and that the powers of attorney granted to agents should extend to carrying out all acts necessary in the course of the war.[64] Despite this, though, the Government of

India generally supported the Chettiars' petition, arguing that repayment of loans in wartime currency that was practically worthless violated the norms of international law. Even as the legislation attempted to settle the question of wartime currency, litigation featuring Chettiar firms continued into the 1960s, taking place before courts in both India and Malaysia.

In January 1942, just as emergency wartime regulations were being enacted, Raja Sir Annamalai Chettiar wrote to M. S. Aney, the member of the Viceroy's Executive Council for "Indians overseas" whom we met in the previous chapter, demanding that the Indo-Burma Immigration Agreement be rewritten: "We have labored in Burma for generations; we have sunk enormous capital there; it is only bare justice that we ought to come and go as we like, as and when we choose."[65] Aney replied, not without a touch of irritation, that both parties were preoccupied with the war and that no decisions on immigration would be taken at that point.[66] Three years later, after the war ended, in cases like *Seethalakshmi Achi*, litigants had begun to demand that they be allowed to recover debts that were repaid using wartime currency. Not only were these cases pivotal to resolving questions about the nature of wartime occupation and the validity of wartime currency, but they had far-reaching implications for whether any of the land or wealth could be recovered in Burma.

Following the end of the war, many Chettiar firms attempted to sever their ties with Burma, while others attempted to get back to claim their wealth. In each instance, they had to make new jurisdictional claims that returned to wartime displacements. Lawyers for Chettiar firms used the language of international laws of war in their submissions—the status of "enemy territory" and "enemy alien"—as national borders replaced imperial ones. Lawyers in Madras, Malaya, and Rangoon employed similar arguments, showing how law circulated—as strategy, precedent, paperwork—with lawyers and litigants like the Chettiars, returning and revisiting the legal implications of wartime displacements. As for Seethalakshmi Achi and Veerappa Chettiar, there is some evidence that their firm survived the loss at the Madras High Court, as well as the restrictions on Indian investment in postwar Burma. The *tozhil vilasam* (trading name) of the firm ("V. T.") appears in a trade directory around 1956, still located on Mogul Street in Rangoon, alongside other Chettiar firms. Following the end of the war, about 5 to 10 percent of the Rangoon firms took on matters other than moneylending, which was no longer a viable occupation. Perhaps the V. T. firm was one of those.

After the war, debt recovery cases like the *Seethalakshmi Achi* appeal reveal the unraveling of financial, geographic, and familial networks across the eastern Indian Ocean. Many Indian migrants who had fled during the war chose to return to Burma, but as we will see, others were unable to return, confronted with borders in the form of new restrictions on immigration. This might have been the situation faced by Seethalakshmi Achi and her family. Perhaps they decided that they could not engage in a long-drawn-out process of reestablishing themselves in Burma; perhaps they decided instead to cut their losses, remain in India, and try to regain what money they could. These cases ostensibly about legal agency—the authority granted to conduct affairs on behalf of another—in fact condensed a whole host of postwar concerns, including the legality of wartime currency, the wartime fulfillment of contracts, and the intertwined legal issues of remittances and taxation. The resolution of these legal issues also had implications for postwar land ownership, cross-border trade, and foreign exchange control more generally.[67]

Coming as they did after a world war, all of these specific legal issues and concerns about the capital and credit that had circulated through migrant networks in Southeast Asia invoked larger questions about nationality and citizenship, and implicitly about national loyalty. Migrant traders and financiers—both the Chettiar firms that remained in Burma and Malaya and those that sought to return to Burma after being displaced by the war—sought to have a continued presence in Burma. But why? The answer seems, often, to have been money. Remittances remained central to recovering some of their prewar prosperity, and Burma and Malaya both mandated that only those who paid tax could make remittances. Thus, as questions of wartime legalities were raised through cases like the *Seethalakshmi Achi* appeal, questions about taxation preoccupied traders, moneylenders, and financiers. In seeking citizenship beyond Indian shores and across the ocean, they were likely less interested in proving political loyalty than in avoiding tax liability. In this first wave of decolonization, it would appear, one could not be achieved without establishing the other.

THREE

TAX RECEIPTS

AFTER THE WAR ENDED, Chettiar firms in Burma and Malaya faced several challenges. As chapter 2 showed, these challenges included rescuing debt repayments from the flood of "banana money" into the economy; this occupation-era currency had sunk in value during the war and left a trail of destruction in its wake. This chapter focuses on how wartime displacements affected encounters with taxation regimes, particularly in litigation around income tax. Changes to income tax legislation in Burma and India had implications for migrant remittances, increasingly restricted by exchange control regulations. Reeling from the possibility of wealth lost to unrecoverable debts, Chettiar firms were now also unable to move money abroad, including to India, unless they paid income tax in Burma. [1] Where Seethalakshmi Achi and Veerappa Chettiar attempted to sever contracts with their agents in Rangoon and recover their debts in Madras, as we saw in the last chapter, many of the Chettiar firms in this chapter sought to establish tax residence in Burma and not Madras to revive circulations of credit because of these legislative changes. As "tax residence" began to be based on temporal limits as well as territorial limits—from a physical presence in the country to the lengths of time spent within its jurisdiction—wartime displacements from Burma meant that for many, their tax residences were in India and not Burma.

While restrictions on travel stopped many partners of Chettiar firms from returning to Burma to attempt to claim the remainder of their fortunes after the war, legal restrictions on remittances determined how much of their Burma fortunes could be salvaged. As India amended definitions of tax residence after the war, migrant remittances that had once remained outside the ambit of Indian income tax became potentially subject to it. So on the one hand, Chettiar firms faced the very real problem of managing tax liability. On the other, whether and where one paid income tax was also critical in postwar Burma and India because it became a means of demonstrating economic attachments and consequently eligibility for citizenship. The specter of income tax thus raised questions of citizenship and national allegiance during decolonization. Amid plans for postwar reconstruction, the British Indian government sought to address tax avoidance and tax evasion, spurred on by rumors of fabulous wartime profits garnered by its wealthiest trading communities.[2] If tax payment is one of the fiscal relationships between states and citizens whose terms are constantly renegotiated,[3] what citizenship would partners in Chettiar firms hold, caught between Indian laws under which they were liable to pay tax and Burmese laws that restricted remittances?

Under these circumstances, Chettiar firms turned—once again—to the courts. Already by 1941, it was possible in India to challenge an official assessment of income tax by "referring" a case to High Courts, like the Madras High Court in the previous chapter that Seethalakshmi Achi had approached to recover wartime debts.[4] These "referred cases" were not tax disputes in the traditional sense, in that they were a means neither of penalizing tax evasion nor of ensuring tax compliance. These "referred cases" or "references" were intended to resolve mixed questions of law and fact in a new field of income tax litigation. The references were also used to educate income tax officials about varied customary commercial practices. The questions that they raised ranged from the obvious—What counts as "profit" in the case of a moneylending business?—to the seemingly redundant—Does theft from a moneylender's strong room count as a "loss" that can be set off against total taxable income?[5] The cases discussing the tax liability of partners in Chettiar firms in Madras were among the first—and, over time, would become the most numerous—cases invoking the reference jurisdiction of the High Courts.[6] The experiences of the Chettiar firms during the war in South and Southeast Asia fundamentally altered how these questions would be answered for other migrant communities. The jurisdictional claims that migrant communities such as the Chettiars made referencing the reasons for wartime displacements and the locations of their income and profits generated during that time would prove consequential for how economic attachments came to be associated with political loyalty.

EMIGRATING CAPITAL

In the late nineteenth century, when the British government first sought to impose income tax in colonial India, it was concerned with raising revenue for the maintenance of the empire, particularly for military purposes.[7] In the 1880s, for example, when the first income tax legislation was introduced, the government was concerned with meeting the expenditure of the Afghan Wars, being fought on the British Indian Empire's northwestern frontiers to counter the influence of the Russian Empire there.[8] These efforts were eventually successful. Historian Ritu Birla shows how over the late nineteenth and early twentieth centuries, owing to the expanding definitions of tax residence, income tax became the fastest-growing category of government revenue.[9]

With World War I, government expenditures rose once again, and to meet the increasing needs, the basis of income taxation was expanded in 1916.[10] In these early decades, principles of taxation were closely linked to territory: if income "arose," "accrued," or was "received" within the territorial extent of British India, then it would be treated as taxable income.[11] In 1918, the law was amended to distinguish between a "resident" and a "nonresident" taxpayer; this allowed "foreign" incomes too to be subject to income tax if they arose, accrued, or were received in British India. These references to "residence" in legal provisions focused not on the geographical location of the potential taxpayer but on the location of "income" itself. In the interwar period, a series of amendments in the interwar period shifted this definition to capture how money moved within migrant networks, defining tax "residence" with reference less to space than to time: "residence" depended on the number of days that one had been physically present in British India in a particular year. In other words, one could be "resident" in British India for tax purposes for a particular year, then be a nonresident the following year.

In this interwar period, many tax references centered on determining tax residence. Lawyers might have categorized some of these disputes as conflict-of-law cases involving double taxation—they might have involved either two different provinces within British India; a British Indian province and an Indian "princely" state, such as Madras and Pudukkottai; or British India and Britain.[12] The determination of tax residence was complicated by the nature of Chettiar banking transactions. Consider David Rudner's ethnography of Chettiar banking practices, which describes the different kinds of deposits that the Chettiars made in the course of their business.[13] Current deposits or *kadai kanakku* were of two kinds: the simple demand deposit (where monies would be paid on demand, along with simple interest), the *nadappu* deposit, and the *thavanai kanakku* (which used compound interest, from other Chettiar firms). When deposits were accepted from non-Chettiars, it was called *vayan vatti kanakku* (paying a simple interest plus a fractional amount depending on the *nadappu* rate). These transactions between Chettiar firms—like the ones between Meyappan and Veerappa in chapter 2—were crucial to the working of Chettiar banking practices, since only a small percentage of their capital came from their own reserves (*mudal panam*). The larger component was what was referred to as *sontha thavani panam* (raised from others in the community). Recall that these transactions were often made across colonial borders—Burma to Madras to Colombo to Ipoh—and across empires, from British India to French Indochina. In addition to these cross-border transactions between firms within the community, Chettiar firms extended credit from British and European banks that operated in Burma, and in this respect they were important financial intermediaries whose wealth was built on transactions between Britain and its colonies in South and Southeast Asia.

Given the many different forms that these banking practices took, Chettiar litigants frequently occupied center stage in disputes over income tax. For example, many Chettiar villages were located in Pudukkottai, a "princely state" with its own ruler and own taxation regime, separate from but adjacent to British ruled-Madras.[14] Community legend had it that the

ninety-six villages that the Chettiars occupied in the area were granted to
them by the local Pandya king; in the twentieth century, their businesses
and homes continued to be located there.[15] Income tax officers in Madras
tasked with examining Chettiar account books complained that the various assessments required to manage these cross-cutting jurisdictions were
so different, and the account books and statements were kept using such
divergent methods, that even arriving at the quantum of double-taxation
relief was a problem.[16] The Chettiar practice of sending "agents" abroad
on three-year terms, as we will see, also complicated the understanding of
tax residence. Thus appeals to the "reference jurisdiction" of the Madras
High Court made by Chettiar firms sharply increased with the new definition of "residence" in the vocabulary of income tax legislation. For instance, in 1920, courts were called on to decide whether interest earned on
a deposit was taxable income and to judge whether money sent from the
Ipoh branch of a moneylending business in Malaya to its Madras branch
was to be treated as profits remitted for the Madras partners.[17] Charting
the course of income in the opposite direction across the Bay, a "referred
case" brought in 1922 concerned a Chettiar firm in Madras that remitted
money to Penang when the exchange rate between British Indian rupees
and Straits Dollars was low and credited it when it was high; the judges
were asked to advise on whether income tax should be assessed on the
"profits" that the firm gained.[18]

Finally, Chettiar banking practices, some of which were explained in
chapter 2, did not seem to fit easily into formulations of British Indian
law on banking, negotiable instruments, and currency, and thus the category of a tax residence. As historians Marina Martin and Ritu Birla have
shown, indigenous forms of banking business were not commensurable
with categories used in colonial law.[19] For instance, like other migrant
trading communities in colonial India, Chettiars used the *hundi* to trans-
mit funds from one place to another, sometimes within the course of a
day.[20] When funds were remitted from one branch of a firm to another
(usually from outside British India to inside), they might be considered
either "profit" or "capital"—and the former could be taxed. *Hundis* were
commonly used in Chettiar banking practices also. However, Chettiars
argued that they used them differently than other groups (the basis of their

claim that the funds should be untaxed). This position was taken by many of the witnesses in the Madras Provincial Banking Enquiry Committee investigations, set up in 1929–30 to investigate agriculture, banking, and credit in the various provinces in British India, including Madras and Burma. During the committee's interviews, representatives of Chettiar firms that operated in Burma and the Federated Malay States could only assert that "it was a different kind of *hundi* business."[21] In another example, the *nadappu* rate—the rate that Chettiar firms operating in a particular locality agreed to charge on deposits once a month—was analogized to the "bank rate," familiar to English systems of banking. These imperfect analogies—of *hundis* to bills of credit or of the *nadappu* rate to the bank rate—led to legal disputes and allegations of tax fraud.

The numerous legal disputes around questions of income tax were themselves blamed for the "emigration" of Chettiar capital. Some observations to this effect are contained in the reports of the Madras Provincial Banking Enquiry Committee. For instance, a witness named Arunachalam Chettiar with businesses in Rangoon and Madras testified before the committee that one of the primary reasons why Chettiar business had moved abroad to Burma, the Federated Malay States, and French Indochina was that it had become very difficult to recover debts lent on mortgages through litigation in India. He noted that suits for debt recovery in India took up to twenty years to be resolved and that during that time the rate of interest awarded by courts was only about 9 percent. He also complained that the Chettiar firms' books, which the courts compelled them to surrender (see figure 3.1 for an example), were kept out of their hands when the cases were pending before the courts: "There are thousands of books locked up in the court and some of our books get lost. Further, a lot of people go through our accounts, and all confidence in regard to them ceases to exist."[22] This was reiterated by the testimony of the assistant commissioner of income tax for Madurai, A. Savarinatha Pillai, who claimed an intimate understanding of the working of Chettiar firms. Pillai opined that reducing rates of income tax would not bring Chettiar capital back to India from Burma, Ceylon, and the Federated Malay States. Instead, he suggested, Chettiar capital could be attracted back to India with better debt-recovery processes.[23] Other witnesses disagreed with the idea that litigation was responsible for the flight of Chettiar capital. Many expressed that they were unlikely to move their businesses back to India even with proposed changes to income tax laws. As the Madras Provincial Banking Enquiry Committee noted in its final report, a special deputy collector and two accountants had been deputed from the Madras Collectorate to deal with the income tax assessments of the Chettiar firms; these officials, who had an in-depth knowledge of the "Chetty" systems of accounting, were appointed to create a "considerable increase of revenue in income tax assessment." The committee estimated that the Chettiars would contribute to an increase in 4.2 million rupees in tax revenue—and this amount, they said, was likely to double over the course of a few years. Given this interest in taxing Chettiar wealth, firms would try to keep their income outside the ambit of Indian income tax law.

In spite of being an increasingly important category of government revenue, by 1938–39 income tax was still only 18.6 percent of the total revenue of the Indian government, with the bulk of its revenue continuing to come in from customs duties.[24] In 1939, following reports submitted by banking inquiry commissions on the eve of the war, amendments to the Indian Income Tax Act made tax residents of India subject to tax on foreign income in addition to domestic income (that is, on their worldwide income), whether or not it was remitted to British India.[25] As a result of this change, those "resident" for tax purposes in India who had an "income" in Burma were taxed on it even if the money itself remained in Burma. Until this period, the Chettiars "resident" in India had not been taxed in British India on incomes earned abroad in Burma, Malaya, or Ceylon. These changes in the income tax legislation threatened to significantly erode their wealth. In response, Raja Annamalai Chettiar, who, as we saw in chapter 2, had tried to secure the place of the Chettiars in Burma during the constitutional separation of the two colonies, once again appealed to the British Indian government. He pointed out that introducing "residence" into the vocabulary of Indian taxation law would cripple the commercial interests of "overseas Indians"—British India's most valued taxpayers.[26] He also noted, appealing to the financial concerns of the British government in London, that in this regard Chettiar concerns aligned with those of British and European firms, and that these non-Chettiar businesses would

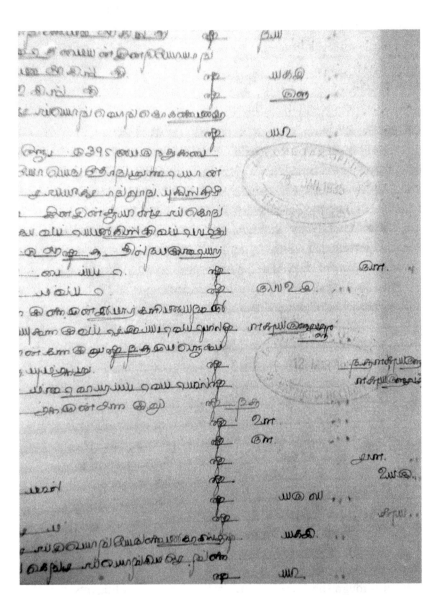

FIGURE 3.1: *Extract from Chettiar ledger with income tax stamp. Photograph by author.*

be similarly disadvantaged by income tax regimes.[27] Thus, even as taxing the wealth of migrants who went back and forth between India and other colonies in the British Empire became increasingly important, it gave rise to a number of legal disputes.

TERRITORY AND TAX RESIDENCE

In Rudner's ethnography of the Chettiars, caste conventions shape commercial relationships, not law. In his view, law is thus not a point of emphasis, representative of how agency and trust have been represented in the context of trading diasporas.[28] Caste tied commercial networks together, and the associated rituals and kinship networks cemented trust among the members of the community, presenting a credible reputation to those outside the community and imposing sanctions on those who violated these norms. Law entered commercial worlds only when there was a need to recover investments from those outside their communities.

But turning to the archive of law fundamentally alters how territory and tax residence relate to each other. As Fahad Bishara has shown for the western Indian Ocean, debt and obligation were recorded and translated through law—among merchants, moneylenders, traders, and plantation owners.[29] Bishara's work represents a move away from viewing networks of financiers or traders as drawing exclusively on caste, "trust," or "reputation." The language of law—and as Bishara shows, not exclusively state law—was critical to the maintenance of these networks.[30] As Mitra Sharafi argues in the case of the Parsis, litigation was a means of shoring up the self-understanding of "minority" communities in colonial India, an argument that could be made about the Chettiars in Burma.[31] Sharafi and Bishara also point to another aspect of Parsi and Gujarati trading/merchant networks: that moving capital across territory was critical. While Bishara uses the *waraqqa* deeds to show how the processes of translation accompanied movements across the "sea of debt," Sharafi points to the "legal India" created through the "jurisdictional jostling" that Parsi litigants were able to achieve. To capture how legal norms sustain and travel alongside movements of people, things, and ideas, Sharafi and Bishara suggest that we must look at legal actors and legal documents in conjunction with each other. In the case of Meyappan Chettiar's promissory note from the previous chapter, for example, traveling from Rangoon to Madras, passing from his agent's hands to the hands of his widow and his lawyers, and crossing paths with Ramani and Braddell's arguments on behalf of the Malaya Chettiars in Selangor and London, we might see how it traces not only the places where Chettiars lived and worked but also the routes and itineraries that Chettiar wealth took. To map these routes, to use scholars Renisa Mawani and Iza Hussin's framing, is to map the travels of law.[32]

But the flow of credits and profits can also be traced through taxation. One way of reading the archive of referred cases before the Madras High Court is to look at how the "legal" is marked off from the "social," as discussed in the context of analogies for the *hundi* and the *nadappu* rate. Like Rudner, historians Ritu Birla and Rachel Sturman show how the particularity of caste-based customary practices was contrasted with the universality of "economic" practices, which were seen as legal or licit. In their view, law is a modernizing force, constituting the Hindu family and their business activities as "vernacular," "traditional," or "illiberal" in contrast to European models of trading and banking. In this vein both Sturman and Birla discuss the Hindu Undivided Family (HUF), which was simultaneously a social and a legal institution. Their arguments, however, are presented in different ways. For Birla, just as legal rules have exceptions, the family firm becomes the cultural exception to universal commercial laws;[33] Sturman argues that economic interests fracture these exceptions rooted in "culture."[34] Eleanor Newbigin's account of the Hindu Code Bill and the development of personal law leading up to and after Indian independence, building on Birla and Sturman's work, shows how debates over the nature of Hindu law in postcolonial India continued debates that took place during the interwar period, constituting Hindu families not only as social but also as economic units through law.[35] However, in these works of scholarship, the Hindu family firm is explored in relation to the making of the nation-state, not in terms of migration of capital and credit. Therefore, questions of territory in the making of fiscal sovereignties are not discussed.

The legal disputes around the definitions of tax residence status of migrant trading and moneylending firms—like those of the Chettiars—were made even more complicated by the interplay between income tax legislation and the law of partnerships in British India.[36] Chettiar firms were often partnerships. Partners in a Chettiar firm could be in more than one place: for example, one partner could be in Madras in British India and another in Colombo in Ceylon, or both partners could be in Madras but do their greatest volume of business in Penang in the Straits Settlements. This was not unusual; Birla notes the many legal forms that Marwari businesses took—a partnership, a HUF, a charitable trust—to carry out business.[37] Partnerships, unlike corporations, did not have a separate legal personality, but income tax legislation regulated partnerships differently. For the purposes of income tax, unregistered partnerships were treated as separate entities, and the partnership itself was designated as having its own residence status; in contrast, in registered firms, partners were assessed on their individual income, even as individual partners could be spread out across South and Southeast Asia.[38] Since many Chettiar firms were registered partnerships with partners in multiple locations, a singular tax residence was difficult to determine.

To resolve this question, a firm's place of "control" or "management" was deemed to be its tax residence. Under the 1922 Income Tax Act (just as in the 1886 and 1918 Acts), the preliminary evaluation for whether someone was a resident or a nonresident was to be made by the collector—the chief revenue and judicial officer in a district—of the "principal place of business."[39] Determining the "principal place of business" as well as "control" and "management" was complicated by Chettiars' practice of operating through "agencies" abroad; recall from chapter 2 that Seethalakshmi Achi and Veerappa Chettiar operated through agents in Burma. Many Chettiar firms were based in their hometowns in Madras and Pudukkottai, sending agents invested with the authority of transacting on behalf of the firm to Burma, Ceylon, or Malaya for a period of three years. Often, these agents were family members, for in yet another complication, many Chettiar firms were family concerns; by 1945, Chettiar firms that operated as HUFs rather than as partnerships were considered "resident" in India if the *karta* (manager) of the HUF was resident there.[40] The various asymmetries and disjunctions between Chettiar businesses' familial arrangements and legal arrangements in India and their branches abroad created a problem for taxation regimes.

The family ownership of Chettiar firms was important, for it meant that location of control and management for Chettiar firms was not only a legal question but also a sociocultural one. Place-making was crucial in the working of Chettiar capital and credit networks. The offices of Chettiar firms tended to cluster together. In Rangoon, most Chettiar firms traded on Mogul Street in downtown Rangoon—recall that Seethalakshmi Achi and Veerappa Chettiar's firm had their offices here as well—and in Colombo the Chettiar *kittangis* were located on Sea Street in the Pettah. In Rangoon and Colombo (as well as in Penang, Ipoh, and Saigon), Chettiars built temples in honor of the Hindu god Murugan (figure 3.2)—temples that hosted monthly meetings of Chettiar associations, where the firms decided on the *nadappu* rate, the prevailing rate of interest.[41] In Singapore, the Sri Thendayuthapani temple on Tank Road also functioned as the "official" address for the Nattukottai Chettiar Chamber of Commerce. These banking and moneylending conventions, which were also familial and social, meant that Chettiar businesses were often difficult to categorize using principles used to determine "residence" for the purposes of income tax.

One of the earliest cases referred before the Madras High Court on the question of "control" and "management" illustrates some of these concerns. In 1919, a young Nattukottai Chettiar, Ramanathan Chettiar, was assessed for Indian income tax on his businesses, which were spread out all the way up to French Cochinchina.[42] In court, his mother, Valliamai Achi, was his legal representative. Ramanathan Chettiar's core claim was that he should not be assessed tax because his business was located beyond the territorial boundaries of British India. This legal challenge caused quite a stir in government circles. Frantic letters were written to and from the government in Madras, for Chettiar firms constituted a significant percentage of Madras's income tax base, and officials, aware of how a precedential finding for the plaintiff would affect government revenue, solicited legal opinions from their best tax law specialists.

Tax law during this period was becoming an emerging area of practice in Madras, as increasingly complicated income tax legislation was being passed. Lawyers experienced in taxation matters commanded an impressive influence over these references from the High Courts. In the Ra-

FIGURE 3.2: *Nattukottai Chettiar Temple, Yangon. Photograph
by author.*

manathan Chettiar case, the lawyer for the government was S. Srinivasa Ayyangar, "thick-set and inclined to stoutness";[43] he occupied the post of the advocate general for Madras and would later be the president of the Indian National Congress. On the other side, M. Subbaraya Aiyar represented Ramanathan's S. Rm. Ar. firm. Although both lawyers lived in Mylapore in Madras City (as many of the prominent lawyers in Madras did at the time),[44] Srinivasa Ayyangar was additionally qualified to assist the government, as he was originally from the Ramanathapuram district, a stronghold of Chettiar families, and he would have been well acquainted with Chettiar banking customs.[45] This expertise lent his legal opinion, included in the papers filed before the High Court, added weight.

Srinivasa Ayyangar was asked, as the lawyer for the government and as an experienced practitioner in taxation matters, to opine before the Madras High Court on the question of what the term *accrue*, used in Section 4 of the act, meant. He stated that control of the business was the operative principle for Section 4 and that in this case the business was controlled in Kanadukathan in British India; therefore, he argued, the S. Rm. Ar. firm could be taxed in British India. In response, the lawyers for the S. Rm. Ar. firm issued a statement saying that the business was not controlled and managed from British India; the partners in Madras were not involved in the day-to-day conduct of the business and instead issued only general instructions to their agents abroad and did not control whom money was lent to entities outside the province. This statement was not false; as Rudner's ethnography of Chettiar networks notes, overseas offices were by and large autonomous in their daily operations as Chettiar agents acted on behalf of their principals. At issue were conflicting customary and legislative interpretations of "control" and "management."

In the end, though, the judges of the Madras High Court sided with the lawyers for Ramanathan Chettiar and his firm, giving an official stamp to Chettiar business practices. Two of three presiding judges, Justices Abdur Rahim and Justice Oldfield, noted that the moneylending business was one that was largely dependent on the discretion of agents who were located outside British India, and the fact that Ramanathan Chettiar issued general instructions from British India did not mean that the business was "controlled" from British India. Issues of "control" aside, they noted that no income had physically accrued or arisen in British India and that no income tax was therefore due. Ramanathan Chettiar's case—one of the first referred to the High Court that addressed income tax legislation's attempt to tax incomes outside the territory of British India—sent a signal to the Chettiar community about the nature of the jurisdictional claims that they must make in income tax cases. However, as we will see, the types of jurisdictional claims needed would change radically with the war.

PARTITIONED ECONOMIES

On the eve of Britain's declaration of war on Germany in 1939, the Indian Legislative Assembly in Delhi was engaged in a much more quotidian task: amending the Indian Income Tax Act of 1922, the federal Indian income tax legislation. The debates were, perhaps most consequentially, about the extraterritorial reach of income tax legislation. Seven years later, as the war formally ended in 1945, the legislative amendments had passed muster. Section 4-A was introduced, extending the reach of income tax legislation. It introduced the category of "resident but not ordinarily resident." Although it was created for European firms, Chettiar firms were also able to take advantage of it, and they would be taxed only on income earned in or remitted to British India. Their profits could continue being accommodated abroad.

The Japanese occupation of Burma during World War II changed the nature of jurisdictional claims around taxation cases. After being separated from India but before the war, Burma set up its own nascent infrastructure for tax collection. Chettiar firms were subject to Burmese income taxes on the income they made in Burma; any double-taxation agreements between two former British Indian provinces now became those across two different British colonies. During the Japanese occupation, as these firms wound up their affairs and moved out of Burma, they left behind promissory notes, loans, land, and homes. Following their wartime displacement, if they had spent time in India, they became potentially liable to pay income tax there, as definitions of tax residence were related to time spent in a particular jurisdiction in addition to physical presence. Indeed, the question of what now constituted their tax residence—given that it was calculated with reference to time as well as territory—had implications not only for their wealth but for inheritance, marriage, adoption, and a variety of other social and economic arrangements, both within their communities and outside.[46] On the one hand, war-ravaged Burma was hardly able to collect income tax; as the *Times of India* wrote of Burma's financial position in 1945, "Exiled for three years in Simla, the Burma Government had no country to rule and no revenue to collect. It was a spending concern."[47] On the other hand, it was relatively simple to challenge tax assessments in India; in 1946, the cost of "referring" a tax case on to the Madras High Court was 100 rupees—not an enormous sum of money for traders, merchants, or business houses.[48] This brought several referred cases on questions of cross-border taxation before the Madras High Court.

With their efforts to recover wartime debts and manage tax liability already in turmoil, Chettiar firms also faced yet another challenge: to gain a measure of control over the postwar economy, the interim Burmese government began to impose legislative restrictions on collecting agricultural debt, foreclosing on prewar mortgages, and carrying on a moneylending business. Soon after a new constitution came into force in 1948 for the Union of Burma, the state was deemed to be the owner of all property, and landholdings were nationalized. This affected Chettiar firms because they had come into land ownership a result of prewar foreclosures on mortgages, in which people had pledged land as collateral. According to scholar Usha Mahajani, even before the war, about three million out of twelve million acres of land—or about 25 percent of all cultivated land in Burma—had thus passed into the hands of the Chettiars, in which their capital was tied up.[49] When these postwar restrictions came into force, many presumed that migrant moneylending communities would be ousted. Andrus Russell, professor of economics at the University of Rangoon, noted in his treatise about the postwar period that "the return of British and Indian investors is assumed, with reservation in regard to Indian money-lenders."[50] Ironically, the return of Chettiar firms to Burma was uncertain because of their outsize impact on the prewar Burmese economy.

In her study of Chettiar economies, S. Sridevi points out that Chettiars themselves saw the end of their time in Burma as a historically significant moment and used it as a milestone to mark the passage of time: in Tamil, *Parma kettatukku appuram* ("after Burma went bad").[51] This phrase captures the relationship between circulations of credit and capital, between place and time, within migrant trading networks such as the Chettiars', which began to unravel after the war ended. In Burma, the export of rice, in which Chettiar credit had played such an important role, came to a standstill; the ships belonging to the Irrawady Flotilla Company that went up and down the rivers, carrying cargo, ceased operation. Many ships and launches had already been destroyed as part of the "scorched earth" policy of both the British Army and the Japanese occupation government. The end of the war brought other sweeping changes to the economy in Burma; postwar economic policies of the government centered on lowering agricultural debt and included offering cash advances or consumer goods in an attempt to increase the acreage of land under cultivation. Building on these official policies, reports in progovernment newspapers exhorted Burman farmers to produce more food to help "fellow Buddhists" in Ceylon and Malaya, who had suffered along with them in the war.[52]

Aware of the changing economic landscape of postwar South and Southeast Asia, income tax administrators in India paid special attention to the Chettiar businesses that had been forced to operate in Japan-occupied territories in Burma, Malaya, and beyond. While the government decreed that tax assessment on these firms would continue, income tax officers were urged to be sympathetic. For example, in response to pleas from Chettiar associations in Burma, Malaya, and Indochina, a Government of India circular noted that copies (rather than originals) of account books sent by Chettiar agents would suffice for official income tax purposes.[53] But this attitude of sympathy and accommodation began to change in 1943, when Japanese troops in Burma retreated. Following this first glimmer of hope on the horizon, talk soon turned to postwar reconstruction in South Asia and the need to increase government revenue through taxation.

The talk of economic and political reconstruction was not restricted to India. For Burma too, the promise of independence from British rule appeared to be within reach. And with the emerging debates over independence came questions of citizenship: "The Burmese do not want any more moneylenders, traders or clerks from India," declared the civil servant B. R. Pearn—a sentiment shared by political factions in Burma, caught up in their own internal questions over territorial sovereignty and self-determination struggles.[54] These discussions of citizenship that would exclude those with an intermittent presence in the country took place within a broader political debate about whose reconstruction would be sustained by Chettiar capital—India's or Burma's. Some Chettiar firms had already declared their intention to move their enterprises back to Madras and participate in the plans for industrialization that were being laid out by Nehru's government. Other firms—including representatives of the Nattukottai Chettiars to the Burmese government, like A. M. M. Vellayan Chettiar—intended to support the return of Chettiar capital to Burma and participate in Burma's industrialization. In the discussions between the Indian and Burmese governments at Simla, Vellayan Chettiar constantly reiterated his belief that to fuel Burma's growth, its government should not emphasize agriculture but should, like India, focus on industrialization.[55] Within this broader framework of postwar economic reconstruction, the question of where postwar Chettiar capital would be invested made tax residence a crucial issue.

TIME AND TAX RESIDENCE

Like the *Ramanathan Chettiar* reference that was instrumental in determining "control" and "management" in the legal definitions of tax residence, the judgment in the *Shanmugham Rubber Estate* case, involving a rubber plantation located in the former Strait Settlements in Malacca, was widely circulated in government circles and among the commissioners of income tax in India. In 1919, the *Ramanathan Chettiar* case had set the precedent that having business interests in a particular location did not mean that one was resident in that location for income tax purposes in India; instead, residency depended on where the control and management of the firm was. In 1945, the *Shanmugham Rubber Estate* judgment of the Madras High Court would rewrite the principles for determining tax residence, changing the way in which income outside the territory of India was treated, once again by way of Chettiar tax references.[56]

In the *Shanmugham Rubber Estate* case, the facts were these: the control and management of a Chettiar partnership firm that owned, among other assets, a plantation in Malacca rotated through six different partners, who split their time between Karaikudi in Madras, the kingdom of Pudukkottai outside but bordering British India, and one of the Federated Malay States. The year of assessment in question was the year preceding wartime displacement in 1940–41, during which one of the Chettiar agents in Malacca wrote to the partner in Karaikudi, asking for instructions on how to invest a sum of 5,000 rupees. Following precedent, the legal issue in the case was where the "control" and "management" of the estate resided. To reach their decision, the Madras High Court examined as evidence letters written from partners in Madras to agents in the Straits Settlements that suggested that "control" and "management" of the firm remained in British India. Indeed, an envelope bearing a British Indian stamp was used as evidence of "control" by partners located in India.[57] Unlike in the *Ramanathan Chettiar* reference, where correspondence of this nature would have been shown to be "general instructions" and not evidence of "control" and "management," the judges held that if there was even partial management from the territory of British India, this would prove tax residence under Section 4-A of the Indian Income Tax Act of 1922.[58] In other words, if the management and control of a firm were not wholly outside British India, that firm would be considered "resident" and subject to Indian income tax.[59] As a result of this ruling, Chettiar firms, which had once been outside assessment of Indian income tax, came under its jurisdiction. After close to a century in which Chettiars had structured their business dealings so as to manage tax liability, it appeared that the "emigration" of Chettiar capital in Southeast Asia was being held to account.

The value of the *Shanmugham Rubber Estate* reference as legal precedent reverberated across Indian diasporic communities beyond South and Southeast Asia: businesses that traded, were invested, or owned land outside India would now be taxed in India. This was especially true for the Straits Settlements and the Malay states, soon to be reconstituted as the Federation of Malaya, where the estate was located. In response, Sir Alagappa Chettiar, a Nattukottai Chettiar who had investments in South India and across Southeast Asia and who was closely associated with Nehru and other leaders of the interim government in India, successfully persuaded the Central Board of Revenue tasked with the administration of income tax to hold off on income tax assessments between 1942 and 1947 for putative assessments from Burma and Malaya.[60] The abatement was to be only a temporary solution, during which Chettiar firms with branches in Malaya struggled to find a solution. "How are we supposed to pay, despaired Manickam Chettiar of Market Street in Singapore who was interviewed by *Malaya Tribune* in connection with the imminent return of income tax assessment, when we can't do any business because of our losses, and our money is tied up by moratorium?"[61]

While the *Shanmugham Rubber Estate* reference was handed down in India, changes to income tax law in Malaya were also under way, with significant implications for Chettiar firms. Under the Income Tax Ordinance introduced in 1948, it was proposed that Chettiar firms in Malaya be assessed as Hindu joint family firms, raising the rate at which they would be assessed, rather than as individual businesses. Many of these firms protested, arguing that they had been carrying on their trade with self-acquired capital and not the funds from the joint family.[62] The proposed rate of 20 percent for nonresidents in Malaya came in for criticism from the All Malaya Chettiars' Chamber of Commerce as being too excessive.[63] The government's response was to demand documentary evidence in the form of separation deeds to show that the Malayan firms were no longer associated with India. Thus, just as in Burma, the first years of the Federation were marked by a sharp animosity to the presence of the Chettiar moneylenders.

In 1947, the pro-British *Straits Times* published a scathing account of the place of the Chettiar in Malaya's economy, critiquing comments by R. Ramani—the lawyer and politician we met in chapter 2—attesting to the importance of Chettiars to the economy of postwar Malaya. In a robust response, the *Indian Daily Mail*, published by G. Sarangapany, writer, publisher, and the founder of the Tamil Reform Association, claimed that these were slanderous remarks that disregarded the Chettiars' steady investments and contributions to the Malayan economy, as well as the philanthropic activities that they had undertaken.[64] Here too, a reference was made to their payment of income tax:

In regard to the allegation that the Chettiars have been conspicuous by their absence from all subscription lists, we would ask our contemporary to go through the present subscription lists in aid of the Malayan Welfare Fund.

Again, the Chettiars have made immense donations to the War Fund and huge subscriptions to the War Loans. In the years 1929–30, when the Straits Settlements Government started a sort of War Fund as an alternative to introducing the income tax, the Chettiar community of Malacca alone had made an yearly contribution of $18,000 towards it. Any number of such examples can be enumerated, suffice to say that the sweeping remark which our contemporary has made about the Chettiars is a deliberate and deplorable distortion of the truth, a baseless aspersion and a calculated insult. It has pained not merely the Chettiars but the entire Indian community beyond measure.

These comments reiterated the importance of taxation as the "founding economic transfer" between states and citizens. Changes to income tax legislation and the jurisdictional claims that diasporic firms were compelled to make in this regard—an unexpected outcome of wartime displacements— would change the nature of citizenship claims made in later years.

In 1945, in the context of significant anxiety about unraveling networks of capital and credit across the Bay of Bengal, Chettiar firms wished to liquidate their landed wealth in Burma and send the proceeds to India without incurring significant tax liability. This, as we saw, was not easily done. The British Military Administration had also taken measures toward agricultural credit reconstruction to alleviate debt: it offered nearly 81 million rupees in cash advances to agriculturists in debt.[65] This changed the dynamics of the economy in Burma where the Chettiar firms operated most extensively; in Lower Burma, the wartime downturn in the import and export of rice meant that most agriculturists in the area were heavily indebted. These restrictions on land transfers (as well as increasing immigration restrictions, discussed in previous chapters) occurred just as legislative provisions were being made to designate more income as taxable. The attempts by the government in Burma to foster domestic agriculture took place against a backdrop of discussions about the place of "Indian interests" in postwar Burma. Here too, the Chettiars fought a losing battle. Burma's attempts at introducing a bank for agriculturists failed; officials privately agreed that the Chettiar firms had far more knowledge of a borrower's repayment prospects than the new civilian government in Burma could.[66]

The general economic situation thus favored the winding up of Chettiar operations outside Madras. At the same time, a widening tax net in India meant that many of them would have preferred to stay abroad. Some of the returning Chettiars invested in educational institutions, others in industrial ventures. Following wartime displacement, the Burma Nattukottai Chettiars' Association itself set up a social welfare branch in Pudukkottai, from which they attempted to carry out social service tasks for Chettiar families returning from Burma.[67] In 1947, the Indian Taxation Investigation Commission had recommended changing the legal understanding of tax residence to include overseas Indians who made remittances home, thus making these remittances taxable in India. However, this was quickly revised because of the major financial implications it would have for displaced migrants following the Partition. In its place, the Income Tax Enquiry Committee recommended in 1949 that the category of "resident but not ordinarily resident" under the Income Tax Act—the legal category that Chettiars had adopted eagerly on the eve of the war—should exclude Indians who had been displaced from South Africa, Malaya, Burma, and Ceylon and who had remitted their income to India because of their displacement.[68]

Section 49, a provision of the Indian Income Tax Act that had not received much attention until then, became the subject of much legislative activity beginning in 1948, owing to these special allowances made for returnees and refugees of war and partition. One account suggests that this was at the behest of Alagappa Chettiar.[69] The provision was originally included to cover situations where there was no scheme for relief from double taxation: this section, intended to be a temporary fiscal arrangement following the partition of India and Pakistan, provided that in the case of double taxation one would pay only the lower rate of tax. This became the model for similar arrangements for double-taxation relief for those in Burma and Ceylon, added through legislative amendment.[70]

But the legislative amendments were not simply a compassionate measure. The Indian government estimated that since this "refugee capital" would amount to twenty or thirty crore rupees, a wider tax net was preferred.[71] Litigation over definitions of tax residence stemming from wartime displacements persisted well into the 1960s in courts in India, Malaya, and Burma.[72] An Indian delegation that visited Burma after the war ended estimated that the Chettiars alone had lost 74.5 million rupees.[73] With the deaths of Raja Annamalai Chettiar and A. M. M. Vellayan Chettiar, the community lost their main interlocutors with the Burmese government; in the year leading up to his death, Vellayan Chettiar had been deeply engaged in discussions on postwar reconstruction in Burma, pushing for improvement of river transport, construction of a better road network, and creation of sound fiscal policy to satisfy Burma's public debt.[74]

By 1951, similar rumors were afloat about capital flight from Malaya. Newspapers in Malaya, and Singapore reported that the government in India was expecting nearly 750 million rupees in remittances from Malaya because of the legislative exemptions granted to overseas Indians. According to the *Indian Daily Mail* again, the main source of this rumor appeared to be a comment made by Malayan Indian Congress founder S. O. K. Ubaidulla that Indian businessmen were transferring much of their wealth to India from Malaya because they were worried that their properties too would be nationalized, as they had been in Burma and Ceylon. In qualifying these remarks, leaders of the Indian Chambers of Commerce hastened to add that there was no such plan afoot and that they were invested in the future of Malaya. The rivalry between the *Straits Times* and the *Indian Daily Mail* was evident once again, as the latter claimed that the former was attempting to foist the blame on the "poor Ramasamy," the South Indian laborers on the rubber plantations, for sending "big sums" away to India. "We have not heard of his category ever mobbing the banks for D/Ds (demand drafts) and T/Ts (telegraphic transfers). It may be that they are sending a few more rupees a month by postal money order to their dependents in India but to construe it as a transfer of capital is simply ridiculous," wrote the newspapers. These rumors of the misplaced loyalties of plantation laborers—arguably the most marginalized among migrants of Indian ancestry in Southeast Asia—would reappear in debates on citizenship; the editorial ended by asking rhetorically: "Who is sending away capital to India?"[75]

The question about capital flight in the aftermath of wartime displacements was tied up with legislative changes around income tax. In 1942, as Japan occupied Singapore, Burma, and Malaya, India's attention had shifted to income tax as a major source of potential income for the British government from those displaced by the war to India, which was struggling to finance a burgeoning war budget.[76] Trading and moneylending communities like the Chettiars formed a significant part of India's taxable base in Madras; they were so critical to the administration of income tax that when they challenged assessments before courts and tribunals, it set the standards for others as well. So it is no coincidence that the legislative changes proposed to income tax legislation around tax residence became a point of crisis for trading communities. Key amendments were made to the Income Tax Act in 1939, 1952, 1955, and finally 1961, particularly around the definitions of "tax residence." In this context, questions of income tax revenue relating to South Asia's "other partitions" continued to come up before courts.[77] In an effort to expand the taxable population beyond the borders of British India, the meaning of "residence" had in the interwar period been understood in temporal terms, with respect to the time periods spent in India. In the aftermath of the Japanese occupation in 1942 and wartime displacements of traders, merchants, and moneylenders from across Southeast Asia, including the Chettiars from Burma and Malaya, and as India was confronted with a possibility of "refugee capital," the temporal understanding of tax residence was further entrenched, as moratoriums on wartime debts also used 1942 as a juridical marker. Even as tax assessments continued to take place and as nonresidents were subjected to increasing rates, businesses, and landholdings were nationalized in Burma, leaving many Chettiar firms in possession of nothing more than worthless title deeds to their erstwhile properties in Burma.

FOUR

APPLICATION FORMS

WHILE THE CHETTIARS FELT the consequences of wartime displacement most keenly in encounters with income tax collectors and the courts as they challenged the changing legal regimes of taxation, ordinary migrants and laborers confronted the consequences of wartime displacement primarily through encounters with bureaucracy. These encounters are documented in application forms. The application forms were for permits, passes, certificates, and the passports that would enable migrants to continue traveling between South and Southeast Asia after the war ended. As we will see, the officials and departments that processed these application forms were constantly being redesignated, and paperwork was not equally recognized and honored across emergent national borders. The paperwork that migrants possessed—both its nature and its value—fluctuated wildly in postwar South and Southeast Asia, changing with the shape and form of borders as they ebbed and flowed, redrawn in law. At a time when principles of immigration and citizenship were yet to be firmly established in South and Southeast Asia, migrants encountered juridical borders like restrictions on travel or remittance limits firsthand through paperwork.

These ebbs and flows in the value of paper took place in the context of surging nationalist movements, with new governments in South and

Southeast Asia trying to separate putative citizens from "undesirable" foreigners. The lack of proper paperwork was thus wielded as a threat. Filling out an application form—or having a form filled up by a clerk, translator, or lawyer—became an act with potentially life-altering consequences. These forms were standardized and provided little space to explain or elaborate on answers, and they were highly fraught: answers to seemingly innocuous questions—such as acknowledging an occasional remittance overseas to family members or explaining absence because of a brief trip to attend a religious festival in one's ancestral village—were seen as a lack of evidence of "permanent settlement." Finally, forms used in different settings were often interlinked, affecting the status of and rate of success with other applications. For example, in Ceylon, where the events in this chapter unfold before turning back to the Madras High Court, signing off on an application form as a "temporary resident" to remit money to relatives in India had repercussions for an entirely separate application for "permanent settlement" and naturalization, as one applicant whose story is narrated in this chapter, Mohammed Ibrahim Saibo, discovered. Although identification and surveillance of migrants were not new—these forms of identification and paperwork built on precolonial and colonial methods of identification and surveillance, such as the *tin ticket* or *tundu* system that had once transported laborers for Ceylon's plantations across the Palk Strait or across the Bay of Bengal to Malaya—travel documents became national identity documents in postwar South and Southeast Asia.

The demand for more paperwork to establish ties to adopted homes had a significant impact on labor migrants. This chapter looks at the applications for citizenship in Ceylon made by laborers who worked on tea plantations in Sri Lanka (figure 4.1), showing how remittance forms, property deeds, letters to loved ones, and travel tickets were used as adverse evidence in legal claims about political belonging. Although these laborers were often in possession of documents establishing their presence in Ceylon, it was considered insufficient to establish permanent settlement and claim citizenship in Ceylon. According to the government, they were migrants, brought over from South India by plantation owners—although they had been in Ceylon for over a century. But neither were these laborers accepted as Indians: the Indian government used this same long period of residence in Ceylon to assert that they should claim citizenship in Ceylon. By altering the value ascribed to the pieces of paper that these laborers produced in support of their citizenship applications, the new nation-states of India and Ceylon wielded application forms as a threat against migrants.

MUTHIAH'S CITIZENSHIP APPLICATION

In 1942, Kandaswamy Muthiah gave up his hawking business in Kandupolle, a small town in Ceylon's Central Province. Kandupolle, located in the heart of Ceylon's plantation economy, was the highest elevation reached by the Ceylon Government Railway, nearly six thousand feet above sea level. Business was not good, and the threat of war loomed on the horizon. Muthiah had a new wife, Karuppayi, whom he had married that year, and he quickly realized that supporting his young family would require a stable income. He therefore found employment as a plantation laborer on the Pundaluoya Estate and by his own account quickly rose to become a kangany, an overseer and recruiting agent for plantation workers.[1]

Five years later, in 1949, the war ended and Ceylon was granted independence from British rule. The new government, headed by the United

FIGURE 4.1: *Two tea pluckers, Ceylon, 1907–17. New York Public Library Digital Collections.*

National Party's D. S. Senanayake, enthusiastically embarked on the project of nation building. Their tactics intentionally deepened schisms between the majority Sinhala and minority Tamil populations on the island, and new citizenship regimes were brought into force. Muthiah discovered that although he had lived, worked, married, and raised children in Ceylon, he was not eligible for citizenship under the new Ceylon Citizenship Act of 1948, as he could not fulfill the requirements of Ceylonese nationality; instead, he was assumed to be of Indian origin. In 1949, a new law was passed—the Indian and Pakistani Residents (Citizenship) Act of 1949 (IPRA or "the 1949 Act")—that provided an opportunity for plantation laborers like Muthiah to become citizens by registration if they met certain requirements. When Muthiah decided to file his citizenship application under the 1949 Act, he likely had no inkling of the legal struggles that were yet to come or foresaw that his fate would be determined by the most mundane form of paperwork: application forms.

Muthiah's application to the Commission for the Registration of Indian and Pakistani Residents (and his subsequent appeal to Ceylon's Supreme Court against the ruling of the deputy commissioner) was one of many hundreds of thousands of applications filed for naturalization by Ceylon's Tamil-speaking plantation laborers. According to the commission's reports, they received 237,000 applications on behalf of nearly 800,000 "Indian Tamils." The Ceylon Workers' Congress, the most prominent trade union in Ceylon's plantation districts, offered resources, including legal representation at the commissioner's inquiries, for plantation workers who would have otherwise been unable to access it.[2] Muthiah's appeal made it all the way to the Supreme Court, but most applications dismissed by the commission never made it that far. This chapter, then, draws largely upon the records held in the commissioner's archive, for these laborers' first and often only point of contact with the government was with the commission, not the courts.

The citizenship applications filled out by these laborers were forms that required applicants' personal details such as places of "origin," and along with these forms their application files included the notes of the investigating officers, the records of the commissioners who heard their cases at the preliminary stage, and the appeals (if any) to the Supreme Court of

Ceylon. These applications were scrutinized by the Office of the Commissioner for Registration of Indian and Pakistani Residents; understaffed and unprepared to deal with the deluge of applications, investigating officers who staffed the bureau were pensioners, pulled back into government service in the postwar period.[3] In 1953, branch offices were opened in Kandy, Matale, Gampola, Nuwara Eliya, Hatton, Bandarawala, Ratnapure, and Kegalle—all plantation districts, where the government expected the most applications to come from. This system was disorganized and inefficient: between 1951, when all applications were due, and 1961, when most of the applications had been adjudicated, numerous applications were mishandled or ignored.[4] However, the officials often blamed applicants for their own mishandling of the documents. In many inquiries where the applicant was unsuccessful, officials informed families that it was because the paperwork was improperly filled out or because the documentary evidence that they had supplied was insufficient, unreliable, or even fraudulent.

MUTHIAH'S TRAVELS

By his own account, Muthiah had come to Ceylon from Madras in 1911, when he was five or six years old, with his parents and many others. During that period, many made the short but perilous journey across the Palk Strait to Ceylon's coastal Mannar district, and from there to the tea plantations in Nuwara Eliya. Men and women from South India had been making these journeys since the mid-nineteenth century, when a plantation economy had been established in Ceylon, with coffee, then tea, as the main plantation crop. Although most of these laborers settled on the island without returning to their villages in India, they were still, in the 1940s, being viewed as "recent arrivals" when immigration and citizenship regimes began to be implemented.[5]

These plantation laborers were often recruited by a kangany—an experienced laborer on a plantation who rose to be an overseer or a supervisor and went back to his or her village in Madras to recruit men and women to the tea, coffee, and rubber plantations in Ceylon. The plantation laborers were "free"—that is to say, there was no contract for indenture, nor were they enslaved. In theory, they could quit their employment with a month's notice and return to their homes in India. Throughout the nineteenth century, historian Patrick Peebles notes, colonial officials framed Tamil-speaking plantation workers as "seasonal laborers" in government reports. They highlighted how different kangany-led migration was from the slavery and indentured migration that were prevalent in other parts of the British Empire—types of migration that entailed permanent stays on plantations.[6] Unlike the indentured migration of Indian labor to Natal, Fiji, the British Caribbean, and beyond, it was presumed that the kangany-led migration to Ceylon, because of the proximity of the island to Indian shores, allowed laborers to maintain their links with their villages of origin.[7]

This "import" of labor by plantation owners from South India had not gone unnoticed in political circles in Ceylon. Beginning in the early twentieth century, electoral politics had coalesced around Sinhala and Tamil nationalism, especially as separate electoral seats for Sinhalese and Tamils were introduced as part of constitutional reforms under the Donoughmore Commission in 1928. Although the Ceylon National Congress, which represented Ceylon's interests to the British government, included both Tamil and Sinhala leadership, these collaborations soon disintegrated, as Ceylon's interests began to be seen as coincident with Sinhala interests. The Congress, acting on the desires of Tamil and moderate Sinhalas, demanded complete independence from Britain. However, a more radical wing of the Congress's Sinhalese delegation, led by D. S. Senanayake, broke away in 1943 to form the United National Party, which sought Dominion status within the British Empire.

In spite of—or because of—the war, simmering nationalist tendencies among both among Sinhala and Tamil political leaders in Ceylon intensified. As Peebles notes, British planters perceived migrant laborers as being more willing to do difficult manual labor—labor that local Kandyan peasants would never deign to do. This was true primarily because there were no socioeconomic reasons for Kandyan peasants and low-country Sinhalese to take up the kinds of wage labor offered by British plantations.[8] However, this perception of innate difference between the two groups— one framed as suited for hard manual labor, the other for less grueling work—heightened the existing tensions between the two communities. Although an official report in 1938 noted that Indian immigration to the plantations in Ceylon had not taken employment away from Ceylonese workers, the discontent surrounding labor migration from India continued. In 1939, the Indian government banned emigration to Ceylon, citing looming war clouds.[9] As we saw in chapter 1, negotiations between the two governments to resume migration began in 1940 but failed to reach a satisfactory consensus around the issue of labor immigration—a failure that set the stage for the difficulties of citizenship applications from after the war.

With the Japanese occupation of Singapore in 1941, the British Empire lost control of its premier plantation economy in the Straits Settlements and its most important source of rubber and tin. Ceylon filled this gap, becoming more important to the British Empire both economically and strategically. But only a year later, in 1942, there was a great need for wartime labor in Ceylon, restarting the flow of people across the Palk Strait. With the end of the war, questions of immigration shifted from the management of labor to the management of putative citizens. In 1945, the year that the war ended, Muthiah's wife, Karuppayi, gave birth to Saraspathy, their first child. Saraspathy's birth would prove crucial to the fate of Muthiah's application before the commission.

THE CITIZENSHIP ACTS

On August 26, 1950, almost a year before the deadline for filing applications for naturalization, Muthiah, Karuppayi, his five-year-old daughter Saraspathy, and his one-year-old son Balakrishnan filed their application for citizenship in Ceylon. There was no word about the status of the application for more than five years, during which Muthiah and his family remained at the risk of statelessness. On October 3, 1955, Muthiah received a notice from the deputy commissioner in Nuwara Eliya, containing the disappointing news that his application had been refused. But the notice also summoned him to appear in person before the deputy commissioner for an inquiry to prove that he fulfilled the requirements. He would have some time before the hearing to gather paperwork and find character witnesses who would speak for him.

The IPRA afforded an opportunity for citizenship by registration for those who could not claim citizenship by descent under the Ceylon Citizenship Act of 1948.[10] It was directed primarily at Indian workers in the plantation districts. Under the 1948 Act, Tamils from Ceylon born in Malaya were eligible to register for citizenship but often experienced challenges to their registration.[11] But the IPRA, directed at Indian or Pakistani residents, could accommodate these cases. It defined an Indian or Pakistani resident as someone who had "permanently settled" in Ceylon but whose "origin" was in British India or an Indian state (a kingdom like Travancore or Hyderabad) before the passing of the Indian Independence Act of 1947 and the territorial partition of the subcontinent. To demonstrate "permanent settlement" and prove "residence" for the purposes of immigration regimes, applicants had to demonstrate that they had been present in Ceylon for seven years before January 1, 1946—that is, from 1939 onwards. This seven-year time period (which came from the draft agreements and proposals put forward during wartime negotiations between India and Ceylon on labor immigration)[12] was referred to as the "minimum period of uninterrupted residence." Applicants also had to prove that they had an "assured income," could conform to Ceylonese laws of marriage and inheritance, and were willing to give up allegiances to any other country.[13]

Although the act claimed to be designed to give a path to citizenship for "Indian Tamils," political leaders at the time were quick to note that these excessively rigid requirements seemed to be designed to exclude the group.[14] Several "Ceylon Tamils" were able to claim citizenship under the 1948 Act on the basis of citizenship by descent, but for "Indian Tamils" (the bulk of immigrant laborers), the only way to secure Ceylonese citizenship was through the IPRA. And with the stringent nature of the documentary proof demanded by the commission, Muthiah's hope for citizenship, like that of many other "Indian Tamils" in Ceylon, appeared to be fading.

By 1950, the definition of Indian citizenship was organized around the territorial partition of the subcontinent into India and Pakistan. According to the new Indian constitution, one had to be born within the territory of India or one's parents or grandparents had to be born there.[15] Dual citizenship was not allowed owing to the partition of India and Pakistan. As with Ceylon (and, later, Malaya), citizenship by registration was possible for migrants to these countries. But the interim government of India encouraged Indians overseas to claim citizenship in their adopted homes, where they had invested their labor.[16] In Ceylon, when the citizenship registers were opened in Kandy and Colombo, very few Indians came forward to claim Indian citizenship,[17] and it is unlikely that many plantation laborers were among those who did. Shut out of both Indian and Ceylonese citizenship, plantation laborers like Muthiah were at the risk of statelessness.

A distinction between "Indian" and "Ceylon" Tamil appears in the official documents of the time. This distinction demand further explanation. The "Indian Tamil," which the census report in Tamil designated one of the separate races to be counted, was an official category with a complicated history.[18] The sense that "Indian Tamil" was a separate category took on a dangerous valence in the 1940s, both during and after the war, as debates over the need for immigrant labor from India entered Ceylonese political discourse. As documents from 1946 show, census officials in Ceylon could not classify the "races" with any degree of certainty. For instance, the Paravars of the Mannar district and the Chettis of Colombo, who had migrated from Madras many centuries prior and intermarried with both Tamil and Sinhalese, were classified in the census as "Ceylon Tamils."[19] Yet these blurry racial designations were important: someone who declared themselves an "Indian Tamil" to a census official or on a census form during the colonial period (often because they did not know the political consequences of that designation) would find the outcome of their citizenship application radically different from that of a "Ceylon Tamil."[20]

Most applicants, however, were aware that the stakes of citizenship applications in Ceylon were high. They knew, for instance, that it was ill advised for potential IPRA applicants like Muthiah to leave the country and go to India; the Immigrants and Emigrants Act of 1948 prohibited travel between India and Ceylon without a passport—a document that could not be obtained without Ceylonese citizenship, something few Indian Tamils had been able to gain under the Ceylon Citizenship Act of 1948.[21] These citizenship laws had other types of important consequences also. For example, they affected political representation. Workers on plantations had first received the right to vote in 1931, as a result of the constitutional reforms recommended by the Donoughmore Commission. This was in no small part due to the efforts of K. Natesa Aiyar and his wife Meenachi Ammal, who had moved to Ceylon from Thanjavur. Natesa Aiyar joined forces with D. M. Manilal, an Indian lawyer who had fought for the rights of the Indians in South Africa, Fiji, and Mauritius and formed the All India Estate Labor Federation in 1931. After the war, the Ceylon (Parliamentary Elections) Order in Council of 1946 disqualified noncitizens from having their name entered in electoral registers, effectively preventing them from voting.[22] Because IPRA applicants, many of them Indian Tamils, did not have citizenship, they did not figure in the registers, which were the basis of the 1952 elections. Thus citizenship status affected political representation and voting rights in the Indian Tamils' chosen homelands.

Perhaps more importantly, these citizenship laws affected mobility for migrants between India and Ceylon. Not only did they prevent those (like Muthiah) who hoped to gain Ceylonese citizenship from traveling to India, they also discouraged people from engaging in traditional economic migrancy. Migrants between India and Ceylon were not forced to choose one citizenship, but for those who did not possess either citizenship, the paperwork began to mount. New bureaucratic categories of documentation—visas and permits—were invented to identify noncitizens or visitors,[23] and a system was instituted to issue Indo-Ceylon passes for those who did not have Indian or Ceylonese passports.[24] Those with non-Ceylonese passports (from India or other countries) could be granted temporary residence permits, issued as passport stamps, that allowed them to continue living or working in Ceylon without Ceylonese citizenship. Identity cards were issued to fishermen in Mannar district, closest to the Indian mainland, who were viewed with suspicion for possibly smuggling Indian immigrants into Ceylon.[25] All of these new burdens of paperwork seemed to be designed to slow the circulation of people between India and Ceylon. Similar changes were taking place outside of the world of paperwork: by 1954, the Ceylon government shut down the quarantine camp at Mandapam in India, the most popular port of embarkation for passengers from India to Ceylon, and stopped providing mattresses, pillows, glasses, or drinking water to the passengers.[26] With the proliferation of these categories of immigration and citizenship, the "illegal" or "illicit" immigrant became a staple of everyday conversation and newspaper headlines.

Even as Muthiah's application wound its way through the commission between 1950 and 1955, the calls for illegal immigration from India to be dealt with using stronger measures grew louder. Newspaper headlines tripped over themselves in excitement and disbelief as they proclaimed that people were swarming across the Palk Strait to Ceylon. "Sly comers," referring to immigrants from India, "they keep coming," noted newspapers in Ceylon in the years following the introduction of formal citizenship regimes. The reporters noted that they could not understand why people would risk stringent immigration control and almost certain detection to come to Ceylon. The controller of immigration and emigration, who claimed that Mannar Island was as crowded with Indians as "South India on a Deepavali day,"[27] wrote of military-strength patrol boats patrolling the northern coastal districts on the island, the Royal Air Force's Airspeed Oxford spying from the air on scurrying immigrants around popular landing spots, and propaganda machines being sent into overdrive.[28] Camps were opened in Mannar and Jaffna to house illegal immigrants until they could stand trial.[29] Vitriolic speeches made by those opposed to migrants from India in Ceylon were printed without editorialization.[30] Cyclostyled anonymous letters were sent to the Indian-origin residents in Ceylon from a mysterious group calling itself the Dutugemunu Secret Society, asking the "blood-sucking *yakas*" to quit Ceylon and threatening them with dire consequences if they did not.[31] The group's name was not without significance—it included a reference to Dutugemunu, a Sinhalese prince of Sri Lanka who defeated the Chola prince Elara in the second century BC.[32]

BEFORE THE COMMISSION

According to the 1946 census, Nuwara Eliya, where Muthiah and his family lived, was the only district where there had been more "Indian Tamils" than "indigenous races," although the district had had only five major tea estates (including Pundaluoya) at its 1920s peak. Note that the categories "Indian Tamil" and "Ceylon Tamil" were used for the census, often reflecting presumptions and/or self-identification, not necessarily an objective truth about ancestral origins. Between 1921 and 1946, the population of self-identified Ceylon Tamils increased by 227.8 percent and Indian Tamils by only 51.8 percent; Ceylon Moors increased by 127.4 percent, while Indian Moors increased by 15.2 percent (more about "Moors" in chapter 5).[33] There were rumors that "Indian Tamils" were self-identifying as "Ceylon Tamils" to qualify for citizenship. In this context, it is not surprising that the investigating officer for Nuwara Eliya, who would have looked at Muthiah's citizenship application form first, was suspicious of his claim that he had stayed in Nuwara Eliya and Ceylon for the ten years required under the act. He referred the matter to the deputy commissioner.

On November 7, 1955, five years after he filed his citizenship application, Muthiah finally had the chance to make his case in person before Deputy Commissioner G. W. Ediriwara, who had until then received impressions of him only via a carefully pieced-together paper trail. Nuwara Eliya was where a large majority of the plantation laborers of Indian origin lived, and the commission likely received many hundreds of thousands of IPRA applications like Muthiah's. Ediriwara's inquiry was conducted in one of sixteen government-commandeered rooms in the St. Andrews Hotel in Nuwara Eliya. He traveled from there to the North Pundaluoya Estate, where Muthiah and his family worked. It was at the "factory office" on the plantation that Muthiah and his witnesses, Arnolis de Silva and A. K. Menon, turned up early in the morning to testify before Ediriwara and the rest of the commission, explaining why there was sufficient evidence for him to be registered as a citizen of Ceylon.

During the inquiry, Ediriwara had what appeared to be a motley collection of scraps of paper before him. The documentary evidence in support of Muthiah's application was a series of shop receipts from his time as a hawker in Kandapulle. These receipts had dates on them, serving as proof that he had been present in Ceylon for seven years prior to 1946, as the act required. However, Ediriwara was not convinced. We do not know his side of the dialogue—the inquiry report notes only applicants' answers, not the commissioner's questions—but the record of Muthiah's "case" reads as a series of desperate pleas about belonging to Ceylon, almost certainly translated and transcribed from Tamil into English. "I have no interest whatsoever in India. I have made no money remittances in India. I have no relations in India. My wife also has no relations in India. My wife was born in Ceylon. I was born in India. I came to Ceylon at the age of seven or eight with my parents. My parents died about twenty years ago." At the end of the interview, Muthiah affirmed that he intended to permanently settle in Ceylon, that he and his wife had no interests in India, and that all of his family—all his "relations"—were on the Pundaluoya Estate.[34]

The commission's procedures for citizenship application represented what David Dery terms "papereality," in which a surfeit of paperwork exceeds the events and persons represented by it, overdetermining reality.[35] According to the IPRA, investigating officers and commissioners had to note if the proper forms had been used and what details included on these forms were supported with affidavits. After an application was received, the commissioner sent it to the investigating officer of the area in which the persons claimed to be "ordinarily resident." The investigating officer looked into the veracity of the claims made by the applicant. If there was no prima facie case, the officer's report was sent back to the commissioner or deputy commissioner, and a notice was issued to the applicant, giving him or her three months to respond. The commissioner, whose legal authority was equivalent to that of a district judge adjudicating a civil case, could also carry out his own inquiry. Muthiah's application had gone through all these stages to reach Ediriwara in 1955.

The grounds on which citizenship was offered or rejected depended largely on the wisdom with which applicants filled out the many required forms. Deputy commissioners had to note whether the right forms had been used and whether they were "in order." Permanent settlement had to be proved, as well as status as an Indian or Pakistani "resident." Any political rights to "the territory from which they emigrated" had to be relinquished. The contradiction between the last two requirements was not lost on the applicants. To claim citizenship by registration, applicants had to first acknowledge that they were an Indian resident, and later in the same process to relinquish that status. Plantation laborers found it difficult to meet the residence requirement because of the amount and types of documentary proof that the act demanded; Muthiah found himself questioned on this point at his inquiry.[36] Many of the first—and ultimately, successful—applicants were those who lived in towns and villages, educated professionals and those who served in Ceylon's government posts. These people had only to provide proof of employment to prove residence.[37] Plantation laborers, however, were entirely dependent on the estate manager and the estate itself to supply them with the details and records that the IPRA demanded. Additionally, this documentation—in the form of school records, pay stubs, check rolls, or the like—had to be produced for the ten years that formed the "period of uninterrupted residence." This onerous standard for documentary proof was a point of contention during the parliamentary debates leading up to its enactment. "I do not know whether the Honourable Dudley Senanayake would ever be able to prove that he is a citizen of Ceylon according to the formal requirements of the law," announced Pieter Keuneman, a member of the Communist Party of Ceylon in Parliament, during the debate on the Indian Citizenship Bill that preceded the IPRA.[38] The controller of immigration and emigration responded loftily, "Collection of proof of residence is not hard."[39] The government claimed that people could use a variety of documents to prove that they were residents: householders' lists available with the Food Control Department, extracts from voters' lists, correspondence with government departments or mercantile firms, certified copies of legal proceedings, vehicle licenses, insurance policy premium payments, purchase receipts, post office savings bank books, or extracts from account books or servants' registers. Even an envelope with a hastily scribbled address would do, they claimed.[40] Yet applicants still struggled to meet the act's demands for paperwork.

The commissioners adjudicating citizenship applications blamed delays on the laborers themselves, saying that investigating officers spent their days scouring over estate ledger entries, looking for applicants' names.[41] This was not the whole truth. On occasion, appeals to the Supreme Court revealed that the deputy commissioners had acted capriciously in dealing with the evidence presented by the applicants.[42] In some cases, for example, applicants never had a chance to respond to notices calling them to an inquiry because the notices had not been delivered to the right postal address;[43] in other cases, deputy commissioners investigated, arrived at conclusions, and presented evidence at inquiries without ever giving notice to applicants at all.[44] In perhaps the most extreme case recorded in legal proceedings, the deputy commissioner concluded—without any basis and with a declaration by the applicant to the contrary—that the applicant had not realized the implications of acquiring citizenship in Ceylon.[45]

At the National Archives of Sri Lanka in Colombo, I looked at over five hundred individual applications like Muthiah's. The "head of household," almost always the oldest male or the husband, filed a single application for the entire household, so the personal and familial histories contained in these applications represented those of thousands of people. During inquiries, many IPRA applicants, like Muthiah, asserted repeatedly that they had no interest in India, that they could hardly remember it, that they had married in Ceylon and had children, and that they would abide by Ceylonese laws. "We are all Ceylonese, and do not know any other country, please," wrote Durai Basheer, pleading with the deputy commissioner to let him know the outcome of his application.[46] Another applicant, M. K. Assan, a shopkeeper in Matale, wrote that both he and his parents had been born in Ceylon, but he could produce only house rent receipts in support of his applications, and the investigating officer noted that his signature was different on the application and during the course of the inquiry. Assan's application was refused.[47]

These suspicions seeped into the official scrutiny of Muthiah's citizenship application as well. The investigating officer looking into Muthiah's application wrote that he had failed to show through documentary evidence that he was resident in Ceylon from 1939 to 1943 and that he had permanently settled in Ceylon. Further, he noted, there was no evidence that Saraspathy, Muthiah's daughter, had lived in Ceylon from 1946 to 1950. From 1946 to 1950, Saraspathy was between one and five years of age and was living with her parents. But this was unconvincing to the investigating officer, as were Muthiah's claims on the permanent settlement questionnaire that neither he nor his wife had any interest in India, that neither had ever owned shares or property in either India or Ceylon, and that none of his family had ever been to India. His affidavit proved insufficient for the investigating officer.

Nor was Muthiah's application convincing to Ediriwara. He wrote that the evidence was simply too "artificial and unconvincing" and that he "refused to believe" that anyone who was hawking goods in Kandupolle would travel to "distant Dickoya" to buy goods when goods were available in Nuwara Eliya or Ramboda, closer to his home. For him, these specifics about Muthiah's family and business did not align with commonly known details about the personal and familial histories of plantation laborers; they cast doubt on Muthiah's paper trail. He also pointed out that the two shop receipts submitted were for one rupee and three rupees respectively. Why, Ediriwara wondered, would Muthiah preserve receipts for sixteen years for such "paltry" sums of money, when notarial bonds for millions of rupees are often thrown away after a period of time? If they were indeed genuine, he asked at the inquiry, why could Muthiah not call witnesses from shops from where they were issued? Ediwara's questions did not take into account other possibilities: these scraps of paper had been preserved only by happenstance. and hundreds or thousands of others had been discarded because they had no significance, legal or otherwise, before nationality and citizenship regimes came into force.

During the inquiry, Ediriwara then turned his attention to the witnesses, Arnolis Silva and A. K. Menon, whom he deemed unimpressive. He noted that Arnolis Silva ought to have kept an account of his dealings with Muthiah and ought to have made a stronger claim about Muthiah's never having been to India. As for Menon, wrote Ediriwara, he was simply a "hired witness," whose testimony was too precise to be believable. Ediriwara wondered why he kept such a close lookout on Muthiah's movements. Using these justifications against the legal proof that Muthiah had supplied, Ediriwara closed the inquiry, stating that neither "permanent settlement" nor "continuous residence" had been established and that Muthiah was therefore ineligible for citizenship in Ceylon.

BEFORE THE SUPREME COURT

Ediriwara's ruling might have appeared bizarre to Muthiah and others like him, familiar with the rhythms and patterns of immigrant life across India and Ceylon. Soon after Muthiah received the final refusal from Ediriwara, the deputy commissioner, in November 1955, lawyers and trade unionists that worked on behalf of plantation laborers' rights, including the Ceylon Workers' Congress and the Democratic Workers' Congress, decided to appeal Ediriwara's order to the Supreme Court. Muthiah's appeal was argued by S. P. Amarasingam, a lawyer born in Ceylon and educated in Malaya. Amarasingam was also a well-regarded journalist with experience reporting in India and Ceylon; he was the founder-editor of the *Tribune*, a weekly newspaper with leftist sympathies, and a contributor to *Congress News*, a periodical published by the Ceylon Workers' Congress.[48] During this period, one of the union's main areas of advocacy was facilitating Supreme Court appeals by IPRA applicants, and in Colombo, Amarasingam became the organization's legal adviser.[49] He also likely authored a weekly legal advice column that appeared in *Congress News* (attributed to "A Lawyer"), which discussed the requirements for immigration and citizenship for people of Indian origin in great detail.[50]

Amarasingam was an excellent choice of lawyer for the IPRA appeals. Even before he became a legal adviser to the Ceylon Workers' Congress, his reporting demonstrated a thorough, on-the-ground understanding of the Indian "exodus" to Ceylon. He spent a considerable amount of time on Mannar in the north of the island, interviewing officials, immigrants, bailsmen, touts, and witnesses for hire. According to him, touts were at fault for most of the "illicit" immigration to the island; the "ringleaders" of the tout system in Ramnad in Madras and the Pettah in Colombo solicited workers to travel illegally to Ceylon for jobs. (He also noted that most of the "illicit" immigrants being demonized in the Ceylonese press were actually mere boys, some not more than fifteen years of age.) Amarasingam also reported on witnesses for hire, who could be procured for 125 to 300 rupees (fairly high sums at the time) to testify to the "permanent residence" status of applicants. He was critical of the demands of the Tamil Congress and the party of its dissidents, the Ilankai Tamil Arasu Katchi (or Federalist Party), led by S. J. V. Chelvanayagam, for Amarasingam believed that the party did not understand the consequences of demanding a separate Tamil state in the north and east of the island, leaving the plantation areas and "Indian Tamils" in the lurch.[51] He worked on the problem of voter disenfranchisement of Indian migrants in Ceylon with prominent lawyers D. N. Pritt and Frank Gahan, bringing test cases from Colombo before the Judicial Committee of the Privy Council in London.[52] Amarasingam knew the "problem" of Indian immigration, and specifically the political situation in the plantation districts, very well.

During Muthiah's appeal before the Supreme Court in Colombo, however, Amarasingham's arguments bore little fruit. The judges shared Deputy Commissioner Ediriwara's suspicion about Muthiah's documentary evidence. If he had moved up in life from being a hawker to becoming a kangany, why would he have bothered to keep those old receipts, they wondered. They also parsed differences between details that Muthiah filled in on the application form and statements that he had made during the inquiry conducted by Ediriwara. Judge Fernando pointed out that Muthiah had claimed during the inquiry that he was doing "odd jobs as a cooly" in Kandupolle, but on the application form he had claimed that he was working as a hawker. Citing these reasons, the judges dismissed the appeal. Six years after Muthiah and his family filed their applications, their hopes for citizenship in Ceylon ended, at least for the time being.

"ILLEGAL" AND "UNDOCUMENTED"

The archival record offers many glimpses like these that demonstrate the vast chasms that divided officials and applicants on the nature of migrant life and work. Muthiah's legal encounters took place within a broader atmosphere of suspicion and fear around questions of immigration and citizenship in India and Ceylon. The Indian government, and the Madras government in particular, were under great pressure to demonstrate that they were doing everything possible to stop "illicit" emigration from India to Ceylon. C. C. Desai, the high commissioner for India in Ceylon, realized that illegal immigration was a "bogey" to deny civic rights to Indians in Ceylon,[53] but there was little he could do beyond reassuring the Indian government that fears around "illegal" immigration were exaggerated and reminding Ceylonese officials of proactive measures being taken by the Madras government to curb illegal immigration.

The archival record also contains reports from the Madras government on its anti-immigration measures. There was a police outpost for every fifteen miles of the coastline from which "illicit" immigrants to Ceylon generally traveled, and police officers had arrested (and the government had prosecuted) all kinds of labor immigrants, including plantation laborers, domestic laborers, conservancy workers, shop assistants, and fishermen. Handbills printed in Tamil were circulated in the coastal towns, and the dangers of illicit immigration were the subject of broadcasts on the All India Radio. In Ramnad and Tiruchirapalli, the districts in Madras that sent the highest number of laborers to Ceylon plantations, lantern slides in rural cinema and radio plays discussed "the futility of illicit immigration."[54] In and around Mandapam, the most important port of embarkation for Ceylon in India, hotelkeepers who were reportedly selling fake embarkation certificates were charged with offenses under the Indian Penal Code of 1860 and were fined for violations of the Indian Emigration Act of 1922.[55] Passports smuggled across the Palk Strait in tins of tea leaves were intercepted.[56] According to the Madras police (echoing Amarasingam's reporting), it was the professional touts, not the potential immigrants, who were at fault.[57]

On the other side of the Palk Strait, Ceylon, too, saw the answer as greater militarization and policing of borders. Patrol boats were deployed, and propaganda machines went into overdrive[58] to combat the "real criminals"—the touts and the agents who promised the illicit immigrants from Madras a better life in Ceylon.[59] To "wage war" on the agents and touts, Amarasingam suggested that the Ceylonese armed forces acquire faster patrol boats. In 1952, when he reported from Mannar, he observed that the only boat being used by the government was the *Lady Lucille*, which was so slow that even the small country craft on which illegal immigrants arrived traveled faster.[60] Before immigration laws were instituted, these catamarans had frequently taken people across the Strait. However, postwar immigration and citizenship regimes distinguished between "legal" and "illegal" travel. To get around these measures, travelers and would-be immigrants claimed to be pilgrims to the sacred site of Kataragama on the island[61] or workers at warehouses in Colombo.[62] Many were so desperate that they walked from Talaimannar on the northern coast to Anuradhapura in the middle of the island without maps.[63]

Local headmen in the islands off the Jaffna peninsula, closest to the Indian mainland, which migrants had to cross to get to Ceylon, were also involved in the fight against "illegal" immigration. In Iranitivu, Sebamalai, a village headman lay in wait to catch migrants coming in from the sea. He claimed before the Jaffna magistrate, Sitharamparapillai, that he had observed thirty-one people wading through the waters to the land with soaking wet Indian currency notes in their pockets. The men, who said that they were from Ceylon, had no valid documents attesting to their immigration status, and they claimed that their travel permits had expired. This was to no avail. They were imprisoned.[64]

Despite these measures—in the face of policing, without passports, permits, or permissions—people continued to journey, as they had for centuries, across the Palk Strait. By 1953, Ceylon had realized that the immigration legislation was having little or no effect.[65] They realized that "illicit" immigration from India was taking place mostly because the structural forces of poverty pushed people to look for a better life elsewhere. Because of aggressive recruitment by the planters' associations, and familial and kinship networks of information across the Strait, Ceylon existed in the Indian imagination as a land of (better) possibility. Illicit immigrants, ranging from toddy tappers whose means of livelihoods had been taken away by prohibition policies to farmers whose lands had been exhausted by famine, came to Ceylon in search of a better future.

The increased policing did not stem the tide of new immigrants, nor did the new documentation requirements capture all the migrants already in Ceylon. Many simply disappeared, overwhelmed by the proof necessary to establish political belonging. At the 1946 Census, the enumerators noted a "rapid decrease" in those who claimed to be born outside Ceylon (from 10.4 percent of the population in 1921 to 5.7 percent of the population in 1946) and estimated that the real figure was around 8 percent.[66] Census officials attributed this trend to "impending political changes,"[67] though they could not verify this, a suspicion that the investigating officer in Muthiah's case must have also harbored. However, it seems unlikely that this decrease was caused by migrants' desire to avoid being sent back to India: in 1946, citizenship legislation did not yet exist, and future applicants could not have known that when it was introduced it would require a period of "continuous residence." Even then, when the stakes were low, most "Indian Tamils" told census officials that they had lived in Ceylon for between twenty-one and thirty years.[68]

BETWEEN CITIZENSHIP AND STATELESSNESS

The challenges of finding the right documents or of aggressive enforcement of national borders for those who did not possess the right paperwork
in Ceylon was not confined to plantation laborers alone, although they
submitted most applications for naturalization. Merchants and traders
who followed the long tradition of traveling between India and Ceylon
for business were also forced to prove, in the course of their application for
citizenship in Ceylon, that they did not have ties to India. For example,
I came across an application from Mohammed Ibrahim Saibo, a "Coast
Moor"—a derogatory term, common in official documents, for a Muslim
of Indian origin in Ceylon—who noted that his monthly income was 500
rupees and that he had a house and a paddy field to his name.[69] During
his inquiry, the deputy commissioner noted that Ibrahim Saibo had been
to India five times, ignoring his claims that he had not stayed more than
three months each time. The commissioner also balked at the fact that
Ibrahim Saibo's wife, who had resided with him until 1942, had left in fear
of the impending Japanese invasion. Perhaps most troubling, in the commission's view, was the fact that Ibrahim Saibo had also remitted money
to India to financially support family members there. Only "temporary
residents" could make remittances, so he had declared himself a "temporary resident" on the exchange control forms. This was a clear example of
how forms interlocked, with declarations made in relation to a particular
application form having a series of cascading consequences for another. It
was difficult to meet citizenship requirements when the evidence from one
form could be used to negate the claims of another. At the inquiry held
by the deputy commissioner, the exchange control forms were held to be
evidence that Ibrahim Saibo did not intend "permanent settlement."

Traders like Ibrahim Saibo likely had a much easier time pleading their
cases than plantation laborers like Muthiah. For one thing, the businessmen who frequently crossed the Palk Strait were able to employ prominent
lawyers to champion their cause and appeal the decisions of commissioners
successfully before the Supreme Court. These merchants and traders also
had other options open to them that plantation laborers did not. Businessmen like Ibrahim Saibo had the option of temporary residence permits,
similar to long-term visas, which allowed them to enjoy the benefits of

trading in both India or Ceylon without being rendered stateless. Securing temporary residence permits proved to be a popular solution. In 1952, nearly 990 out of the 1,106 new permits issued were for wives and children of those who lived on the island; by 1953, 90 percent of all temporary residence permits issued by the Ceylon government had gone to "Indian nationals."[70] However, even for this privileged group, there were rumblings about immigration fraud. The controller of emigration and immigration claimed that a storm of "fake" evidentiary materials was brewing, with "Ceylon Muslims" at the center.[71] He accused them of using the birth certificates of Ceylon nationals to apply for emigration certificates from the Ceylonese government, claiming that nearly four hundred certificates had been fraudulently issued. By the 1970s, the system of temporary residence permits would be wound down, forcing long-term residents of Indian origin on the island to make a permanent choice between their adopted home and their home of origin.

In 1954, as the inquires and appeals on the citizenship question dragged on, India and Ceylon announced a joint solution known as the Nehru-Kotelawala Pact, which changed the immigration and citizenship policy between India and Ceylon for the first time since 1949. India's prime minister Jawaharlal Nehru and Ceylon's prime minister John Kotelawala announced several changes in immigration policy and practices between the two countries. First, the Mandapam quarantine camp in India for Ceylonese immigrants was to be slowly shut down. Second, a Cabinet subcommittee under the Ministry of Justice would be set up to consider amendments to India's Immigrants and Emigrants Act of 1948. Third, Ceylon would consider abolishing residence permits altogether and replacing them with short-term visas; they would also implement stricter sanctions for illegal immigration and implement progressive "Ceylonization" of all sectors of the economy.[72]

Soon after the signing of the Nehru-Kotelawala Pact, the percentage of citizenship applications accepted in Ceylon went down from 45 percent to 7 percent. Kotelawala attributed the previous large number of acceptances to corruption that had plagued earlier inquiries and was quick to note that many IPRA officials had been dismissed on these grounds.[73] Despite this success, though, the pact left many matters relating to "Indian" and "Ceylonese" citizenship unresolved, including labor repatriation, separate electorates, and methods for control of illegal immigration, all of which were points of negotiation in later years. The chaos and confusion continued.[74]

The decade after the 1949 introduction of the IPRA saw a wave of legal challenges to commissioners' rulings, with many cases being appealed to the Ceylon Supreme Court.[75] The sheer number of appeals evidenced a problem of legal procedure—one so acute that the Judicial Committee of the Privy Council ruled that although the deputy commissioners had wide-ranging discretionary powers, they had to act in accordance with principles of natural justice in order to reduce the number of appeals.[76] Throughout the 1950s, the Ceylon Supreme Court followed this principle, setting aside the lower courts' decisions in cases that obviously violated principles of natural justice: for example, those where the applicants were revealed to have been wholly unaware of the investigations by the deputy commissioners and the conclusions that they had reached.[77] In 1955, the same year as Muthiah's unsuccessful Supreme Court appeal, another bench of the Supreme Court made another ruling on the legal process around immigration applications, deciding that deputy commissioners could no longer invalidate witness testimony on the grounds that the witnesses were IPRA applicants themselves.[78] What if Muthiah's case had come up before that bench? As the processes of naturalization had become more standardized in terms of procedure, they had increasingly seemed to turn on the whims and fancies of an unnamed official somewhere in the recesses of the government. The 1950s changes to the process sought to make it more fair and equitable and to ensure that it was applied more consistently across cases.

As appeals of citizenship decisions became common, Ceylonese newspapers carried accounts of the pathologies of the legal bureaucracy created by the 1949 Act. The stories they reported reflected the public fears that the citizenship process was being hijacked for political reasons. They erroneously stated that those who had received citizenship in Ceylon were also legally able to apply for and receive citizenship with India at the same time. They often reported on malfeasance in the application process: they noted that detectives were investigating whether applications were forged (the Ceylon government was convinced that applications were being filed only at the behest of the Ceylon Indian Congress) and that fraudulent applications had mysteriously disappeared from the offices of the commission, raising the question of an inside job. The "duplicity of paper," as Bhavani Raman puts it, was at work: the burden of legal proof required for legitimate citizenship applications was so high that it invited—indeed, seemed to some to require—deception. The rice ration books of return emigrants were being sold in South India to those who wanted to come to Ceylon,[79] and birth certificates of Ceylon nationals were being submitted by "non-nationals" in support of their applications.[80] Political belonging was now solidly a matter of legal proof, not of attachments or desires.

The immigration and citizenship regimes in India and Ceylon were part of a larger system that made similarly onerous demands for documentary evidence from migrants. In the transition from empire to nation-states in South and Southeast Asia, newly independent nations used documents as proof of political belonging—and loyalty. For example, to return to Burma after the end of the war to resume business or work, migrants had to secure a "temporary permit," often called a "B" permit (figure 4.2). To secure this temporary permit, they needed to produce an evacuee identification card, which was available only to people whose names appeared in a badly mismanaged evacuee census—recall the evacuee census from chapter 1—carried out in India between 1943 and 1945. Prominent Indian businessmen and traders, including the Chettiars, managed to get hold of these cards, but the laborers—sweepers, conservancy workers, rickshaw pullers—who were at the heart of Rangoon's economy did not. Without this documentation proving that they had been physically present in Burma in the key years, the citizenship legislation of 1948 made them ineligible for Burmese citizenship. A signature, stamp, or thumbprint on documents generated at a time when nation-states had not yet been imagined shaped how belonging and loyalty would be measured and perceived.

For Indians in Burma, citizenship processes in both India and Burma were fraught with difficulties. Both the Union Citizenship Act and the Union Citizenship (Election) Act were passed in 1948. Those who had fled Burma during the occupation—people of both Indian and Chinese descent—found themselves after the war falling afoul of the residence requirement under the Union Citizenship (Election) Act of 1948.[81] The

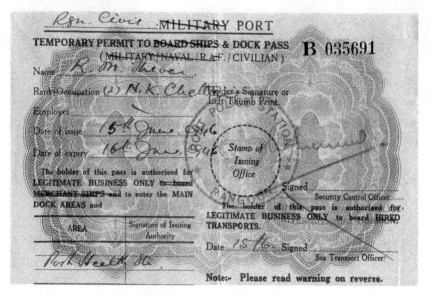

FIGURE 4.2: *A "B" permit to visit Burma. Photograph by author.*

Constitution of 1951 specified in Section 11 that citizenship was automatically extended to everyone who belonged to one of the indigenous races of Burma and whose grandparents had lived in the territory of Burma. Section 12 decreed that citizenship would be traced through descent and that children born to female Burmese citizens would automatically have Burmese citizenship; however, children born of fathers who were aliens had to renounce foreign citizenship within one year of attaining majority, for dual citizenship was not allowed for adults. A certificate of citizenship could be issued to those whose citizenship was in doubt, but the certification process was extremely slow. The physical citizenship certificate (not the mere approval of the citizenship application) was required for many purposes, including buying or selling land.[82] Many who had applied and approved for citizenship found their land-related transactions voided because they had not had a physical citizenship certificate in hand.[83] In addition, the certificates of registration had to be renewed multiple times, with an associated fee each time—in 1957, the fee was fifty kyats per head. After the land was nationalized, smallholder peasants without certificates were left without a means of collecting their rents or incomes, and residents of

Burma who had not paid income tax in the country were not allowed to remit any amount to their dependents in India.[84]

After the war ended, paperwork became essential to piecing back together the networks of labor, capital, and credit that had been severed by the war. In the early years of decolonization, borders were both territorial and juridical. We can see in the fate of Muthiah's application how, in Ceylon, plantation workers were presumed to belong to India, because India was where they were "from," although they had come to Ceylon before the idea of the nation-state, territorially bound and separate from its neighbors, had emerged. The assumption was that national origins mapped onto the territory of one's "proper" residence and that geographical mobility—the back-and-forth across the Palk Strait engaged in by many traders and merchants—reflected a similar meandering in the migrants' political loyalties. This distrust of the recent arrival was reflected in the skeptical scrutiny of rent receipts and bank accounts, but also in the kind of questions that judges and officials asked, often about decisions made precisely because residency laws demanded it: Why did (or did not) the applicant maintain a paper trail of his presence on the island? Why did a co-linguist appear as a witness? Why did the applicant visit family in India or send them money? Where was "home"?

The violence of the banal legal encounters in Muthiah's story shows postwar legal regimes' suspicion of personal and familial histories that aligned too closely with official or state-sanctioned histories. In Ibrahim Saibo's case, officials were suspicious because documents showed that he had sent remittances to India and had returned there five times; in Muthiah's case, officials were suspicious of his claim that he had never left Ceylon because he had only sparse documentation of his uninterrupted residence in Ceylon. For these immigrants, paperwork was both opportunity and threat. As scholar Kamal Sadiq notes, immigrants are very rarely "undocumented."[85] On the contrary, like Muthiah, they often had documentation chronicling their personal and familial histories. States simply deemed that documentation legally insufficient.

Outside the world of forms, signatures, and paperwork, plantation workers held a *satyagraha*—a nonviolent protest—in Colombo (figure 4.3), traveling from the plantations to the capital city of Colombo. A "ballad" reprinted in *Congress News* articulated the desires and stakes of Ceylon citizenship for applicants like Muthiah:

> We cared not for photos in papers
> Hoped not for names on bronze plates
> And aspired not for medals and titles
> Not for us these things
> We only wanted our names in the lists
> And votes in the hands
> We wanted our men in the Parliament.[86]

Other matters at stake for economic migrants from India—being able to return to an ancestral village for an annual religious festival or to remit

FIGURE 4.3: *The first issue of* Congress News, *announcing the Ceylon Indian Congress–led* satyagraha *in Colombo.*

money to support aged parents or relatives in India while continuing to live, work and raise a family in Ceylon—remain unspoken and unsung.

In the end, when Muthiah's appeal was denied in 1955, hostilities were escalating between political parties representing Tamil and Sinhala Buddhist interests, and nationalist movements were gathering strength on the island. During this period, there was increasing violence against the *malaiyaha thamilar* on the plantations—minorities deemed perpetual migrants. When the civil war finally broke out in 1983, many of the *malaiyaha thamilar* fled to the Vanni in the north of the island; many remain there even today, internally displaced from their homes for almost forty years.[87] As for the IPRA applicants, many remained stateless, unsuccessful in gaining citizenship on either side of the Palk Strait. Ceylon sought to address this problem with two sets of legislation, the Grant of Citizenship to Stateless Persons Act of 1986 and the Grant of Citizenship (Special Provisions) Act in 2003, both of which allotted states to stateless citizens. But even those migrants who did not end up stateless lost their homes: out of nearly 800,000 IPRA applicants, nearly 445,588 had by 1960s been repatriated to South India, "settled" in a "home" that they often had no connections to and had no memory of.[88] Muthiah and his family might have been among them.

FIVE

WOMEN WHO WAIT

AS JURIDICAL BORDERS ROSE UP in service of new immigration regimes between India and Ceylon, investigating officers and commissioners appointed under the Indian and Pakistani Residents (Citizenship) Act of 1949 scrutinized familial ties for evidence of intention to permanently settle in Ceylon. Even occasional visits to India to see family were viewed with suspicion and as proof of divided loyalties. As we saw in chapter 4, in an inquiry following an application for citizenship, a "Coast Moor" named Mohammed Ibrahim Saibo testified to the deputy commissioner that he had a monthly "assured income" of 500 rupees as well as a house and a paddy field to his name—evidence that he would be able to financially support his wife and children in Ceylon as the 1949 Act required.[1] However, what caught the attention of the deputy commissioner in the paper trail before him was that Ibrahim Saibo had been to India five times since 1942. The deputy commissioner ignored Ibrahim Saibo's explanations that he had a reason to visit India periodically—to visit his wife, who had lived with him in Ceylon but had evacuated in 1942, fleeing to India in fear of the Japanese invasion of the island. He had not stayed more than three months during any of the visits. Although these visits illustrated that Ibrahim Saibo's family fit within the normative family framework privileged by the new citizenship laws, the geographic mobility of Ibrahim Saibo's wife—her travel between the two now-separate countries—was cause for suspicion about the family's (and thus Ibrahim Saibo's) loyalty to Ceylon.

The circulation of money between the countries was also cause for suspicion about Ibrahim Saibo's loyalty to Ceylon. He had remitted money to India, and he admitted as much when filling out forms to comply with foreign exchange control regulations; to make remittances, he had to declare himself a "temporary resident" in Ceylon, because only "temporary residents" could make remittances abroad. These funds were sent to support not only his wife but also his extended family, including his aging father in India. It seemed, then, to the commissioner that just as members of his family were spread out on both sides of the Strait, so was his loyalty split between India and Ceylon: the deputy commissioner considered these remittances to be evidence that Ibrahim Saibo did not intend "permanent settlement" in Ceylon.[2] Although signing off as a "temporary resident" on the form was the only way to financially support any family members in India, this sign of financial support was used as legal evidence of partitioned loyalties, which spoke against Ibrahim Saibo's intentions for "permanent settlement" in Ceylon. His application for citizenship was denied.

Beginning with Ibrahim Saibo's dismissed citizenship application, this chapter explores how immigration regimes illustrate the ways the question of citizenship was an economic problem for the two newly independent nations of India and Ceylon. Who would enjoy the fruits of the labor and investment of migrant traders like Ibrahim Saibo? Citizenship is described as conferring legal status with attendant rights and privileges, but the concepts that underpinned citizenship in these new nations also emerged from banal legal encounters where the formation of national economies was worked out in intricate detail. But as chapters 2 and 3 showed, the roles of families, economies, and the states were deeply intertwined with each other on the eve of decolonization in South and Southeast Asia, and the postwar partitioning of territory—and the separation of economies that attended it—unraveled a long history of trading networks and connections across the Palk Strait.

Whereas immigration regimes in India and Ceylon assumed the family to be patrilineal, taxation legislation mapped onto a more extensive understanding of familial "attachment"; taxation and immigration regimes, as we saw by way of the legal cases thus far, were braided together.

THE FAMILY IN LAW

Familial and marital attachments were central to the mythmaking of nation-states during South and Southeast Asia's decolonization. During the territorial partition of the subcontinent into the separate nations of India and Pakistan, stories of families broken apart by political machinations on both sides and spirited across the new border became common: rumors circulated of Hindu women "abducted" by Muslim men and taken to Pakistan, as well as of Muslim women kidnapped by Hindu men and carried off to India. These rumors had such power that the Abducted Women (Recovery and Restoration) Act was enacted in 1949 by the provisional Indian government, intended to "return" women to their "rightful" places. As Veena Das notes, invoking Carole Pateman's notion of the "sexual contract," it was as if India and Pakistan could not come into being until women were restored to their rightful states, Hindu women to India, and Muslim women to Pakistan.[3] Das's reading of the legal measures that responded to "abducted women" invokes debates over the nationality of married women and whether the wife's "domicile" must follow that of the husband. Farhana Ibrahim shows how these debates that emerged in the context of the Partition continue to inflect present-day debates on citizenship.[4] Although Das's reading allows us to explore the familial through the lens of the marital, we can also explore the familial through the lens of the political. New nation-states in South and Southeast Asia, working in a context of "other partitions," translated familial—not just marital—attachments into political and economic attachments. However, these translations and legal fictions were at odds with the realities, rhythms, and patterns of migrant life.

Scholars of gender and sexuality have shown how the "family" is not a transhistorical category. This is a critical insight for understanding familial relations that were geographically dispersed because of the gendered workforces on plantations or because of transnational trade and commerce. As Mytheli Sreenivas notes, the "family"—especially in Dravidian discourse in mid-twentieth-century Madras—was defined by kinship alone, excluding other possibilities.[5] Sreenivas notes how the "family" became the site of revolutionary ideas, a place where the political was performed.[6] This chapter highlights the glimpses of personal and familial histories revealed through legal encounters, showing how the realities of circular migration—sojourn and return—led to multiple reconfigurations of the "family" after the war.[7] These encounters, where migrants made jurisdictional claims rather than leveraging juridical categories, undid the legal fiction in immigration regimes that families must necessarily live all together in one place. Law's encounter with the familial within nationalist frames is characterized by epistemic violence, disavowing customs, practices, negotiations, and anxieties over sexualities and overturned social hierarchies. However, it also speaks to possibilities and plausibilities in migrant worlds of reinventing familial hierarchies.

The legal fictions of a "family" connected through blood and kinship can clearly be seen in the notion of *jus sanguinis* citizenship laid out in the Ceylon Citizenship Act of 1948. It can also be seen in the gendered notions of citizenship—the idea that citizenship was awarded to a male head of household and was then passed along to his family—reflected in the debates over the Indian Citizenship Bill (which later became the Indian and Pakistani Residents [Citizenship] Act of 1949) in Ceylon's Legislative Assembly. The debates also touched on race and family: N. M. Perera, of the Lanka Sama Samaja Party, called D. S. Senanayake, Ceylon's prime minister, "the last racialist in the world" for his citizenship policies but also noted that the proposed exclusive policies were not only about race; they also reflected the interests of the "capitalist elements" in the country, who wanted to exclude non-Ceylonese workers—even those whose "fathers" had labored on this land.[8] The importance of lineage (which implicated familial racial and religious identities as well as geographic location) in proposed citizenship policies was also discussed by Colvin de Silva, a member of the Bolshevik Samasamaja Party in the Parliament, who wondered aloud if the only objective of the government's policies was to provide "ample occupation for genealogical researchers and family tree constructors."[9] As Perera's and de Silva's comments showed, the decision to choose *jus sanguinis* citizenship as the dominant model in Ceylon as well as the decision to disallow dual citizenship in South Asia was not accidental. It was a result of anxieties over overlapping religious, social, and ethnic identities that blurred the bright lines that citizenship legislation needed in order to "fix" people in their places.

These presumptions about family structures in immigration regimes existed uneasily alongside the realities of migrant families. As Dennis McGilvray shows, Sri Lankan Muslims on the eastern coast around Batticaloa and Amparai practiced matriliny—a legacy of the island's connections with the coasts of South India—which existed even as patrilineal structures were embedded in laws.[10] Similarly, the practice of polygamy in some Hindu and Muslim communities was treated as a "disability" that had to be disclosed under the 1949 Act's provisions; the deputy commissioner had to fill out forms attesting that the applicant was not under any legal disabilities that violated "Ceylonese law."[11] However, there was then no singular system of "Ceylonese law." Like British India, Dutch and British Ceylon recognized systems of "personal" law that governed various aspects of the familial: marriage, divorce, and adoption in religious communities, including the Thesawamalai for Tamils in the northern provinces including Jaffna, and customary law for Muslims. However, many applications under the 1949 Act were rejected on the grounds of polygamy or indeed familial intermarriage: uncles were denied citizenship for marrying their nieces, and brothers-in-law for marrying their sisters-in-law.

Family structures and practices increasingly became the basis for citizenship decisions, and the new nation-states began to consider familial attachments as reflecting political attachments and being evidence for national "loyalty." The Ceylon Citizenship Act of 1948, for example, contained provisions for naturalization if one married a Ceylonese citizen. But there was a dissonance between the legislation being introduced and actual sentiments about familial relations. For instance, in the 1948 debates over the Indian Citizenship Bill, J. R. Jayawardena, at the time Ceylon's finance minister but later to be president and prime minister of Sri Lanka, commented that all the Indians "hankering after" citizenship should marry women belonging to Sinhala, Tamil, Burgher, or Ceylon Moor communities on the island, a fact that would be considered favorable evidence of permanent settlement.[12] This seemed a simple enough solution to him, but in practice, those who had intermarried across racial or ethnic lines—for example, a Tamil Hindu married to a Sinhala Buddhist—often found that this did not necessarily have a favorable effect on their applications for citizenship: the applications took longer to process, and their temporary residence permits were often rejected.[13]

ACROSS THE PALK STRAIT

Immigrants to Ceylon from India were not only plantation laborers; they also included wealthy merchants and moneylenders like the Chettiars of chapters 2 and 3, as well as small-time traders and businessmen. Trade and commerce across the Palk Strait were part of a long-standing Indian Ocean trade stretching from the Persian Gulf to China. Muslim trading communities from the Indian subcontinent, including Bohras from Gujarat, Memons from Kutch, Tamil Muslims from the southeastern coast, and Mappillas from Malabar on the southwestern coast, were fixtures in this trade, which imported and exported rice, arrack, areca, spices, and ivory, among other commodities.[14] Like the Chettiars, who were involved in both long-distance trade across the Indian Ocean and "coasting" trade between the smaller ports on its littoral since at least the sixteenth century, "Tamil" or "Malabari" Muslim merchants had long anchored the trade between India and Ceylon, and indeed, across the Bay of Bengal to Malaya and Singapore.[15]

Like other colonial port cities of this time around the Indian Ocean, Colombo's Pettah was home to people of many ethnicities, races, and origins. The Pettah was the base of operations for many migrant Muslim traders; indeed, some went so far as to say that by the early twentieth century, Colombo was a "Moorish city."[16] By the 1860s, the Pettah hosted jewelry stores, and its street names reflected its ethnic makeup: Old Moor Street, New Moor Street, and Arab Street.[17] Muslim traders and merchants who had grown wealthy from Indian Ocean trade built "palatial houses" in the area,[18] and alongside these merchant families, traders and merchants carried out short-distance trade between India and Ceylon. These people, whose businesses large and small depended on migration across the Strait, all worked and prospered in Colombo.

In Ceylon, the use of the term was drawn from the Portuguese *maura*, which the Portuguese traders used for Muslims on the Malabar coast, where they first arrived in the fifteenth century.[19] At least one popular legend credits Moors with having brought the Portuguese to the island, noting that a boat laden with the rich spices of Lanka was pursued by the Portuguese, caught in a strong gale, and driven by the winds to the island.[20] In twentieth-century political discourse about citizenship and belonging in Ceylon, these legends about arrival and settlement were revived to discuss the place of migrant traders in Ceylon. As with the discussion over the Chettiars in Burma, the "origins" of Muslims in Ceylon became a heavily debated topic in discussions of citizenship, national loyalty, and economic investment.

Despite the long history (both territorial and familial) that this origin story conveyed, its associations were not favorable, for Tamil-speaking communities were becoming increasingly marginalized in politics dominated by majority Sinhala Buddhist political parties. Ceylon's "Moors" were considered not only a religious category but also an ethnic one, like Tamil or Sinhalese. According to the 1911 Census in Ceylon, most of the country's "Moors" were shopkeepers and merchants, trading in textiles, rice, and coconut.[21] Muslims in Ceylon spoke multiple languages, including Malay, Tamil, Malayalam, Urdu, Arabic, and others, with the use of Tamil becoming particularly salient in the increasingly ethnonationalist climate of Ceylon as it cemented its independence.[22] Some argued that the Muslims of Ceylon were descendants of Arab traders who had traded, converted and intermarried with Tamil- and Malayalam-speaking communities in South India and Ceylon.[23] By the end of the nineteenth century, elite Muslims, particularly those in Colombo, began to call themselves Ceylon Moors, or *sonakar*, to distinguish themselves from small traders and establish themselves as natives of Ceylon, with their claims to be descendants of the first Arab settlers on the island in Beruwala. They sought to distinguish themselves from other Tamil-speaking Muslims, especially small-time traders like Mohammed Ibrahim Saibo, who had family in India and frequently traveled there. These migrant Muslim traders were called "Coast Moors," "Indian Moors," or *sammankarar*.[24] The *sonakars'* insistence on separate origin myths for these two groups created and reinforced political distinctions between the Indian and Ceylon Moors for their economic and political benefit; they wanted to maintain their citizenship, residence, and businesses in Ceylon.

The ethnic and linguistic categories shaped Colombo's cityscape and began to appear in official documents like the census and court filings. For example, separate mosques were built for the "Ceylon Moors" and the "Indian Moors": the Ceylon Moors built the Grand Mosque, while the "Indian Moors" congregated at the Jami ul-Alfar Mosque (today called "the Red Mosque") in the Pettah.[25] In 1946, just as the flood of cases involving Muslim traders on either side of the Palk Strait was about to crash down onto courts in Madras and Colombo, the distinctions between Ceylon and Indian Moors became officially enshrined in policy and law.[26] According to the well-known scholar of Islam in Sri Lanka M. A. Nuhman, the controversial presence of "Coast Moors" was washed away by the stringent citizenship regime; in the aftermath of the citizenship laws and the legal cases they engendered, the Coast Moors "silently vanished or submerged leaving their imprint as a past history."[27] But the archive of law suggests otherwise: many of these traders remained, and even those who were pushed out left important legal and political traces behind them. These migrant traders, and the jurisdictional claims that they made, were thus critical to how Ceylon and India worked out notions of citizenship in the age of decolonization.

TAMIL AND MUSLIM CITIZENSHIP

On the eve of decolonization, with the reality of the territorial partition of India and Pakistan looming, India grappled with whether Muslims could be, as Gyanendra Pandey has put it, reliably Indian.[28] These tensions reverberated differently across the Indian diaspora in different places.[29] Across the western Indian Ocean, in East Africa, there were separate Hindu and Muslim electoral rolls; in Ceylon, the Donoughmore Constitution in 1928 introduced communal representation in the legislatures on the basis of Tamil and Sinhalese electoral rolls.[30] Subsequently, schisms between Sinhalese and Tamil nationalisms in Sri Lanka widened, coming to a head with the introduction of citizenship regimes that excluded migrant families. Ceylonese politicians asked: Could a Tamil-speaking migrant Muslim be a loyal Ceylonese minority citizen? In the 1940s Ceylon's anxieties were primarily linguistic: Sinhala Buddhist nationalist groups in Ceylon attributed an Indian origin to communities on the island that spoke Tamil, irrespective of religious identity. In Ceylon, language was taken as a proxy for national and ethnic identity.

For the Tamil political leadership in Colombo, the "Coast Moor" presented an electoral opportunity: with this large group of Tamil-speaking traders added to their political base, they could build a coalition of minorities against a Sinhala Buddhist majority.[31] They thus decided to exploit the separate origin stories that had been promoted by the *sonakar* to legitimize their citizenship. In 1888, Ponnambalam Ramanathan, the prominent Tamil leader from Jaffna, published a lecture titled "Ethnology of the Moors of Ceylon." In it, he argued that the "Coast Moors" were Muslim members of the Tamil race, since they spoke the same language and had similar familial customs. He noted that Muslims in Ceylon had migrated from Kayalpatanam on the coast of Madras and that Beruwala, which was often cited as one of the first Arab settlements in Ceylon (and the source of the *sonakar* claims to a Ceylon identity since time immemorial) was an "offshoot" of Kayalpatanam.[32] Ramanathan's claims were strongly rebutted by the Muslim leadership, including I. L. M. Abdul Azeez, the leader of the Colombo-based Moors' Union. Azeez wrote that Ramanathan's paper had been written with a "prejudiced" mind and that the Moors were unequivocally descendants of Arab settlers in Ceylon. He claimed that they spoke Tamil only because they had entered "business relations" with the "Malabars" in Ceylon and that those business connections had fostered familial connections; many of them had married Tamil women. Was it not natural, he asked in his reply speech, that children would "cherish and adopt the thoughts and habits of their mothers rather than of their fathers"?[33] Azeez emphasized that the racial origins of the Ceylon Moors—the *sonakar*—were to be traced through blood, not language.[34] Many Muslim political leaders in Ceylon viewed these claims about connections between India and Ceylon with suspicion and as a way for the Tamil political leadership in Colombo to dominate Muslims.

The "Coast Moors," or migrant Muslims from India to Ceylon like Ibrahim Saibo, whose citizenship application was denied on the basis of his ties to India, did not fit easily into the categories and affiliations that grounded most Muslim political associations like the Moors' Union in Colombo, which Azeez led. With the exception of the All Ceylon Muslim League, there were no claims to a pan-Islamic identity in Ceylon—one that included both the Indian Muslims and the Muslims who had migrated to Ceylon from the Malay-speaking world in Indonesia.[35] Indeed, Azeez's speech explicitly made a distinction between these two groups. Unlike the *sonakar* or the Ceylon Moors, who, he said, had settled in Ceylon from the first century onwards, he noted that the Tamils or the Malabars had instead "invaded Ceylon" from South India. So Ramanathan's account establishing familial links between Tamils and Muslims in Ceylon, he said, pertained only to the "Coast Moors," who had come to Ceylon from Madras. The Ceylon Moors, he wrote with pride, were not only petty traders, peddlers, boutique keepers, boatmen, fishermen, agriculturists, and coolies—stereotypes of the Coast Moors—but also wholesale merchants, large shopkeepers, planters, and wealthy landed proprietors. These distinctions positioned the Ceylon Moors as wealthy contributors to Ceylon's economy whose political interests were not to be easily dismissed.[36]

These two versions of "origin myths," politicized as they were in the above debate between Ramanathan and Azeez, can be placed in conversation with the legal discourse on citizenship based on patrilineal descent. As Torsten Tschacher writes, origin myths about Arab origins and settlement in South and Southeast Asia began to be spread in the nineteenth century to serve the needs of colonial-era structures of political representation.[37] In Ceylon, these debates, grounded in competing notions of bloodlines, had been on the ascent since the 1920s as efforts to create a constitutional structure for elections and representation gained momentum.[38] As the Indian Muslims' fortunes (and their sense of shared ethnic and class identities) grew, so did Sinhala Buddhist nationalism. Ethnic strife simmered below the surface in the last quarter of the nineteenth century, and in 1915 it broke loose in the form of violent conflict.

The official narrative of the 1915 riots against Muslims in Kandy pins the cause of the riots on Muslim men's threat to Sinhalese women. The riots, which would be the subject of a legal prosecution popularly known as the Gampola Perahera case, targeted Muslim property and were severe and violent enough to prompt the imposition of martial law. In his dispatch to the Colonial Office, Robert Chalmers, the governor of Ceylon, expressed the nationalist resentments in play when he said that the Muslims, the "Coast Moors" who were targeted in the riots, were "transitory aliens" who profited from selling and lending money to the local peasants, incurring their ire.[39] There was, however, another possible explanation, which Chalmers mentioned only in passing: some said that the local Sinhalese traders, who had a nascent rivalry with the Muslims, had instigated the former to riot.[40] This budding commercial rivalry, stemming from an envy of "Coast Moor" fortunes, is the explanation that most scholars espouse. Edward Perera, the lawyer who defended the rioters in the case, penned an opinion on events that was printed for audiences in London in anticipation of an appeal to the Judicial Committee of the Privy Council. In this publication, he attributed the riots not to economic resentment but to the need to protect the family unit: he speculated that the "Coast Moors" had attacked Sinhalese women in Colombo. However, the investigating authorities seemed to place the blame elsewhere, for once martial law was declared in Ceylon following the riots, some noted, the homes of well-known Sinhala political leaders were searched, and the women of their household ordered to stand outside in the sun.[41] Ramanathan and his allies, who had earlier attempted to consolidate minority support by arguing that Muslims in Ceylon were descendants of traders from India, now changed their tune, quickly blaming the 1915 riots on the errant "Coast Moors."[42] For those who were seeking to consolidate a pan-Islamic identity in Ceylon, this betrayal was evidence that the Tamil political leadership was not genuinely interested in their fate.

Both the Ramanathan-Azeez debate and the 1915 Gampola Perahera case positioned the Coast Moors as sojourners—people who did not intend to settle, politically or socially, in Ceylon and had only a passing commercial interest. Their wives and families did not accompany them, adding further credence to this stereotype. The traders' circular migration was a discordant note in the narrative of the nation that was taking shape on the eve of decolonization. Because the dominant understanding of the ethnic conflict in Ceylon was that it was between Sinhala and Tamil political interests, the Muslims were categorized alongside other Tamil speakers that included Hindus and Christians, simply because of their language, which classified them as being of Indian origin. Even the Muslims who had lived for many generations on the island spoke Tamil and were thus at a disadvantage during the debates over national citizenship.[43] For Ceylon Moors, excluding the itinerant Indian Moors allowed them to define themselves as belonging to Ceylon.[44]

In both cases, the place of the Muslims in Ceylon was disputed, as though their homes were elsewhere—in Kayalpatanam in Madras or in Calicut on the Malabar Coast. In the legal archives of tax, property, and citizenship cases, we can trace the ways that ordinary migrant Muslim families were constructed in law. As Nuhman notes in his analysis of the 1911 census, most "Coast Moors" were men; only 6,500 of the nearly 32,000 "Coast Moors" on the island were women.[45] Most of the migrant Muslim traders were men, and most of their families were likely back in Madras. As with Ibrahim Saibo's citizenship application mentioned at the beginning of the chapter, all these factors came together to create a perfect storm as the Ceylonese nation-state sought to make a decision in the postwar period on who belonged to it and who had to go back "home." Central to this resolution would be the presence of "wives."

AFFECTIONS AND AFFILIATIONS

In 1942, Sayed Abdul Cader, a trader and merchant who owned a business in Colombo and had married a "Ceylonese lady," fled back across the Palk Strait to his hometown in Madras, fearing the imminent Japanese invasion of the island. He rode out the occupation in Madras, and when the threat appeared to have passed, he made his way back to Ceylon. A few years later, in 1950, he found himself back in Madras, this time at the Madras High Court. Income tax authorities in India had noticed that he had remitted nearly 60,000 rupees to his father during 1942. As we saw in chapter 3, as time rather than territory became central to the ideas of tax residence, wartime displacements could make one subject to income tax in India. And indeed, because Abdul Cader had been in India during the year, they believed that the sum was subject to Indian income tax.[46] He disagreed with the assessment and appealed to the Madras High Court but was ultimately unsuccessful. Not only had he stayed for over six months and rented a house in Tirunelveli, but the court also observed that he, not his father, was likely the recipient of the 60,000 rupees.

This legal case is ostensibly, as with the discussion in chapter 3, about tax residence. But following references in the legal archive, the arguments put forward in cases like these are glimpses into how, in negotiations over citizenship in postwar South and Southeast Asia, familial attachments were treated as evidence of economic ties and of political loyalty.[47] The family—a traditional constellation of male head of household, wife, and any children born of the marriage—emerges as a legal fiction with real political and social consequences in the world, as it was used to answer (or raise) questions of political allegiance. Around this legal fiction, which posited one territorial location for the family, migrants were compelled to make their own narratives about how places and families were connected. Immigration laws in Ceylon and India assumed the familial to be patrilineal; taxation legislation mapped onto a more extensive understanding of familial "attachment" and geographic location. Abdul Cader lost his taxation case because his travels to Madras were used as evidence that his family and his business were rooted not, as he claimed, in Ceylon but in India.

Sayed Abdul Cader's taxation case faded away from institutional memory. Not a single judgment made after the case was decided has used it as precedent. From the perspective of a legal practitioner, then, this judgment is relevant only to the parties to the case, not to the development of legal doctrine on the question of tax residence. But in a strange twist of fate, in 1951, two years after Sayed Abdul Cader's case was decided, the same set of judges in the Madras High Court—Justice Satyanarayana Rao and Justice Viswanatha Sastri—were assigned to hear a very similar case on the question of "tax residence."

Like Sayed Abdul Cader, Zackariah Sahib, a "Muhammadan merchant" who "usually resided" in Ceylon, had gone to Madras in 1942 and 1943.[48] Perhaps he was visiting his parents, as he claimed, but it is more likely, given the years, that he fled to India in fear of the Japanese invasion, just as Sayed Abdul Cader had. His wife, whom he had married in 1940, had never lived with him in Ceylon, remaining with her parents and in-laws in Madras. When he visited in 1942, Zackariah stayed in his maternal home. Indian income tax authorities claimed that under Section 4-A (a) (ii) of the Indian Income Tax Act of 1922, which we looked at in chapter 3, Zackariah Sahib was thus "resident" in British India for the purposes of income tax because he had a "dwelling home" maintained for him there. This, income tax authorities ruled, meant that the income from his business, earned in Ceylon, could be taxed in India.

In his judgment of the case, Justice Sastri leaned on the problem of how families were constructed in Indian law. He noted that the house in India that Zackariah Sahib lived in was his mother's and that it was neither owned, rented, or mortgaged by him. The Hindu Undivided Family (HUF), he pointed out, was defined in Hindu law as a separate entity, composed of a "common ancestor" and his male descendants, wives, and unmarried daughters, which possessed a common home, owned by all family members (recall a similar discussion in chapter 3) In contrast, the "Muhammadan" family had no common home whose maintenance benefited each one of its members. Zackariah Sahib's home in Madras, therefore, was not a family home that could be construed as partly his. Even the remittances to his family could not be construed as being for the upkeep of a home for him in Madras, wrote Justice Sastri: "The assessee goes to his mother's house as a visitor. It is not as if he goes there as going home." The judge found for the plaintiff, not only setting aside the income tax assessment but also awarding 250 rupees in costs to a jubilant Zackariah Sahib.

Justice Sastri's invocation of the differences between Hindus and Muslims—and specifically of differences in Hindu and Muslim families and their living arrangements—was not uncommon within the context of taxation cases. Under Indian law, the HUF was treated as a separate entity for the purposes of taxation, much like a corporation, and the law recognized an "ancestral home" to which members of the HUF had a right to return. Sastri's statement did not mean that Muslims did not live in joint families, merely that Muslim personal law had no legal equivalent of the HUF; the Muslim familial arrangement was not recognized as being a coherent and distinct legal entity, and there was therefore no family "home" for Zackariah Sahib to return to. Recall from chapter 3 that the HUFs, as legal entities, were also business entities, used by Chettiars as trading firms; there was no such legal and commercial structure for

Muslim trading families, which were not treated as separate legal entities for the purposes of income tax. As discussed in chapter 3, if these Muslim firms were registered under the Indian Income Tax Act of 1922, they could gain certain concessions, though these concessions were nowhere near as generous as those accorded with the HUF. As this case shows, the provisions of the beleaguered Section 4-A of the Indian Income Tax Act of 1922 that discussed tax "residence" in fact translated familial attachments into commercial and economized attachments that shaped notions of political belonging.

The same judge—Justice Sastri—had decided differently on two similar cases, those of Sayed Abdul Cader and Zackariah Sahib. Although both Sayed Abdul Cader and Zackariah Sahib had probably fled Ceylon in fear of a Japanese invasion in 1942, Sayed Abdul Cader had to pay income tax in India and Zackariah Sahib did not. Then again, 1949 and 1951 were vastly different political moments for migrant Muslim traders between India and Ceylon. In 1949, when Sayed Abdul Cader was asked to pay income tax in India, the possibility of Ceylonese citizenship for immigrant Indians was still alive, with the introduction of legal regimes offering citizenship by registration to those who could "prove" an intention to permanently live in Ceylon. In 1951, it was becoming increasingly clear that this was only a law on the books that marginalized migrants without an extensive—even unreasonable—paper trail. By 1952, the Ceylon government noted that there had been an approximately 100 percent increase in remittances from Ceylon to India.[49]

The presence of wives and families along with traders in Ceylon was thus critical to the success or failure of a citizenship application, enough to warrant a legislative amendment to the 1949 Act. Take the case of Shahul Hameed and his family. Shahul Hameed's case, like Sayed Abdul Cader's, turned on the judicial understanding of what a loyal citizen's family ought to look like: a Ceylonese citizen's entire nuclear family belonged in Ceylon, even through hardship and danger. In 1953, two years after Shahul Hameed had filed an application for his family and himself to be registered as Ceylonese citizens, the deputy commissioner informed him that his wife's residence in Ceylon had not been satisfactorily proved.[50] Shahul Hameed did not take this lying down. He was a prominent Muslim merchant whose business supplied meat to the Dehiwala-Mount Lavinia Urban Council, and he owned a large house and vast amounts of property in Dehiwala, a suburb of Colombo. He appealed to the Supreme Court, employing prominent lawyers Shanmughanayagam and N. K. Choksy to appeal his case.

The lawyer for the other side was M. Tiruchelvam, then-deputy solicitor-general and a prominent Colombo lawyer who had been involved in the drafting of the Soulbury Constitution. When the case came up before the Supreme Court in Ceylon, Tiruchelvam appeared for the Commission for the Registration of Indian and Pakistani Residents. He argued that the 1949 Act had been amended in 1952 to specify that the wife of an applicant had to be present in Ceylon with her husband not later than one year after her marriage. According to Tiruchelvam, these were the grounds on which the deputy commissioner had (correctly) turned down Shahul Hameed's wife's application: Shahul Hameed had married his wife in February 1941, but she had not come to Ceylon until June 1942. This meant that he had not demonstrated legally that he and his family intended to settle in Ceylon permanently.

As Shahul Hameed's lawyers pointed out, his family had filed their application in 1951, a year before the act was amended. His lawyers pointed out that the amendment to the 1949 Act had a proviso that could help Shahul Hameed and his family. If the wife was absent from the island from December 1941 to December 1945, then it would not be counted against her because it would be attributed to the fear of "enemy action." This loophole put Shahul Hameed in a quandary: he had already sworn an affidavit in 1951 that his wife was unable to come to Ceylon because of her "delicate health," having given birth to a child in May 1942 and then immediately becoming pregnant again. How could he reconcile this affidavit with the claim that he had not brought her over because of the threat of air raids on Colombo?

Fortunately for Shahul Hameed, he had competent lawyers and sympathetic judges. Justice Nagalingam, the first "Ceylon Tamil" appointed to the Supreme Court, wrote eloquently: "Can it be said that the applicant was devoid of all tender feelings towards his wife and child, that he remained unaffected by the announcement of the headman that those who wished to evacuate to the interior may do so, and that he was so callous as not to care for the welfare, not to speak of the lives, of his wife and child?" The judge also further added that the wife had come over in June 1942 and had not waited until December 1945, which the act would have allowed. He could not be penalized for bringing her over sooner. Indeed, the judge commended him: "But because he or rather the wife braved the perils of enemy action, because the wife was herself prepared to stand by the husband and share the hazards of war, his conduct is penalised, but to my mind such conduct is worthy of commendation; in fact I find that the applicant has had certificates granted to him by more than one Chairman of the Urban Council lauding him for remaining behind when a number of shopkeepers had left the area." This was an exceptional case, for which the reward was Ceylonese citizenship. Shahul Hameed had deserted neither his family nor his adopted country. Within the courtroom, his leaving one would have been tantamount to leaving the other.

These three legal cases of Sayed Abdul Cader (1950), Zackariah Sahib (1951), and Shahul Hameed (1953), litigated on both sides of the Palk Strait, offer a snapshot of how familial attachments were translated into political attachments in the wake of wartime displacements. As we saw earlier, these cases unfolded in a climate of distrust of migrant Muslim traders and merchants in Ceylon, who were perceived as having escaped to India during the war. This chapter does not look to these taxation and immigration cases in terms of the plaintiffs' religious or social identities alone but invokes those identities to show how familial attachments were interpreted as political and economic attachments. Whereas immigration regimes in India and Ceylon assumed the familial to be patrilineal, taxation legislation mapped onto a more extensive understanding of familial "attachment"; taxation and immigration regimes, as we saw by way of the legal cases thus far, were braided together. The realities of migrant families across the Palk Strait differed from the law's understanding of "the family," and the distinction between juridical categories and the jurisdictional claims made by Muslim traders underscored the hollowness of these legal fictions.

THE MIGRANT FAMILY AS LEGAL FICTION

As Shanmughanayagam, Shahul Hameed's lawyer, had noted, the legal restrictions on families staying together changed in the postwar period to account for wartime displacements, though the new laws favored reuniting families. By 1950, the controller of labor for the Ceylon government noted that the Government of India allowed all wives married after 1942—at the height of wartime threats in Ceylon—to proceed to the island despite the ban on emigration at the beginning of the war. The Ceylon government demanded that they be granted separate permission, but in 1950, 908 out of 953 wives who applied for permission received it.[51] Families who did not apply for citizenship in Ceylon sought to stay together in other ways; it is likely that many families stayed together by applying for temporary residence permits rather than applying for citizenship (as discussed in chapter 4, anyone traveling from India to Ceylon had to have a passport or an Indo-Ceylon pass, which were difficult to obtain, especially for wives and children). In 1952, nearly 990 out of the 1,106 new residence permits issued were for wives and children of those who lived on the island.[52]

In the chaos of postwar attempts to straighten out legal paperwork, reunite families, and decide citizenships while building a newly independent nation, Muslims were singled out as engaging in fraudulent practices to gain citizenship. This group received a significant number of the permissions and permits that were granted in Ceylon during this period,[53] and the controller for emigration and immigration in Colombo saw "Ceylon Muslims" at the heart of the problem of "fake" evidentiary materials for citizenship (see chapter 4). He accused this group of using the birth certificates of Ceylon nationals to apply for emigration certificates from the Ceylonese government. Nearly four hundred certificates, he claimed, had been issued in this manner. The fear that their paperwork would be adjudged fraudulent continued to haunt families into the first decade of independence in Ceylon. The physical presence of their families perhaps seemed a hedge against these possible accusations: families that stayed all together in one place rather than on opposite sides of the Strait were strong evidence that applicants did indeed intend to live permanently in Ceylon. The influx of what the controller of immigration termed "new wives"— women newly married to migrant traders—across the Palk Strait during this period suggests that resident families were becoming "proof" of political belonging and of political loyalty in postwar South Asia. Both taxation and immigration legislation operated on assumptions that the family had one location. This was not customary for traders who traveled across the Palk Strait, placing them at odds with postwar legal regimes. These conflicts had implications for citizenship.

Immigration regimes skewed toward patrilineal descent. The fact that "family" and "marriage" were defined in heteronormative terms in taxation and immigration legislation was unsurprising, since the legal construction of "family" is integral to the constitution of "race" and "nation"; these definitions of family (which mapped most neatly onto nonmigrant, non-Indian-descended families) served the political interests of Sinhala Buddhist nationalism in Ceylon. The legal fiction that citizenship was to be claimed by the male head of household also suffered from another disadvantage: it relied on the assumption that families were racially, ethnically, and religiously homogeneous—exclusively Tamil, Sinhalese, Muslim, or Hindu, never mixed. For comparison, anxieties around mixed marriages existed in Burma as well. As historians Chie Ikeya and Rajashree Mazumder show, anxieties over marriages between Indians and Burmese (often sidelined in the colonial record because they did not threaten the superior position of Europeans in the colonies) were reflected in legislation.[54] In Burma, Mazumder shows, fear of mixed marriages was mobilized for anti-immigrant sentiment.[55] While Indian laborers were believed to be hard-working partners to the Burmese women they lived with, they were seen as "sojourners" who had other families back "home" and would thus eventually leave Burma.[56] In Ceylon, a similar sentiment against migrant traders who married local women manifested in the general public's responses to the Soulbury Commission's 1945 constitutional reforms, which posited that marriage between the different "races" had brought these communities into the same "family." But the legal fiction of the "family," which was structured around a set of corporeal, knowable markers, occluded these realities from official notice.[57] In citizenship legislation in both Ceylon and Burma, marriage exemplified the familial relationship par excellence; other types of familiar relationships were excluded from the definition of family, in part because of the fear of the Indian immigrant man. Denying the potential for full legal citizenship to parties in nonmarital relation-ships (aging parents, cousins, etc.) indirectly censured these other types of family structures.

KATHEESA BI'S WAIT

Narratives of women who wait—as wives, daughters, or lovers staying behind while men venture forth—sit uneasily alongside the family as ter-ritorialized legal fiction. Women wait, historian Caroline Brettell writes, while men migrate. In histories of trading families, men are often por-trayed as sojourning cosmopolitans (a stereotype that, as we have seen, can also be used against them), while women stay behind in charge of aging parents, children, and the home.[58] This fiction can be quickly dismantled. One can reasonably speculate about the lives of women like Seethalakshmi Achi, who took on the recovery of her husband's debts in Burma after his death and after the end of the war, as we saw in chapter 2, or the women in colonial-era photographs advertising Ceylon Tea in chapter 4 (figure 4.1), who were the primary earners for the home, women who on citi-zenship applications were listed only as dependents on the male head of household.[59] Historian Arunima Datta describes the experiences of coolie women in the Malayan plantations with what she terms "fleeting agency." They continued to labor on the plantation and tended to their own homes even as their husbands, brothers, or sons were recruited by the Indian Na-tional Army or the Japanese forces; they also joined the Rani of Jhansi regiment of the Indian National Army themselves to ensure that they had access to opportunities.[60] In the case of Muslim trading families whose business crossed the Palk Strait, as we saw from the legal cases above, wives often lived in their husbands' natal homes with parents and other dependents while the men traded or labored beyond the shores of the Mal-abar and Coromandel Coasts. But we can see glimpses into the lives of these women in the margins of legal texts that document litigation around familial attachments as political attachments: in taxation and immigration cases around "casual visits" or in cases where families maintained "dwell-ing houses," we can see that these women did not merely wait for men to return from lands across the ocean but lived and thrived.

The legal battle over the will of Puthen Veettil Umbichi Haji, a merchant from Calicut in Madras who lived and worked in Colombo, reveals the many paradoxes of these formulations regarding "women who wait while men migrate," as well as the ways in which familial attachments translated in law as political attachments.[61] In 1934, Umbichi wrote a letter to the mayor of Colombo, noting that he intended to spend the rest of his days in Ceylon and wanted to be buried in the city, on the premises of the mosque that he had funded and built. The mayor wrote back saying he had no objections, and when he died two years later, Umbichi was accordingly buried there. In the year of his death in Ceylon, his cousin Moideen Kutti Haji contested his will, which left a considerable amount of his wealth for charitable purposes in Ceylon. In this conflict-of-law case, the judges of the Madras High Court had to decide which country's law would apply to what portion of his assets. In the end, the judges ruled against Moideen Kutti. Umbichi's will was interpreted per the provisions of law in Ceylon, and his wealth was left to charities there.

Umbichi was born in a small town near Kozhikode (former Calicut on the Malabar coast, in present-day Kerala). He left home at a very young age, according to his unofficial biographer, jumping aboard an *uru*—a kind of *dhow* or boat manufactured locally—that was bound for Cochin to seek help from his relatives who lived there. He found nothing to improve his fortunes in Cochin, so he borrowed money to travel to Madras, from which he boarded a steamer for Colombo. From then on, his story is a classic rags-to-riches tale. In Ceylon, he set up businesses exporting cured fish, much in demand there and cheaply available from the Malabar Coast and the islands of Lakshwadweep, and built up a vast import-export business that expanded beyond dried fish to bullion and money exchange. In the bustling streets of the Pettah in Colombo, the mosque that was ostensibly built with charitable contributions from Umbichi Haji and houses his remains still stands today, *a jumma masjid*. On an August afternoon in 2018, I spoke to the sole remaining chief trustee (name withheld) of the mosque about Umbichi. The elderly trustee told me that Umbichi's family lived in Kozhikode (Calicut), part of British Madras before 1956 and that his descendants used to visit Colombo, but that their interest in maintaining the family connections between the two places had trailed off in recent times. He confirmed that Umbichi's wealth had not gone to his wife, children, and other kin in Malabar but had remained in Sri Lanka, benefiting Sri Lankans.

But the legal dispute surrounding his will tells a different story, one in which Umbichi's loyalty to Ceylon was challenged before the Madras High Court. His nephew Moideen Kutti Haji argued before the district court in South Malabar, where the will was first contested, that Umbichi had never intended to leave India. In legal terms, he claimed that his uncle Umbichi Haji had never abandoned his Indian "domicile" to adopt Ceylon as his permanent home. After all, Moideen Kutti pointed out, Umbichi's wife Katheesa Bi and two daughters continued to live in Calicut; unlike wives who applied for permissions to travel across the Palk Strait after being displaced by the war, his family never followed him to Colombo. If his domicile was still in India, his will had to be interpreted according to Muslim law relating to inheritances in India.

Moideen Kutti and his lawyers presumably knew that the way that this legal argument translated familial attachments into legal attachments was not grounded in custom. Umbichi and his wife Katheesa Bi belonged to Koya families in Malabar. Koya families were uxorilocal: the husband resided with the wife after marriage in a home built for them by the bride's family.[62] So it was for Umbichi and Katheesa. Umbichi, born in 1865, moved to Calicut and to the *Ponmanichintakath tharavad* (ancestral home) when he married Katheesa Bi. Over the years, Umbichi also built a new house in Calicut for his wife and daughters, Ayesha Bi and Umbichamina Bi, known today as "Ceylon House" (see figure 5.1). This was the grounds for Moideen Kutti and his lawyers' legal strategy, which argued that the patriarchal, nuclear-family-based legal conception of family should not decide the case; instead, the decision should define family as it was understood in matrilineal Koya custom. This argument reflected the realities of migrant traders' and laborers' postwar citizenship in India and Ceylon, a sharp contrast to how taxation and immigration regimes imagined familial and political loyalties.

Ultimately, Moideen Kutti Haji's appeal failed. The judges of the Madras High Court ruled that Umbichi's will clearly stated that he intended to remain and die in Ceylon and had "no intention" of abandoning it. Umbichi's vast estate was divided mostly in compliance with the terms

FIGURE 5.1: *Ceylon House, Calicut. Photograph by author.*

of his will (because of a legal loophole, discussed below, the plaintiffs did receive small bequests), including the charitable contributions he wished made in Ceylon.[63] Yet in spite of this legal decision, his influence shaped both the home where he was born and his adopted home: today, his name is emblazoned on both a street in the Pettah and a school in Calicut. Only at the time of his death was the hidden jurisdictional border between the two countries revealed.

The stakes of Moideen Kutti Haji's argument that Umbichi never intended to relinquish his "domicile" in India are revealed by a close examination of these legal borders between India and Ceylon. By the late nineteenth century, as Umbichi was making his way from India to Ceylon, several legal codification projects in British India were adjudicating the growing conflicts between law and custom. These projects aimed to delineate questions of marriage, divorce, and inheritance according to "personal law," which was determined by one's religion. (In Ceylon, there was no similar national project to codify the relationship of personal law and national law, but since Ceylon was a Crown colony, several ordinances were passed laying out the boundaries of personal law for different communities there.) The various spheres of personal law that overlapped and competed within the patchwork of Ceylon's legal system, as we saw earlier, included Roman-Dutch law, introduced by the Dutch in Ceylon's Maritime Provinces; British law relating to various criminal laws; the customary law of the Kandyan Sinhalese; the Tesavalamai for the Hindu Tamils in the Northern Province; and Islamic law. The ordinance relating to Umbichi's case was passed in 1844. Known as the Wills Ordinance, it discussed the scope of testamentary power held by Muslims in Sri Lanka. Most importantly, the ordinance noted that it was applicable throughout the territorial extent of Ceylon: in other words, this ordinance about personal law turned on the question of territorial jurisdiction. (This is the loophole mentioned above; because of this ordinance, the family contesting Umbichi's will did receive small bequests, though the bulk of his fortune was disposed in the way he had requested.)

A similar legal reform project to delineate the scope of Islamic law in Malabar was under way at the same time, championed by representatives of the Mappilla community. Their claims were the opposite of those put forward by Umbichi's nephew: they claimed that *marumakkathayam*—a system of inheritance that followed matrilineal descent as espoused by Koya families—was "un-Islamic" and had to give way to codification. In other words, they asserted that when Koya custom came up against Islamic law, there needed to be a legal precedent for how to settle the conflict. Umbichi and Katheesa's legal fates would be marked by these efforts to codify and reform Islamic law in both India and Ceylon.

It is likely that Umbichi, a wealthy merchant and businessman, would have had (and taken) excellent legal advice when drawing up his will. In the archival records, there is a mention of an "Advocate Wilson" who handled his affairs in Colombo, and his legal advisers in Madras included some of the top lawyers of the day, including B. Pocker Sahib, who would later go on to join the Constituent Assembly of India, and B. Sitarama Rao, a celebrated jurist who wrote the definitive book on Malabar law. One of the key provisions of the Wills Ordinance was that, notwithstanding any principle of "Mohammedan law" (the Muslim "personal law"), one could dispose of one's entire property through a will. In other words, in Ceylon, it was possible to disinherit by means of a will those who, under Mohammedan law, would be one's automatic legal heirs. Under British India's Mohammedan law, Moideen Kutti was a legal heir in Malabar, but under the provisions of Ceylon's Wills Ordinance, Umbichi could bequeath all his property away from Moideen Kutti, leaving it to his wife Katheesa Bi and his daughters Ayesha Bi and Umbichinaminabi and their children—or to the charities and mosques in Ceylon that he had named.

Indeed, some of Umbichi's actions in his last years seem to show that he was trying to make his will unchallengeable. He first wrote up his will in 1933. In 1934, he applied for permission to be buried on the premises of the mosque that he had supplied funds to build and was granted permission by the mayor of Colombo. Over the course of the next two years, right up until a few months before his death, he amended his will three times. He also left behind a paper trail that would allow the executors of his will to prove that he had a Ceylon domicile. This was an attempt at what historians have termed "forum shopping"—choosing a territorial jurisdiction that is more sympathetic to one's claims as a legal strategy.

As we have seen, Umbichi's work to make his will watertight was successful: the charitable bequests were distributed and he was buried at the mosque. So how did Moideen Kutti and his heirs still end up with a share in Umbichi's properties? The judges of the Madras High Court, which made the final decision on this litigation, ruled that Ceylonese law did not apply to all of Umbichi's properties everywhere; in other words, in this case (unlike in the income tax cases), domicile was not all-important. Instead, they ruled, Ceylonese law could apply only to the part of his properties that was actually located in Ceylon. This meant that his extensive holdings in British Malabar were subject to Mohammedan law for British India. Considering the scope of Umbichi's wealth, this would have still been a considerable amount. In a strange twist, the courts both granted and thwarted Umbichi's last wishes.

Today, Umbichi's final resting place, the Wolfendahl Mosque (figure 5.2), is easy to miss amid the bustling streets of Colombo's Pettah. The trustee of the mosque told me that during Umbichi's life he never cared for Malabar: he had lived and died for Sri Lanka—*ellavum Sri Lanka-*

FIGURE 5.2: *Wolfendahl Mosque, Colombo. Photograph by author.*

vukku thaan (everything was for Sri Lanka). But Umbichi almost certainly also cared for Katheesa Bi and his daughters in Malabar. A descendent of Umbichi's, whom I will call Abdul, told me that that Umbichi created several *waqfs* with his wife; under one of these *waafs*, each of the two hundred members of the *Ponmanichintakath tharavad* receives a thousand rupees per month. Abdul told me that no one was particularly interested in Umbichi's Sri Lankan properties, for there was plenty to go around in Malabar—although he joked that if my research uncovered any means of recovering those properties, it would bring the entire family together. But when I asked pointed questions about the old postwar litigation he was referring to, he categorically denied any knowledge. So perhaps for Umbichi, not *everything* was for Sri Lanka. Katheesa and her daughters were not simply waiting for Umbichi but living and thriving.

We can see Umbichi's and Katheesa's legal lives as reflecting migrant Muslim families' complex histories and legacies, both in India and in Ceylon, and as challenging the notion of women who waited while men migrated.[64] At the same time, migrants were aware that familial attachments were translated into political attachments, and they planned accordingly. In the 1940s and 1950s, as the countries' governments created separate immigration and citizenship regimes for India and Sri Lanka, Muslims in Sri Lanka were seen as sojourners and had to prove that they belonged to the island. Of course, not all Sri Lankan Muslims spoke Tamil—there were also speakers of Malayalam, Malay, and Urdu among them who hailed not from India but from other parts of South and Southeast Asia. But Ceylon's conflation of Muslims with Tamils meant that their claims to belong in Sri Lanka had to be made more vociferously. These jurisdictional claims were a means of narrating personal and familial histories. This was the climate in which Katheesa Bi and Umbichi's family in Malabar brought their suit, which grappled with the assumptions of legal regimes that translated familial attachments as political attachments.

According to the citizenship regime that Ceylon enacted, several things were entangled with the right to citizenship: family structure, geographic location, economic contributions, and race, ethnicity, religion, and culture—the last set of concerns being particularly relevant for minoritized groups in Ceylon. We can see this in the cases of Sayed Abdul Cader and Shahul Hameed, who needed to prove their intention to be permanently resident on the island by convincing the court that their families were not only located in Ceylon but also in possession of an "assured income" that would not prove to be an economic burden to the new nation-state.[65] Sayed Abdul Cader and Shahul Hameed were fortunate in this: unlike the Tamil-speaking laborers who worked in the tea plantations in the hill country, these traders were able to generate evidence for their claims in the form of character witnesses including prominent political leaders, as well as documents proving their economic contribution to the country.

For migrant traders to Ceylon with families in India, like Sayed Abdul Cader and Zackariah Sahib, familial ties and the physical locations of family also became important. These men, who did not live in British India, were claimed as Indian "residents" for the purposes of Indian income tax, and they had to prove that the visits to their families were indeed visits, not periodic returns to their true homes. But their cases present an interesting contrast too. Sayed Abdul Cader, who had married a "Ceylonese lady," lost his case, while Zackariah Sahib, whose wife remained in their natal village in Tirunelveli rather than joining him in Ceylon, won his case. Familial attachments went beyond immediate relationships, and the complexities of family structures revealed in these cases unraveled legal fictions of the family.

Ultimately, the question of family structure and location—whether wives and husbands must have lived together during the years before they filed citizenship applications—was finally laid to rest by the Judicial Committee of the Privy Council in 1952.66 If wives and husbands stayed apart, they said, this fact could not be used as proof against their application as a family.

Migrant traders like Abdul Cader, Zackariah Sahib, Shahul Hameed, and Umbichi Haji posed a problem for the ways in which newly independent India and Ceylon could claim and exercise sovereignty. States perform sovereignty in many ways, including the imposition of taxes and the control of immigration processes. But the fragmented families that emerged from the legal records of migrant Muslim traders disrupted the seemingly easy logic of legal bureaucracies, which are both a means for and an example of, state sovereignty. We might, then, begin to see how a legal archive of "ordinary" cases can record challenges to governmental assertions of territorial sovereignty.

PART II

SIX

RED FLAGS

IN LATE 1948, the SS *Vasna* reached the shores of Madras City from Singapore, on a routine voyage across the Bay of Bengal.[1] For six of the passengers on board, the journey would be far from routine. As soon as they disembarked, they were detained by police officials under the Madras Maintenance of Public Order Act (MMPOA) on the suspicion of being communists, potentially capable of inciting violence and disorder in the province. These unexpected detentions were a sign of a storm that would touch down on both shores of the Bay. An intense suspicion of "communists" was rapidly brewing, with counterinsurgency operations in Malaya leading to a period that historians would later label "the Emergency," strikes on Ceylon's plantations in 1946–47 that spilled over into trade union support for the citizenship rights of plantation laborers, and insurgencies and unrest in Burma in which the Communist Party of Burma was involved. The SS *Vasna* had docked in Madras amid this perfect storm.

As we have seen in previous chapters, the major political parties leading the movements for independence in Burma, Ceylon, and Malaya did not envision a place for labor migrants in their countries' postwar futures. These political parties found common cause with ethnonationalist movements that demanded homelands for the countries' "original" inhabitants and excluded those who were perceived to be newer settlers. The exclusions were not restricted to legislative and constitutional frameworks or to the terms of political debate. In this chapter, we see how postwar nation-states mobilized legal regimes of banishment and deportation to expel migrants, often labeling them "communists." In response, trade unionists as well as writers and journalists with leftist sympathies began advocating for the rights of working- class migrant laborers on plantations and in port cities. These advocates included prominent labor leaders and trade unionists such as S. Nadesan and lawyer-journalist S. P. Amarasingam, whom we met in chapter 4, and journalists and writers G. Sarangapany and R. Ramanathan in Malaya, whom we will meet in this chapter. They also included lesser-known figures like the lawyer V. G. Row, who represented the "Malayan Detenus"—as the detainees from the SS *Vasna* came to be known—before the Madras High Court.

The ill-fated men detained upon embarkation from the SS *Vasna* were banished from Singapore (at the time part of British Malaya), where they had been dockworkers at Singapore Harbor. Some of the men were de-scendants of Indian indentured laborers and were born in Malaya. They had been sent back to a "home" that they had never seen or been to. Rely-ing on lawyers like Row for representation, they filed habeas corpus appli-cations at the Madras High Court and wrote to their families and leaders of various political parties, pleading for release. These labor migrants had been barred from returning to Singapore but were now detained in pris-ons in their perceived "home" in Madras, forced to navigate deportation, detention, and exile because of their political sympathies and the circum-stances of their birth.

A PERFECT STORM

The MMPOA, the legislation under which the six men were detained, was enacted for the first time in March 1947 in Madras. It allowed for preventive detention, censorship, and control of essential commodities in the name of "public safety." Legislation of this sort was not peculiar to Madras. Several other provinces in British India had enacted, or were in the process of enacting, similar legislation, ostensibly designed to deal with the inevitable violence predicted to follow the territorial partition of

the subcontinent into India and Pakistan.[2] That the MMPOA was antici-
patory in nature was borne out by the first six weeks of its existence on the
books: over 145 people were arrested, and thirty-five warrants were issued
for searches and seizures.[3]

Although the intention behind enacting the MMPOA was aligned
with national politics, the passage of the Act in Madras also anticipated
electoral outcomes in the province. In the first postwar provincial elections in 1946, the Communist Party was aligned with the Dravida Ka-
zhagam, the Indian National Congress's main opponent. In the 1946
elections, the Communist Party had secured nine seats in Madras and
organized the railway workers of the Southern Indian Railway and at the
Coimbatore Mills—an electoral outcome and an industrial action that
had gathered popular support.[4] The Communist Party of India members
believed that the act was a measure directed against them rather than one
meant to serve the law-and-order interests of the province.[5] The passage
of the MMPOA therefore provoked an intense debate in the Madras legislature. "Members of the Congress Party," thundered P. Venkateswarlu,
a prominent Communist Party representative in the Madras Legislative
Assembly, "you are all members of this ordinance raj. We have struggled
against these repressive measures and were able to achieve this much of
civil liberty we are enjoying now. With this Ordinance goes all your previous labor to waste. Do you allow the Ordinance to pass into law?"[6] The
Communist Party representatives invoked the ongoing process of decolonization, accusing the ruling Indian National Congress government in
Madras of "playing into the hands of the blue-eyed imperialist" with the
passage of the act.[7] But criticism of the act was not restricted to the Communist Party. Some of the pro-Congress Tamil-language newspapers
opined that the government had taken more powers than necessary in
the proposed bill.[8] In spite of these objections, the MMPOA was passed
in 1947.

Venkateswarlu's allegations about the disproportionate impact of the
MMPOA on communists were not untrue. The confidential files of the
Madras government's secretariat note that the MMPOA was indeed being
introduced to combat "the Communist menace," which, the Secretariat
said, had reached alarming proportions in the province and along its bor-

ders.[9] Although communists were not the only political workers detained under the MMPOA, the available numbers indicate that they made up the bulk of the detainees. For instance, at the end of March 1949, 7,145 communists were detained, but only 2,837 Rashtriya Swayam Sevak workers were detained.[10] Other political workers were affected as well, including the Red Volunteer Army and the Muslim National Guards, who served as the foot soldiers of non-Congress political parties; however, the numbers of detainees in these groups were also lower than those of suspected communists.

Although it came under attack from opposition parties for the harshness of its provisions, the MMPOA was not the first law to disproportionately affect the Communist Party; the party was no stranger to legal restrictions on its activities. In Madras, it had been subject to surveillance from its inception in the 1920s: for example, M. Singaravelu Chettiar, a trade union leader from Madras, was implicated in the infamous Kanpur conspiracy case that brought widespread attention to the activities of the Communist Party in India.[11] M. N. Roy, the émigré communist who traveled to Germany and Mexico, was reportedly in touch with Chettiar and communists in Madras City from its earliest days.[12] B. P. Wadia and N. M. Joshi, prominent trade unionists in Bombay, were frequently part of meetings called by communist-controlled labor unions in Madras. Between 1934 and 1942, the party was declared an "unlawful association" and was forced into clandestine operation: many of its leaders went underground, and others became part of mass front organizations including trade unions, civil liberties unions, and labor protection leagues. But the party worked the ban to its advantage, and its membership grew steadily. At the beginning of 1934, it had a paltry membership of 20, which grew by the end of the year to 150.[13] It recruited heavily during the war years, going from 4,000 members in 1942 to 15,000 in 1943 and 53,000 in 1946. Similarly, the membership of the communist-led All India Trade Union Congress doubled, going from 250,000 to 500,000 between 1942 and 1944.[14] As Sanjoy Bhattacharya notes, while public processions and meetings were subject to legal action, actions such as door-to-door pamphleteering and street theater were far more difficult to police.[15] Through these street-level recruitment and mobilization efforts, the Communist Party quietly grew in strength.

In 1942, following the attack of German forces in Russia, farther afield than the threats of a Japanese attack on the shores of the Bay of Bengal that we discussed in chapter 1, the Communist Party began referring to the World War as a "people's war." They had once labeled it "an imperialist war," which targeted "bourgeois nationalist parties" in addition to British imperialism. In response, the Central Government in India lifted the ban on the Communist Party after it promised to support the Allied forces in World War II. However, the party's goal remained not just defeating imperialism but overturning all types of class oppression—including the existing political and economic systems in India that persisted after independence. In 1947, the Constituent Assembly (which also doubled as the interim Indian government) adopted a hard line with the Communist Party in India.[16] The Indian government's anticommunism strategies framed the party as a threat to safety and security, arguing that communism (whether home-grown or imported from violent "communist revolts abroad") caused violence and unrest. However, the real threat posed by communism was electoral: the ruling class and existing politicians saw the party gaining traction among the working class and sought to retain their power.[17] Fully aware of the party's stance toward them, postwar Congress governments in various provinces, including Madras, struck back, in part through legislation like the MMPOA.

As mentioned above, the first legislative measures against the working of covert communist organizations were passed between 1930 and 1939 because of peasant agitations in the Thanjavur and Malabar districts of Madras. But the most elaborate surveillance measures were reserved for communist threats from outside the province: the peasant agitations brewing across the land border in the princely states of Hyderabad, Travancore, and Cochin and the plantation labor strikes taking place across the Bay of Bengal in British Malaya and across the Palk Strait in Ceylon.[18] The threat of the communists across the territorial borders of British India in the princely states was made plain in 1946, when Travancore witnessed the Punnapra Vayalar uprising, organized by Communist Party workers against the oppressive agrarian policies followed by the diwan (prime minister), C. P. Ramaswamy Aiyar.[19] The Communist Party leaders in Madras formed alliances across other borders as well: for example, they connected with V. Subbiah, the most prominent Communist Party leader in Pondicherry in French India.[20] Other French enclaves, including Mahe and Karikal, were just as worried as British India and were seeing similar conflicts between the Congress and communists arise. Jessica Namakkal shows how Communist Party leaders like Subbiah were named in French Indian reports as "goondas," disruptors and disloyal political actors, who were keen to overturn efforts at the referendum over whether to join India or the French Union following Indian independence.[21] The fear of communism within and beyond the territorial borders of Madras played into the enactment and implementation of the MMPOA.

The fear of communism in Madras was further stoked by the fact that prominent leaders of the Communist Party in India traveled back and forth between India, Ceylon, and Malaya, where they supported working-class causes, including the rights of migrant laborers from India. In his autobiography, the Praja Socialist and later Communist Party leader A. K. Gopalan wrote of traveling between these countries in the late 1930s, organizing the Malayali Mahajana Sabha in Ceylon and addressing large crowds of Malayali workers in Wellawatte in Colombo.[22] Nira Wickramasinghe notes the rising tension between local and migrant workers in Colombo and elsewhere, exacerbated by the migrant workers' communist sympathies: in her discussion of the racial tensions between "Indians" and "Sinhalese," Wickramasinghe argues that the presence of Malayali workers for the Public Works Department and in various industries contributed to the resentment that the Sinhalese-led labor movement in Colombo felt toward immigrant workers. Like worker coalitions, political coalitions also allied with the communists. The Lanka Sama Samaja Party (LSSP), which we encountered in chapter 4, and which had influence over plantation workers, had connections with the Communist Party in India.[23] Members of the LSSP, including N. M. Perera and Philip Gunawardena, had escaped to India after the crackdown on the labor movement on the plantations that they had led. S. C. C. Anthonypillai, one of its other prominent leaders, was externed from Ceylon and lived in Madras City for many decades with his wife Caroline Anthonypillai, where they both remained deeply involved in the trade union movement in the city.

But the fear of "communists"—and use of banishment and deportation ordinances—was by this time widespread in Malaya, where emergency rule was announced by the British administration in June 1948. The report on the administrative measures associated with the emergency that were undertaken in Singapore was then circulated to places with large urban populations such as Mombasa, Accra, and Zanzibar. Those of Chinese descent in Malaya were labeled "aliens" and "repatriated" to the mainland, and others were "resettled" in villages where they were subject to strict surveillance. Although it was labeled "repatriation," in reality, the British high commissioner had sweeping powers to detain or banish those who were suspected of being "communists." As Low Choo Chin notes, these administrative measures and emergency regulations that sought to maintain law and order became a form of immigration control.[24]

The MMPOA imposed collective fines and strict limits on the freedom of movement for people, information, and commodities. It also took control of the distribution of essential commodities such as food.[25] The food control policy arose from the emergency legal regimes of World War II, and government reports noted that the MMPOA was designed to help put down disturbances and riots arising during the harvest season, for it mandated sanctions for violations of its provisions.[26] This might be the specific reason why the Congress feared the Communist Party as political opposition: the communists in Madras attacked the food control policy, and the ruling Indian National Congress government feared that this struck at the heart of their credibility. In at least one case that Row would take up, an attack on the government's food control policy was explicitly given as the reason for detention.[27] Further, the agricultural districts most affected by the MMPOA's food control policies were also historically the districts from which people migrated to Southeast Asia.

The Madras government therefore likely feared that returnees like the "Malayan Detenus," who were influenced by communist ideas and who were able to speak in Tamil and employ local idioms, could inspire violence against the state in their villages. It was their potential to stir up these types of violence or dissent that marked them as "communists." So by 1948 when the SS *Vasna* docked in Madras, a "communist" was not necessarily a card-carrying member of the Communist Party but someone who had the potential to generate political dissent around poverty, famine, and inequality; for the Indian National Congress–led Madras government, the label "communist" became a placeholder for any sort of political opponent. The term even entered the mainstream, denoting anyone whom someone did not like: several Malayalam newspapers noted that neighbors tried to "settle scores" by handing over their enemies as "communists."[28]

FROM MALAYA TO MADRAS

In contrast to India's measures against communism, Malaya's were spearheaded by a returning British military administration, which took over after Japanese forces surrendered in 1945. Soon after the takeover, a wave of strikes swept Malayan rubber plantations. On June 16, 1948, Malaya, fearing a violent communist "revolt," declared a state of emergency, requiring everyone to carry identity cards and empowering the Federation of Malaya to "banish" political opponents.[29] Similar measures were in force in Singapore, where the commissioner of police reinstituted the country's emergency regulations from the prewar period.[30] Trade unions were at risk of being labeled as communist organizations and were issued instructions to their members on how the emergency regulations would affect them. By September 1949, about eight hundred Indians were being detained in camps on suspicion of aiding and abetting a communist rebellion.[31] According to Federation of Malaya–era documents, in 1950 alone, 887 Chinese nationals and their families were deported to China and 225 Indian nationals were deported to India.[32]

The Special Branch of the Criminal Investigation Department of the Madras government reported that Ramiah, one of the six detainees, had been born in Singapore to Indian parents who were indentured laborers and had studied up to the fifth standard. Recall that the labor migration to the Straits Settlements took place, at least in part, under conditions of indenture. Singapore, as part of the Crown colony of the Straits Settlements, was, as Sunil Amrith points out, a "mobile city" in the imagination of aspiring emigrants, promising better fortunes and futures.[33] It was also alleged that Ramiah was a part of the "Singapore Harbor Labor Union Thondar Padai" and a personal bodyguard of P. Veerasenan, the president of the Singapore Harbor Labor Union at the time.[34] Intelligence agencies also noted that during the Japanese occupation of Malaya, Ramiah was a *sepoy* in the Indian National Army led by Subhas Chandra Bose (referred to in chapter 1). Ramiah admitted that he was a member of the SHLU but denied that he was a communist.

The police officer who investigated the Malayan Detenus case concluded by saying that "reliance could not be placed on his [Ramiah's] statements,"[35] although no reasons were given for why he was deemed unreliable. Inferences about his politics and motivations were made during detention and from the fact that he spoke Tamil. For instance, Ramiah was one of ten prisoners who asked to be removed from the general enclosure and wanted to be housed together with the other local communists—a request that the jail authorities understood as an admission of guilt. The officers feared that the if the communist group were housed together in the prison, they would find a sense of camaraderie with communists from India, Malaya, and Burma and that the men—who all spoke Tamil—would then spread propaganda in Madras about the "heroic exploits" of communists in other countries. They also worried that the men would be more likely to resort to "antisocial" activities upon release.[36] For these reasons, police officials decided they should be treated as a grave threat to "public order."

To understand Ramiah's statements and actions, we might revisit Indian immigration to Singapore from the mid-nineteenth century onwards. Labor immigration from India to Malaya included not only plantation workers under the indenture system, as was the case with Ramiah's parents, or as part of kangany-recruited migration, but also moneylenders, traders, dockworkers, railway workers, and restaurant workers. Workers from Madras were stereotyped as "docile," cheap, and poor; in addition, they were easily transportable from one part of the British Empire to another, unlike, say, Javanese labor, which involved negotiations with the Dutch. For these reasons, migrant laborers from Madras were a fixture on plantations in the Straits Settlements, particularly in Perak, Selangor, and Negri Sembilan.[37] In the 1890s, as coffee plantations in Ceylon died out, plantation owners moved from Ceylon to the Malay States, where they planted rubber. By the turn of the century, rubber was the dominant plantation crop on the Selangor estates,[38] and by the interwar period, much of the crop produced in the region, including from the Netherlands East Indies, passed through Singapore Harbor.[39] But during the Japanese occupation, as Paul Kratoska notes, many estate workers were forced to leave the plantations and seek employment in towns.[40]

Ramiah's involvements in wartime and postwar Malaya were also shared by many of the young men who had joined Ras Behari Bose's Indian Independence League and Subash Chandra Bose's Indian National Army in Malaya, Thailand, and Singapore. As we saw in chapter 1, some had joined for patriotic reasons, others to escape the brutalities inflicted on Indians by the occupying Japanese.[41] Following the end of the war, as Rajeswary Ampalavanar Brown describes, some joined the Pan-Malayan Federation of Trade Unions (PMFTU), and others joined the Thondar Padai movement. Ramiah followed the latter path. The Thondar Padai was initially started to curb the toddy-drinking habit among Indian laborers on estates in the former Federated Malay States.[42] In the postwar period, however, the Thondar Padai morphed into an organization that encouraged and engaged with trade unions, although most of its support came from plantation workers.[43] In 1945, the Malayan Union authorities arrested K. A. Chandran, a member of the Malayan Communist Party, who confessed that the party planned to infiltrate the Singapore Harbor Labor Union. At the same time, P. Veerasenan, who was connected to the Singapore branch of the PMFTU associated with the Communist Party, was involved in negotiations with the Singapore Harbor Board for improved wages for wharf workers.[44] Because of Chandran's confession and Veerasenan's association, anyone linked with the Singapore Harbor Labor Union was likely suspected of being a member of the Communist Party. Additionally, the Thondar Padai was banned in Malaya, and its founder, A. M. Samy, was exiled to India. Thus Ramiah's various affiliations were suspect in postwar Malaya.

Both working-class migrants like Ramiah and middle-class migrants including traders and professionals were often forced to comply with occupation forces during the war, but the differential treatment that they received after the war was stark. Although the Indian National Army men who fought in Burma were at first court-martialed for treason in India, they were eventually heralded as "patriots" for wanting to drive out the

British from the subcontinent. Others who were professionals or politically engaged "overseas" Indians pursued diplomatic careers after the war. For instance, K. P. Kesava Menon, lawyer, politician, and one-time member of the Indian Independence League who parted ways with Subash Chandra Bose over the alliance with Japanese forces, became high commissioner to Ceylon; similarly, John Thivy, once a member of the Indian National Army, was appointed ambassador to Mauritius in 1950.[45] The Malayan Detenus, on the other hand, were not only banished from Singapore but detained without trial in Madras.

Months after they were first detained, the six men from the SS *Vasna* were still at the Vellore Jail in Madras City, their cases still unreviewed by the Advisory Council tasked with looking into the reasons and conditions for detention and determining the length of detention. In this age of panic about communist sympathizers, MMPOA detainees like Ramiah and his comrades were fully enmeshed in the machinery of legal procedures around immigration and detention. The MMPOA, like other preventive detention legislation, was built on suspicion and speculation about political loyalties. Orders were issued by district magistrates and police commissioners, then cancelled the next day. Advisory Councils, which were constituted under the act to review detention orders, were often not fully staffed and met infrequently. Impassioned petitions were written to the governments in Madras and Delhi. Interviews were granted to curious journalists. Not all detainees went through identical procedures, but most of them likely consulted a lawyer, who would have almost certainly suggested that they file habeas corpus applications in the Madras High Court.[46]

Before the Madras High Court, the lawyer for the Malayan Detenus, V. G. Row—about whom we will soon learn more—argued that the men were being illegally detained. The government had taken account of the detainees' events and activities outside Madras, such as their former membership in trade unions in Singapore.[47] He argued that since the MMPOA was restricted in its operation to the province of Madras, anything beyond its territorial borders should not have been considered. But Judges Rao and Sastri were not persuaded. The detention orders, they ruled, stated that the detainees were members of a violent communist-controlled labor union in

Malaya, responsible for assaulting Chinese laborers, and that they continued to take orders from communist leaders in Malaya.[48] The judges ruled that even if the grounds for detention came from events and activities outside Madras, the men were within the jurisdiction of Madras when they were detained. In any case, the court would not, they ruled, scrutinize the Madras government's "subjective satisfaction." If the governor of Madras was convinced that there was a need for preventive detention, judges could not decide otherwise. The court dismissed the applications. The Madras High Court did not question the government's power to detain a suspected "communist"—a decision that gave sanction for the Madras government's authority to take stock of people, ideas, and events beyond its territorial jurisdiction.

HABEAS CORPUS

The legal archive of habeas corpus applications, such as the ones that V. G. Row filed on behalf of the Malayan Detenus, gives us a valuable look into the contemporary understandings of territory, loyalty, and political belonging in the period—a record that is especially valuable because many Intelligence Branch files about this period were destroyed or deliberately misplaced.[49] As Nasser Hussain shows in his study of emergency legislation in colonial India, the writ of habeas corpus ran as far as the sovereignty of the king extended and thus was a way of marking out through jurisdiction and extending colonial territory.[50] However, as Hussain notes, this was not the initial understanding of the writ: it was intended to produce the subject before the king, to hold him or her to account. This older understanding of the writ was at work in the habeas corpus applications involving the "Malayan Detenus." When the government forced the detainees to come before the High Court on a habeas corpus application, it was attempting to ascertain political belonging and to test political loyalties. It clearly believed that communist political workers could galvanize support beyond Madras's land borders. The habeas corpus hearings for the Malayan Detenus, from the perspective of the Indian state, would be an opportunity for the detainees to publicly disavow these claims and swear allegiance to independent India.

Habeas corpus applications filed by MMPOA detainees reveal details about the contemporary political climate and its fear of communism. Many detainees were not even told the grounds upon which they were being detained until they requested access to the government's case to file habeas corpus applications in court.[51] The reasons offered by the Madras government were varied, but all demonstrated a fear of communism: some individuals were detained for being "close friends" of known or detained communists;[52] others were imprisoned for supplying food to underground communists;[53] still others were charged with possessing literature that made references to the "capitalist" Congress government (these detainees pleaded that they were engaging in "legal public political work").[54] One office clerk in the offices of the South Indian Railway was told that he was responsible for instigating a strike, for no reason other than that the labor union of which he was a member had given a strike notice.[55] Guilt by association was rampant, and the public fear of communism swelled with every new detention order.

The grounds supplied to these detainees all contained an identical paragraph describing the Communist Party in general terms and suggesting that the violent methods followed by the party were the reasons for the detention. In the draft detention orders, officials even directed typists to "insert general paragraph on Communists." In the fair copies, the paragraph read:

> The Communist Party to which he belongs is now indulging in violence and subversive activities and is likely that he will also indulge in violent and subversive activities. Most of the important members of the Party have gone underground from where they are guiding various crimes such as arson, loot, murder etc. committed by Communists. Communists are also extorting money from the public by illegal means for party purposes. Leaflets are also published praising the work of Communist hooligans and encouraging the ignorant to follow them. He, being an important member of the Party will be guided by the instruction of the underground leaders and is likely to indulge in crimes etc.[56]

Since this paragraph was repeated verbatim in every detention order, there appears to have been no application of mind before these orders were issued.

The facts in the case of the Malayan Detenus were identical to those of a case that had been decided a year earlier by the Madras High Court. In May 1948, R. Ramanathan, a suspected "communist" in Madras City, was detained for his alleged membership in the communist-controlled Madras Provincial Trade Union Congress and for his previous attempts at organizing workers. He was said to have distributed "objectionable" literature to textile and railway workers and to have made several speeches accusing the Madras government of colluding with the capitalists and ignoring the demands of labor. As in the Malayan Detenus case, the grounds for detention communicated to Ramanathan made several generalizations about the Communist Party, such as the fact that it was "out for violence" and that it was "engaged in subversive activities"; these were ambiguously worded, reflecting the government's growing fear of communist influence.[57]

Like Ramiah, Ramanathan had a connection to labor movements on plantations in Selangor in British Malaya. Ramanathan's brother, R. H. Nathan, was reported to be the leader of a "small group" of labor agitators like the Klang Indian Association, who organized plantation laborers on the Selangor estates in Malaya, supposedly "against their will," to ask for an increase in wages. The propaganda against Nathan was relentless. Secret government communiques referred to him derisively as a "seditionmonger . . . [who] posed as the champion of oppressed labour against the employers."[58] The government noted that although the workers' wages were increased, this "group" continued to protest and was even prepared to resort to armed violence.[59] Soon after a wave of strikes on Selangor estates, Nathan was arrested and deported to British India in May 1941.[60] Nathan's brother, Ramanathan, attempted to forge a career in Tamil journalism in the Straits Settlements. His attempt failed, and Ramanathan followed his brother to British India soon after his deportation.[61]

Justice Ali, who presided over the case at the Madras High Court, pointed out that Ramanathan's membership in the Communist Party, a legally constituted organization at the time, could not be a valid ground for detention. There could be no guilt by association. In a concluding paragraph that the judges in later cases seemed to have missed, Justice Ali stated: "It need hardly be pointed out that this special enactment is directed not against organizations or parties or groups of persons but against

particular individuals and it is their conduct, their attitude, their tendency
which has to be borne in mind in coming to the conclusion whether they
are persons who should be held under detention in the interests of public
safety."[62] But by 1949 the tides had turned.

A CONDITIONAL RELEASE
The habeas corpus applications on behalf of Ramiah and his comrades were
filed by the law firm of Row and Reddy. The firm, which had its offices
on Thambu Chetty Street, across the road from the Madras High Court,
played a significant role in challenging the unfair impact of "public safety
laws" like the MMPOA on communists, trade unionists, and members of
the working class. The firm was founded by V. G. Row and A. Ramach-
andran, both of whom had qualified as barristers in England. Legend has
it that they were sent to London to prepare for the Indian Civil Service
examination, which was considered the pinnacle of success for young men
from well-to-do Indian families at the time. In London, Row and Ram-
achandran contacted the Communist Party of Great Britain, which was
an outspoken critic of the British government in India. (Ivor Jennings, the
architect of Ceylon's 1945 Soulbury Constitution and legal adviser to D. S.
Senanayake, whom we met in chapter 4, would later write of men like Row
that "in the thirties, it was fashionable for the England educated to turn
Communist.")[63] The two decided not to sit the exam, vowing not to be part
of an imperialist institution like the Indian Civil Service.

Unlike the Communist Party in India at the time, which had come
under the influence of the ultraleft Ranadive line, Row and Ramachan-
dran were willing to engage with courts and legislatures. In the early years,
their law firm represented only labor, and Row represented the interests
of the working class in the Madras Legislative Council. There he championed workers' rights under the Shops and Establishments Act, which
allowed nonindustrial workers to legally fight dismissals from their places
of employment.[64] MMPOA detainees in 1949 probably approached Row
and Reddy because of their links to organized labor movements in the
city. When the 1950 Constitution came into force in India, he filed a test
case before the Madras High Court challenging the ban on the People's
Education Society, a semilegal front that the party had begun during the

ban (which lasted from 1947 to 1952). Through their advocacy, Row and Reddy shaped legal precedent on the nature of transitional preventive detention laws, as well as the fates of thousands of political prisoners under the MMPOA.

Row and Reddy launched an all-out offensive on the MMPOA. As one affidavit in the habeas corpus applications noted, "This [referring to the allegations in the detention orders] is pure political bluff intended only to add weight to the otherwise vague grounds on which people were detained." Another claimed that the detentions under the MMPOA were a result of "vindictive persecution of political opponents" as well as "a negation of all democratic rights and a wholesale violation of accepted civil liberties in any civilized country."[65] After all, these petitions reiterated, the Communist Party was a legal organization, and people could not be detained simply because they were affiliated with it.[66] Row and Reddy made public statements about the disproportionate impact of the act and the delays in releasing detainees whose orders had been struck down as a result of litigation. For example, a letter in the *Indian Express* suggested that the enforcement of the act was not overly aggressive: only three hundred people had been detained under the act, they said, and most of the detainees were in fact threats; the High Court had released only twelve out of the seventy-six habeas corpus applicants before it. Row and Reddy countered with their own statistics indicating that many of these detentions were wrongful ones, by the government's own decision: in 1949, they had appeared for seventy-six applicants, twenty of whom had successfully won release in court; in fifteen further cases, the government had released the detainees when it learned that litigation was in the offing.[67]

Filing habeas corpus applications was only one arena where Ramiah and his comrades made jurisdictional claims. In their representations to the governments of India and Madras, Ramiah and his comrades made it clear that they had been repatriated to India as "freemen"[68]—they had not been deported, as R. H. Nathan was, nor were they suspects in an active investigation. However, news reports and a reading of banishment ordinances show that this was not entirely the case: Ramiah and comrades were told that they could stay in a Malayan prison or return to India if they did not come back to Malaya. Although both countries' governments were concerned that they would incite "the masses" because they knew Tamil, the detainees claimed that they "knew nothing of India"—indeed, several of them had never been there before. The men said that they wanted to start a "law-abiding citizen's life in India." In this way, of the twenty-four that had been detained, ten produced undertakings before the superintendent of the Central Jail in Vellore that they neither were communists nor had anything to do with the Communist Party.[69] Ramiah did not proclaim his communist sympathies, but neither was he one of those who renounced it.[70]

Another one of the detainees, Duraiswamy, admitted to being a member of the Malayan Communist Party. He defended his association with the party and pleaded for his release. He recounted the plight of trade unionists in Malaya who were fighting "British imperialism" and claimed that "Japanese Fascists" persecuted workers; only the Malayan Communist Party, he argued, had taken a strong stance against both. He put forward three lawyer-style arguments against his detention, echoing Row and Reddy's submissions before the Madras High Court but going even further. First, he noted (as the news reports confirmed) that Malaya had offered him a conditional release: he was to be "freed" provided he did not return to Malaya. Second, he argued that he could not be prosecuted for posing a threat to public safety twice, and he had already been prosecuted for his "crimes"—arguably those of participating in activities led by the Communist Party—in Singapore, a principle that lawyers would recognize as the principle against double jeopardy. Third, he noted, his knowledge of Tamil could not be held against him and leveraged to claim jurisdiction—and it was the only ground for detention offered by the Madras government in his papers. Duraiswamy's petition pointed out, in no uncertain terms, the legal irregularities of his detention. The government sought to justify in legal terms its widespread detentions, but detainees like Duraiswamy were quick to see the discrepancies in their claims.

When Ramiah's habeas corpus application was dismissed in April 1949, his case was yet to come up before the Advisory Council, and final orders for detention had not been issued. The High Court litigation must have put pressure on the council. When it finally considered his case on June 20, 1949, it was clear that there were insufficient grounds for his detention. Ramiah's release was ordered on the condition that he produce an undertaking that he would not "take part in subversive activities."

Unlike the habeas corpus applications filed by the Malayan Detenus, which would have gone relatively unnoticed outside Madras, the legal trials unfolding in Malaya and London in the context of "the Emergency" at the same time garnered much attention. Chief among those was the Sambasivam case in 1950: an appeal against a death penalty handed down to a "Indian Tamil" clerk and teacher under Section 4(1) of the Emergency Regulations of 1948 for carrying unauthorized ammunition in Johore Bahru. The allegations against Sambasivam were that he had pulled out a revolver and attacked three Malay men; the men escaped and reported that they had been attacked by "communists."[71] While the Federation of Malaya government had privately agreed in Sambasivam's appeal to the Judicial Committee of the Privy Council in 1949 that it would not do to "overemphasise the part played by Indian communists," the attention that the Sambasivam appeal, supported by John Thivy, whom we encountered in chapter 1, garnered in both Madras and Singapore made this difficult.[72] Equally infamous were the death by hanging of S. A. Ganapathy, the leader of the PMFTU, in 1949.[73] In the same year, P. Veerasenan, the "notorious" trade unionist whose bodyguard Ramiah had allegedly been, was shot dead by the British Military Administration.[74] He was twenty-two years old, and by most historians' accounts, he was never a member of the Malayan Communist Party.[75]

WAITING, WRITING, WITNESSING

Ramiah's case, as well as other MMPOA habeas corpus decisions of the Madras High Court, prompted much debate in the Madras Legislative Assembly.[76] The members, mostly belonging to the ruling Congress party, were concerned about the rising number of detainee releases that the government had ordered. However, in the *Ramanathan* case, the court had ruled that it would not investigate the "subjective satisfaction" or the discretion of the government in issuing detention orders. This allowed the government to confidently assert that there was no mala fides in its orders for mass detentions of the kind that had been taking place since 1947. It also allowed the government to say, without fear of retribution, that detainees had been released because police officers and magistrates had been "misapprehending" the scope of the act,[77] but that the officers would not be punished; as the government argued, even the High Court had not said anything to the effect that police officers ordering illegal detentions ought to be held accountable.

In June 1949, the government reported that around six hundred to seven hundred detainees were being housed in various jails all over the province and that three hundred or four hundred cases were under investigation; a substantial number of these detainees were suspected of belonging to the Communist Party.[78] These mass detentions seemed to unnerve the government far less than the court's many releases. In a debate on how the act was being implemented, a member of the Madras Legislative Assembly pointed out that the government was not prioritizing releases that had been ordered by the High Court; judges in these decisions had noted that delays at the level of the government and the Advisory Council ought to be avoided. Representatives for the government replied that the district officials had been "preoccupied" with more "urgent" and "more important" work.[79] Pressed for details on the relationship between the government and the Advisory Council (the body that conducted the review of detention orders to ascertain whether there was sufficient grounds to continue detention), the government merely replied that it was "confidential."[80] Since the High Court judges could rule only on the basis of the material placed before them and on the arguments made by the lawyers, habeas corpus petitions like Ramiah's continued to be adjudicated on the basis of half-truths and presumptions.

It is also worth mentioning that by this time Madras's reputation for its harsh response to the communist threat had spread far and wide. The Colonial Office in London noted that "Indian statesmen, including the Prime Minister, have publicly made it known that they are fully aware of the danger with which they are confronted, and its character, and have made it clear that they are determined to meet the challenge with all the powers that they possess. Where these powers are not considered sufficient, there has been no hesitation in taking others, and Madras, for example, has reinforced itself by ordinance and other means in a degree that was not surpassed by any previous government in India." The Colonial Office also oversaw the British administration in Malaya; if the MMPOA and In-dia's other anticommunist measures were greatly admired by the Malayan government, which in retrospect has been denounced for the severity of its counterinsurgency measures, the magnitude of India's detention, censor-ship, and repression (including those acts that left no archival traces) can only be imagined.

Three of the six men, apart from Ramiah, who arrived aboard the SS *Vasna*—Sevu, Paulraj, and Subbiah—were detained for months after the Madras High Court ordered their releases.[81] Having exhausted available judicial remedies, they continued to wait for their release from jail.

Take the case of Paulraj, who was suspected of being a member of the Communist Party. He was also believed to be a member of the Indian Democratic Youth League, a group led by K. A. Chandran, a trade union leader who confessed to the Malayan Union intelligence agencies in 1945 that the Malayan Communist Party planned to infiltrate the Singapore Harbor Labor Board.[82] But Paulraj claimed that these were affiliations of convenience: he had desperately fled India for Malaya under an alias to escape "domestic trouble," and he was in fact an Indian National Congress supporter, who had worked as a typist in the Indian National Congress Office in Malaya even as late as March 1948.

These claims of political loyalty to India were to no avail. Paulraj's telegrams asking to be interviewed about his detention went unanswered, and although he produced undertakings before the district magistrate in which he stated that he was not a communist and had no intention of participating in communist activities, he was not released—not even after the Government of India finally decided to release all the remaining de-tainees from the SS *Vasna*. He sent multiple petitions to the governments of India and Madras, and tellingly, to the leaders of the Malayan Com-munist Party, alternating between precise legal arguments and emotional appeals to the officers to show him mercy and release him from jail. In his final letter to the Indian government in May 1949, he noted that he and his two acquaintances Sevu and Subbiah had been singled out for "Cinderella treatment." It concluded: "Like a schoolboy whose name does not appear in the examination pass list, we do not deserve such treatment."[83]

The government was aware of the unconscionable delays in processing the paperwork of detainees under the MMPOA, and they knew well that the Communist Party could not be stamped out by any number of detentions. The chief minister of Madras, P. S. Kumaraswamy Raja, asked the Legislative Assembly in June 1949: "How long are we to put a man in detention without trial in the name of a danger to public safety?"[84] Raja pointed out that if someone had resigned from the Communist Party and regretted his past actions, there was little reason to continue doubting his bona fides or to judge him, as the district magistrate had, by his past. The blame for the blanket rejections of petitions for release was squarely laid at the door of the district magistrates and the police officers, and the Legislative Assembly reexamined several cases for "comparatively insignificant" detainees whose petitions had been initially denied.

Under this new government policy, the cases of Paulraj, Subbiah, and Sevu were reconsidered.[85] But Paulraj was not released until nearly a year after he was first detained in August 1949, when some relatives volunteered to stand security for him. Shortly thereafter, the Madras government closed the detention files of the last of the Malayan Detenus. But banishment and deportation under emergency regulations and ordinances in Malaya continued well into years leading up to Malayan independence in 1957.[86]

BANISHED FOREVER

In September 1949, Annamalai Chettiar, the president of the Indian Estate Owners' Association in Malaya, stepped off a ship from Malaya, entering Madras along with forty-three other Indian passengers. At the time, as we saw from chapter 2, Chettiar landowners constituted 3 percent of all estate owners in Malaya, and Annamalai Chettiar's reception was quite different from that of the "Malayan Detenus," despite the rumors that the Nattukkottai Chettiars had paid protection money to the Malayan Communist Party. Battling rumors that the Chettiars had evaded the worst of the Japanese occupation and wartime displacements because they had bribed soldiers on both sides of the war, the All Malaya Nattukottai Chettiars' Chamber of Commerce had been forced to pass a resolution at a public meeting in February 1949 affirming that they would not pay "protection money" to anyone working against the interests of law and order in Malaya.[87] In a news conference upon arrival, Chettiar stated to assembled reporters that the Malayan government was making indiscriminate arrests on the grounds of curbing communism, putting both Indians and Chinese laborers into detention camps. He also claimed that the police were protecting European estate owners and allowing Indian owners to be arrested along with their workers. Annamalai Chettiar reaffirmed what Duraiswamy, one of the Malayan Detenus, had mentioned in his petition. Once in the camps, the owners could choose to stay, or they could accept a "conditional release" like that described by Duraiswamy: they would have to give an undertaking that they would not return to Malaya without the permission of the Malayan administration. Annamalai Chettiar reported that 150 Indians out of a possible 800 had given the undertaking and returned to India.

Annamalai Chettiar's statement pointed to a bigger dilemma, one that would trouble all of the present and former British colonies in South and Southeast Asia and would not be resolved in Malaya until its own independence: that of jurisdiction. What was the legal authority under which British subjects—as all of the inhabitants of the former Straits Settlements were—could be banished from a British colony? If the subjects were citizens of the Federation of Malaya, they could not be deported. The Banishment Ordinance by this time was restricted to the Malay States; it did not apply to Singapore, whose emergency regulations were already under fire. Across the Bay of Bengal, India's own ambiguous citizenship provisions in the 1950 Constitution left former migrants like Ramiah and his comrades at the risk of statelessness, without access to Indian nationality and deported from Singapore, set adrift.

In the years following, much would be made of India's reluctance to accept these "undesirables."[88] On the other hand, perhaps the cases of Ramiah and his comrades, and the plight they described in their petitions, forced the Madras government to rethink their policies on preventive detention. For instance, in a habeas corpus petition filed before the High Court in April 1949 and heard in November 1949, nearly six months after the dismissal of Ramiah's habeas corpus application, and after the collapse of the PMFTU in Singapore, the court dismissed the applicants on the grounds that they were "dangerous communist workers" who had arrived from Malaya.[89] Ramiah's legal legacy continued. By 1950, the membership of the CPI had declined from eighty-nine thousand to twenty thousand.[90] In Madras, the Communist Party became a part of the "parliamentary left," participating in the 1952 general elections and largely following a constitutionalist approach.[91]

Habeas corpus litigation under the MMPOA demonstrated the punitive nature of preventive detention—punishment that was not limited to the detention itself, for the maze of legal procedure that migrant detainees, their families, and their lawyers had to negotiate was as punishing as (or more punishing than) the simple prison stints. In the era of decolonization, complex legal systems were becoming increasingly bound within national borders—questions of jurisdiction. In contrast, people's lives—political, familial, ideological—stretched across these emerging national borders; the answers they sought could not be captured through juridical categories and could only be narrated as personal and familial histories through jurisdictional claims. The governments invoked the notion of "public order," but in fact this notion was a legal fiction—one around which governments were constructing their notions of territorial sovereignty. Habeas corpus applications became a means of extending territorial sovereignty and calling putative citizens to account before the law, testing one's political loyalty.[92] The consequence, of course, as we saw in Paulraj's case, was to wait, write, and continue to wait.

The labyrinthine legal procedures traced in this chapter—detention without trial, the habeas corpus litigation that was engendered, and the "jurisdiction of suspicion"—were not exclusive to the postwar period, nor did the demise of the MMPOA signal the end of executive detention regimes in India.[93] However, in in June 1948, probably around the time that it planned the deportation of Ramiah and his comrades, the Colonial Office in London spoke of the virtues of detention without trial: "Trials do harm because of the publicity that accompanies them and the martyrs they make. If they fail because of the terrorist tactics the Communists adopt, they do more harm still. Detention without trial is therefore the remedy. This action has the additional advantage that it creates opportunities for the examination of the persons detained, and in this way hitherto unknown, but often important accomplices, are disclosed."[94]

The legal and bureaucratic logic in the habeas corpus applications filed by six men aboard the SS *Vasna* reveals that the political context and ambiguity of political borders were very much on the minds of the government. In each of these cases, the government seemed to have formed their impressions of the detainees from several sources: their previous legal encounters, secret intelligence and rumor regarding their "communistic" activities in lands far away, and (perhaps most salient) the general mistrust of communism as a political alternative to liberal democratism. This was the primary grounds for detention presented in the heavily redacted records placed before the courts.

In the records relating to the habeas corpus applications, we see the slow rise of Cold War tensions across Asia.[95] Colonial records from this period indicate that the government in Malaya was convinced that a communist takeover of Southeast Asia was in progress, based on the capitulation of China to communist forces, the establishment of U Nu's government in Burma, and the rising levels of violence carried out by guerrilla forces in Malaya. Discussions over the fate of Malayan "communists"—members of the party and otherwise—were discussed in the context of secret (and not-so-secret) meetings of Yugoslav and Russian communists in Calcutta that were attended by communists from all over South Asia.[96] The discussions were far removed from the lives and concerns of Ramiah, Paulraj, and others, but these men's fates were caught up in the fear, uncertainty, and anxiety created by the looming communist threat to South and Southeast Asia. Thus the archive of habeas corpus litigation under the MMPOA is not merely a record of a single repressive "colonial-style" piece of legislation in a postcolonial republic. It also documents a moment of political transition from imperial to national geographies, offering us a glimpse of how people experienced this geopolitical transition as they attempted to navigate the stormy legal seas of postwar South and Southeast Asia.

SEVEN

1962

IN 1962, RANGOON ONCE AGAIN became the scene of displacement, this time because of legal measures around taxation, immigration, and expulsion, adopted following a military coup. Led by General Ne Win—formerly fellow traveler to U Nu and Aung San as part of the Burma Independence Army during the war—military forces overthrew the civilian government and took power, ending five years of a gradual decline in military and civilian relations in independent Burma.[1] Following the coup, General Ne Win instituted what he termed the Burmese Way to Socialism, in aid of which there was nationalization of trade and business, the demonetization of high-value Burmese kyat notes, rapid tightening of restrictions on remittances by "foreigners"—including Indian, Pakistani, Nepali, and Chinese migrants who lived and worked in Burma—and the criminalization of a growing number of economic offenses under which foreigners could be detained without trial or deported. Once again, Rangoon, city of migrants, began to empty out.

These displacements from Burma following the coup and owing to economic restrictions were part of a broader wave of expulsions, resettlements, and repatriations that took place in former colonies in South Asia and Southeast Asia and across the Indian Ocean in East Africa during

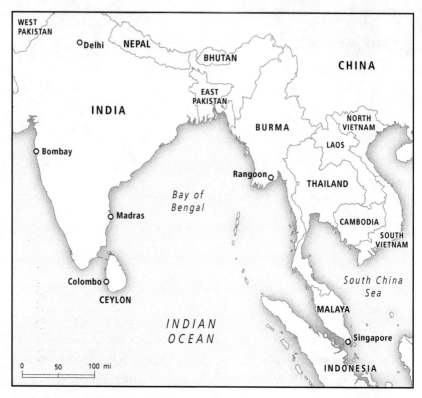

MAP 2: *South and Southeast Asia in 1962*

the 1960s. In Ceylon, Sirimavo Bandaranaike's government, itself newly recovered from a failed coup, was in the process of negotiating "repatriation" agreements and population transfers between India and itself for the *malaiyaha thamilar*, who worked on plantations and whose immigration and citizenship status had not been settled since its independence. These negotiations resulted in a formal agreement between Bandaranaike and India's prime minister, Lal Bahadur Shastri, in 1964, referred to as the Sirima-Shastri Pact, which sought to remedy the failures of earlier agreements signed between Ceylon's John Kotelawala and India's Jawaharlal Nehru in 1954.[2] As chapter 6 showed, detentions and banishments of "migrants" from Malaya because of counterinsurgency operations against communists took place even as protections for minorities within proposed constitutional frameworks were heavily contested.[3] Although formal repatriation schemes affected only a small minority of migrant laborers, many others struggled to cope with the requirements of Malaysian and Singaporean citizenship. Beyond South and Southeast Asia, a "second wave" of decolonization in the British Empire brought hard-won independence to former East Africa (Tanzania, Kenya, and Uganda) between 1961 and 1963. Independence for these new states was accompanied by a reckoning on the place of immigrant Asians in their countries.[4] At the time, many Indian migrants to East Africa held British subject passports and had not chosen Indian citizenship because of the confusion surrounding its terms; they soon also discovered that the British immigration and nationality regimes were increasingly hostile to British subject passport holders. A decade later, when they were expelled from Uganda in 1972, they would find themselves unwelcome in Britain. These displacements from East Africa, Algeria, and Burma beginning in 1962 took place as former imperial centers in Britain and France reworked their immigration, nationality, and citizenship laws, reconciling obligations to former colonies with the demands of anticolonial movements.[5] In Britain, the Commonwealth Immigrants Act was passed in 1962, putting an end to people's free movement between Britain and its former colonies as "citizens of the United Kingdom and the Colonies"—a status that had been available under the British Nationality and Status of Aliens Act of 1948 to many in Burma, Ceylon, and Malaya. Instead, the 1962 Act instituted a system of work permits for highly skilled immigrants. Reflecting the waning possibilities for migrations between and across empires, and increasing legal regulation of travel, movement, and residence on racial lines, the space to retain the rhythms and patterns of migrant life between South and Southeast Asia appeared to be dwindling.

In the twenty years between 1942 and 1962, the legal questions that had arisen in postwar Ceylon, India, and Burma about the validity of wartime contracts, as in Seethalakshmi Achi's debt recovery case discussed in chapter 2, or the scope of government powers to detain and deport migrants, as in V. G. Row's habeas corpus applications in chapter 6, remained or reappeared before courts, commissions, and legislatures in South and Southeast Asia. In returning to 1942 as a juridical marker, these disputes reestablished the relationship between displacement and emerging citizenship regimes. Set against the background of this second wave of decolonization that brought questions of self-determination into sharp relief, these disputes pointed to still unresolved questions about belonging in a shared political future not restrained by national borders.[6] In 1962, even as new constitutional and legislative frameworks defined citizenship as a legal status, deportations, resettlements, and repatriations exposed the limits of political belonging. Jurisdictional claims and counterclaims around taxation, immigration, and detention by which people navigated a spectrum of legal statuses from citizenship to statelessness, attempting to retain the rhythms and patterns of immigrant life, began to take on new forms or be eclipsed by concerns around citizenship.

CITIZENSHIPS, 1942–62

A brief discussion of national and international debates around citizenship in South and Southeast Asia will make these positions clear. As the negotiations toward the end of colonial rule in South Asia had made clear, the terms of national citizenship would be left to the new governments themselves and not overseen by retreating British imperial administrations. Since the formal end of the war in 1945, the Indian government's official policy had consistently been that Indians "overseas"—a category used to refer to the Indian emigrants after the eponymous government department and to which many in the previous chapter belonged—should seek to become citizens of the places where they lived and worked.[7] By this time, as previous chapters showed, many of these "migrants" were second- or third-generation immigrants in Burma, Ceylon, and Malaya and considered these places their home. Following the Partition and independence in 1947, the interim provisions for citizenship in the Indian Constitution noted that those whose parents or grandparents were born within the territory of unpartitioned India according to the definition in the Government of India Act of 1935 (which did not include Burma) would be able to register as Indian citizens abroad.[8] Although this was directed not primarily at Indian migrants to Southeast Asia but much more likely at Indians in East Africa, Indian High Commissions—consular posts—across South and Southeast Asia maintained registers for those who wished to become Indian citizens. But this official stance of encouraging Indian emigrants to seek citizenship in their adopted homes and places of work and the confusion around the variety of citizenships available to Indians overseas all but guaranteed a lukewarm response to this registration drive.

Sunil Amrith argues this response was not a surprise: the terms of Indian citizenship, drafted and debated between 1947 and 1955, were based on the "disavowal" of migration from India to Southeast Asia.[9] But as the previous chapters have demonstrated, the time factor was also critical to this disavowal. Since Ceylon and Burma's national citizenship regimes came into force in 1948 with the Ceylon Citizenship Act and the Union Citizenship Act respectively, seven years before India would finally pass its own Citizenship Act, there was some panic among Indians "ordinarily resident" in Ceylon and Burma as to whether they would relinquish their Indian citizenship if they opted to register as Ceylonese or Burmese citizens. As the communal politics surrounding the Partition made dual nationality and dual citizenship in India an impossibility, this group of overseas Indians—the group to which many of the migrants in the previous chapters belonged—had to make their decisions about Ceylonese or Burmese citizenship without knowing whether they would later be able to relinquish it and acquire Indian citizenship. At the same time, citizenship legislation in Ceylon and Burma also prohibited dual nationality, further complicated by the problems of nationality accompanying interracial and interethnic marriages. There was some discussion about alternate political possibilities that came from the affected migrants themselves: trade union workers representing the *malaiyaka thamilar* in Ceylon discussed the possibility of a joint citizenship for India and Ceylon.[10] Evacuee associations proposed the same for India and Burma in the postwar period.[11] There was no venue or opportunity to explore these possibilities; consider, by contrast, in Frederick Cooper's scholarship on French West Africa, the different alternatives to the territorial nation-state explored by political leaders and anticolonial thinkers.[12]

The sole exception to widely known political possibilities beyond the nation-state was the incipient British Commonwealth, which held out one possibility of a common and reciprocal citizenship. This was an attractive proposition for India. As Kalathmika Natarajan and Raphaëlle Khan show, India's own inclination toward Commonwealth membership was influenced by the possibility of reciprocal obligations from Burma and Ceylon, which had by then enacted exclusionary citizenship legislation that affected Indian migrants.[13] Burma opted to remain outside the Commonwealth and initiated a different set of anxieties around the question of citizenship for overseas Indians. In response to panicked correspondence from its High Commissions abroad, India's Ministry of Home Affairs clarified that those who registered as Ceylonese citizens were not to be barred from later acquiring Indian citizenship under Article 8 of the Indian Constitution. Consulting leading authorities on international law like Dicey, Cheshire, and Oppenheim, the ministry considered it a "remote contingency" that Ceylon would follow Burma's example and exit the Commonwealth.[14] While Natarajan notes that officials within the Indian government attempted to keep the possibility of statelessness at bay for overseas Indians by encouraging them to seek citizenships abroad, the different temporal horizons within citizenship regimes and diverging trajectories of decolonization that countries in South and Southeast Asia followed rendered many of these attempts futile. With General Ne Win's coup in 1962, which further resulted in deprivation of citizenship rights, this official position became increasingly untenable for Indian nationals in Burma, who had registered as "foreigners" and were restricted from seeking Burmese citizenship.[15] By 1962, time was running out for many Indian nationals abroad.

Malaya, which would not gain independence from Britain until 1957, presented a somewhat more complicated situation than Burma or Ceylon. By 1948, the constitution for the Federation of Malaya laid down the contours of citizenship. Those eligible could register themselves as citizens, following a process like that described in chapter 4 for Ceylon. Travel, movement, and residence to the Federation was restricted. Not only was a very small percentage of Indians—135 out of 700,000—given citizenship rights under the Federation of Malaya's citizenship provisions by 1952, but the Immigration Ordinance of 1952 and the Immigration (Prohibition of Entry) Ordinance of 1953 controlled entry to Malaya.[16] Entry to the Federation was restricted to British subjects born or naturalized in Malaya, subjects of the ruler of a Malay state, federal citizens, British subjects ordinarily resident in Malaya, aliens who were holders of Residents' Certificates, and wives and children under eighteen who were dependents. Also allowed was immigration of professionals, business owners, and holders of passes. These immigrations were not to be prejudicial to Malayan interests, and professionals had to command a salary of 1,200 Malayan dollars a month.[17] In spite of these restrictions, clerks, teachers, engineers, and lawyers continued to journey across the Bay. Many Indian nationals in Malaya held British subject passports when Malaya gained independence in 1957; they were eligible for citizenship in Malaysia, or later Singapore, and simultaneously also for citizenship of the United Kingdom and the Colonies.[18] Confusion thus reigned over the question of diasporic nationality and citizenship legislation even in former British colonies and Commonwealth countries.

As India's Ministry of External Affairs noted, the possibility of British citizenship for migrants from India living in Malaya turned on the postwar changes to British nationality legislation.[19] Under the British Nationality and Status of Aliens Act in 1948, a new category of citizenship was created: citizenship of the United Kingdom and the Colonies, which would offer formerly imperial subjects the opportunity to acquire British nationality and allow them to travel to and reside in the United Kingdom. The creation of a citizenship of the United Kingdom and the Colonies was different from approaches to the question of citizenship in the French and Portuguese enclaves of the subcontinent. The French and Dutch models of postwar citizenship for former imperial possessions offered both nationality and citizenship in former imperial centers; note, by contrast, how in the same instance French Algerians, as Todd Shepard shows, were stripped of citizenship in 1962.[20] In India, Jessica Namakkal shows how French Indian territories like Pondicherry, Mahe, and Karikal were given the option to join the French federation by voting in a referendum.[21] They voted no, but not before a debate on the nature of citizenship in the two colonies. Portuguese rule over Goa, which the Indian government had sought to end, had come to an uneasy solution only a year prior to the military coup in Burma; as Pamila Gupta notes, this resulted in dispossession for Goans who were displaced to Angola, South Africa, and Mozambique, with citizenship a matter of contention.[22] Neither benefits flowing from Commonwealth membership nor the British Nationality Act in 1948 offered an equivalent, which shaped the difficulties that overseas Indians experienced in their adopted homes and places of work.

Indeed, this sort of half-citizenship—among the other legal statuses provided by the British Nationality Act—raised a major question for Indian migrants to Malaya (and, later, former Indian migrants to Uganda in the 1970s): Would holding a British subject passport available under the British Nationality Act bar them from holding Indian citizenship under Article 5 (1) (b) of the Indian Constitution? In 1957, on the eve of independence for Malaysia, India's Ministry of External Affairs decided that it would not, as British subject passports did not amount to British nationality—although the holders were labeled British subjects without citizenship under the British Nationality Act —though it did offer the possibility of eventually naturalizing as British citizens.[23] For those who had already registered as Burmese or Ceylonese citizens, this option was not available, as they already subscribed to a national citizenship regime. Many would remain, or choose to migrate to the United Kingdom, Europe, or, after changes in 1965 to the Immigration and Nationality Act, the United States. This was indeed a route that some followed: for example, after 1948, some former British subjects, including Indian and Pakistani nationals in South and Southeast Asia who were born in Malaya, Singapore, or Ceylon, took up Britain's offer, traveling to the United Kingdom and later naturalizing as British citizens.[24] But these opportunities for multiple citizenships—some more-than-national, others less-than-imperial citizenship—for former British subjects collided with efforts of emergent nation-states to define their own populations, as well as with the British government's simultaneous attempts to restrict immigration from its former colonies.[25]

The question of citizenship across South and Southeast Asia for diasporic communities that were now splintered across new nation-states was made even more difficult by the fact that diplomatic negotiations between them—some independent, others British Dominions, yet others still colonies—were less than successful in aligning nationality, immigration, and citizenship. At international gatherings such as the Asian Relations Conference in New Delhi in 1947, the Commonwealth Conference in 1954 in Colombo, and the Bandung Conference in 1955, representatives from governments in Asia and Africa focused not on specific issues but on self-determination struggles and broader stances toward anti-imperialism and anticommunism.[26] U Ba Swe's Asian Socialist Conference held in Rangoon in 1953 and in Bombay in 1956 sought to chart a neutral path through the growing schisms of the Cold War.[27] In other words, these international conferences also reflected the dominant geopolitical divides of the time. As Cindy Ewing shows, the politics of "minority" populations was discussed at these gatherings.[28] But the relationship between migrant futures and minority politics was relegated to bilateral negotiations and agreements. A unified "regional" or interregional response to the question of migration and citizenship was still lacking, fraught as a result of South Asia's "other partitions." None of these international or diplomatic meetings was able to bring about a resolution to the unraveling of migrant networks of trade, capital, finance, and labor, and proposed forms of citizenship as legal status appeared to be unable to settle the issue of wartime displacements. Even as states fashioned different postwar futures and networks of solidarity, wartime displacements continued to cast a long shadow over the legal proceedings around taxes, citizenship, and other issues that were brought and decided in the early 1960s.

In 1962, with increasingly complex immigration, nationality, and citizenship regimes, the space for Indian migrants around the Indian Ocean to negotiate the spectrum of legal statuses between citizenship and statelessness—explored in the previous chapters—began to shrink. Unlike Uganda and Kenya later in the 1970s, Indian nationals excluded from citizenship were not physically expelled in Ceylon or Burma.[29] In Ceylon, as Valli Kanapathipillai notes, expulsions took place under the guise of diplomatic negotiations.[30] Renaud Egreteau too observed from interviews with Burma "repatriates" in India that there were no physical expulsions.[31] Instead, the unraveling of labor, capital, credit, and trade networks continued through cascading legal consequences stemming from postwar legal regimes' decisions around taxation, immigration, and detention, the lesser-known "other partitions" of South and Southeast Asia. Even so, many, as we saw in the previous chapters, chose to keep waiting at the risk of statelessness rather than return to a home that they had never known.

IN THE COUP'S WAKE

In Burma, the years between 1942 to 1962—between Japanese occupation, the formation of the Union of Burma, and its eventual takeover by military forces—there was intense political debate over the form of government and the relationship between majority and minority communities. Ne Win had led a military campaign against "communists," which had been in the making since 1948, when Burma gained independence. Many Indian and Chinese nationals living or working in Burma were caught up in these rising tides of nationalism and separatism.[32]

Burma had chosen not to join the British Commonwealth in 1948. Soon after independence in 1948, the Union Citizenship Act and Rules in Burma described a citizen as one whose parents belonged to any of the indigenous "races" of Burma—Burman, Mon, or Kachin, for example—or who had at least one grandparent who belonged to these specific races and was born in the territories that made up independent Burma, or who had been granted a certificate of citizenship under the Union Citizenship (Election) Act of 1948 or a similar certificate of naturalization under the Burma Naturalization Act.[33] Indian migrants who were eligible for Burmese citizenship—having resided for eight out of ten years since 1942 in Burma—had to actively choose it, which many did not. As a result, they lost ownership of lands available only for Burmese citizens or were denied compensation for land that was taken away from them.[34] Because of the confusion surrounding Indian nationality and citizenship legislation described earlier, many Indian nationals did not elect to become Burmese citizens or Indian citizens, remaining "foreigners" in Burma. Recall that to apply for citizenship, applicants approached the district court with affidavits. After a period of six weeks, and if no one had objected, a citizenship certificate would be issued. To remain a foreigner but stay in Burma, applicants above the age of twelve registered with the local police station and got an identity pass with a photograph attached, which cost thirty-five rupees. The certificate lapsed if the holder did not return for sixty days.[35] Following the coup, in what Ne Win's government described as "economic insurgency," migrant Indian and Chinese nationals in Burma were forced into litigation to fight for the renewal of their foreigner registration certificates. Many of the deportations from Burma for nonrenewal of these certificates were successfully challenged in court, but only after a lengthy judicial process—a long period of waiting to discover whether one would be deemed a foreigner or a resident, and whether one's paperwork was necessary or not. Mahajani terms these amendments "a virtual banishment order."[36] Many who had migrated from India and opted for Burmese citizenship found their citizenship revoked with retroactive effect in 1963.[37]

Confronting these jurisdictional borders was not only a question of getting one's paperwork for citizenship applications in order. It was also increasingly difficult to live or work in two places, in India and Burma. For instance, by May 1963, even foreign money orders of relatively small sums of up to twenty rupees, which migrants used to remit money from Burma to India for family expenses or for children's education, were restricted. Two years later, controls on trade were imposed. In an echo of emergency wartime legislation in British India that prescribed commodity controls, those who violated these controls were arrested on charges of "economic offenses" and detained without trial; if they were convicted or pled guilty, their properties were confiscated and they were deported.[38] Those perceived to be foreigners were prohibited from engaging in any work, including street hawking or rickshaw pulling, a significant percentage of which used to be, as we saw in earlier chapters, carried out by migrant labor from South India. Many were deported and were not allowed to sell land or take jewelry or sums of more than 75 rupees out of the country.[39]

By this time, Burma's postwar system of issuing temporary visit visas or "B" permits—with which many Chettiars returned to Burma after the end of the war, as chapter 2 described, without acquiring Burmese citizenship—ended; conversely, anyone who wished to return to India from Burma was supposed to collect a departure form in person from an office outside Rangoon and then wait for a suitable means of repatriation.[40] Indian passports, mandatory for overseas travel, were not issued to "unskilled labor"—mostly lower-caste and landless laborers—to return to Burma.[41] For migrants, travel, movement, and residence in both directions were thus severely restricted even before the coup. Following the coup, to enable Indian nationals to leave Burma without going through the Burmese government's regime relating to foreigners, the Indian Embassy in Rangoon began to register Indians under the Indian Citizenship Act of

1955. Those Indian nationals who had registered themselves as "foreigners" in Burma—and therefore were neither Indian or Burmese citizens—were granted "emergency certificates" to travel to India. Those who had opted to wait out a decision on citizenship found that they could wait no longer. The number of applications for Indian citizenship rose by 300 percent, and over 300,000 Indians in Burma were classified as refugees.[9] By 1967, the Indian Embassy in Rangoon estimated that 275,000 "Indians" in Burma held "no documents of any kind"—they were de facto stateless.

In this second wave of displacement that began with the military coup in 1962, many Chettiar firms gave up their Burma wealth for good because by this time income tax ordinances in Burma imposed a penalty on migrants, defined yet again by temporality as much as geography; Burma imposed a 65 percent tax on the income of "nonresidents," defined as those who spent less than three hundred days in Burma. By 1958, it was clear that compensation for the land nationalization schemes would not be forthcoming—according to one estimate, a mere 1,500,000 rupees had been received as compensation for the nearly three million acres of land owned by Indians in Burma.[42] By 1963, nationalization and demonetization wiped out any opportunity for final reassessments of income tax in Burma, and petty traders and business owners alike simply waited and hoped for compensation for their seized assets. A year later, in 1964, the Indian Embassy in Rangoon wrote to Delhi: "We have during the year taken up a number of cases of delay in assessment both in general terms and in individual cases. So far, we have had no final reply about it, not even in a single case."[43] Many former Burma repatriates, housed in "Burma colonies" in Tamil Nadu today, continue to wait for compensation.[44]

Meanwhile, seemingly far removed from the anxieties surrounding Rangoon in 1962, litigation over "banana money"—demonetized wartime currency in Malaya—and its implications for income tax reached the Indian Supreme Court on appeal from the Madras High Court, championed by Chettiar firms in Malaya with links to India.[45] At issue was the question of income tax: whether the special scheme introduced by the Malayan legislature to reinstate wartime debt discussed in chapter 2 would constitute "income" under taxation regimes. Twenty years later, the outcome of this litigation—which had traveled between Kuala Lumpur, Madras, and

London—continued to have implications for the wealth of Chettiar firms that remained in Burma, Malaya, and Singapore. The Judicial Committee of the Privy Council in London—which still heard appeals on civil matters from Malaysia until 1985—had also considered the issue of "banana money" and its implications for income tax assessments.[46] But the military coup in Burma brought these questions into sharp relief—there was suddenly much more at stake—and it affected many more migrants than the Chettiar firms who pursued litigation as a strategy to retain the rhythms and patterns of immigrant life. Jurisdictional claims faded away in the light of citizenship claims.

REPATRIATION AND RETURN

In 1963, seven years after an inquiry was held into his citizenship application at which he produced birth certificates for himself and his parents showing them to be "Ceylon Tamils," Nallan Ramaswamy, an employee of the Kandy Municipal Corporation, wrote to the commissioner for the registration of Indian and Pakistani residents in Colombo. He wrote: "I beg most humbly to state that I have been an applicant for registration under the above [the Indian and Pakistani Residents (Citizenship) Act of 1949]. Thus I presume that I have no right to be registered under the above Act from your letter dated 29th August 1956 [informing him of insufficient evidence to be registered as a citizen]. Therefore could I crave to be registered under the Ceylon Citizenship Act. Please let me know early, as I am in very difficult circumstances and stateless at the moment."[47]

Ramaswamy's seven-year wait for citizenship in Ceylon—seemingly because of a confusion about the law under which he was eligible for citizenship in Ceylon—was not unique. In 1961, the Commission for the Registration of Indian and Pakistani Residents declared that it had completed its inquiries into the nearly 750,000 applicants for Ceylonese citizenship; they ultimately approved only a meager 10 to 12 percent for citizenship. As with Muthiah's case in chapter 4, we do not know what happened to Nallan Ramaswamy and his family and whether his wish to be recognized—not registered—as a Ceylonese citizen was honored. By 1963, as Nallan Ramaswamy's letter indicates, more than a decade had elapsed since the deadline to file applications for Ceylonese citizenship; like him, many faced the prospect of statelessness. Many denials were appealed to the Supreme Court of Ceylon in Colombo and to the Judicial Committee of the Privy Council in London, and citizenship litigation swelled, alleging that procedural norms in citizenship inquiries had not been followed.[48] During this time, the numbers of persons at the risk of statelessness grew.[49]

Alongside Ceylon's citizenship legislation, the Immigrants and Emigrants Act was introduced in 1948, under which the government began to keep track of "illicit immigrants" and "overstayers"—those who remained on the island even after their visas or temporary residence permits expired. As people neared the end of their visa periods, officials issued "quit notices," but these often proved futile, for no one wanted to leave before they had exhausted all avenues that might allow them to stay, without deciding on citizenship. In 1964, Wilton Jayasinghe, the commissioner for the registration of Indian and Pakistani residents, noted that "coercive means" were being used to deport such overstayers.[50] So widespread was the concern around the citizenship status of plantation laborers in Ceylon that Bandaranaike consulted with Clive Parry, eminent jurist and professor of international law at the University of Cambridge, for his opinion on the rights of Indian immigrant workers in Sri Lanka; Parry at the time had just completed a two-volume work on nationality and citizenship laws across the Commonwealth and the Republic of Ireland. Even as these developments took place on an international stage, people were engaged in worldmaking projects of their own, weighing the costs and benefits of staying or leaving; as Valli Kanapathipillai notes, many Indian-descended plantation laborers in Ceylon were willing to run the risk of being rendered stateless to avoid being sent back to a home they had never seen.[51]

By the 1960s, even though the lack of "assured income" was used to justify rejection of the naturalization applications of plantation laborers, Ceylonese government officials feared losing not only the labor but also the economic assets of Indian-descended laborers who were part of official repatriation programs. Officials worried that plantation laborers being repatriated would take their savings with them, collapsing the already emaciated tea industry in Ceylon and causing a run on the banks. Up to 75,000 rupees could be taken out without being subjected to foreign exchange controls, and the reports hastened to reassure the people that even if every plantation worker withdrew the maximum amount, it would not topple the Ceylonese economy, for the plantation laborers being forced out made up only 0.1 percent of the population on the island.[52] By 1964, all but three applications for Ceylonese citizenship had been adjudicated by the Commission for the Registration of Indian and Pakistani Residents. However, the question of legal citizenship—and, by extension, of access to employment, housing, and other services—was far from being settled. The Indian prime minister, Lal Bahadur Shastri, and Ceylon's prime minister, Sirimavo Bandaranaike, began to negotiate the terms of diplomatic agreements about citizenship. However, time was running out for these agreements; the Indian assistant high commissioner in Kandy was at that time organizing repatriation programs for plantation laborers.[53] In 1976, when the immigration agreement between the two countries, known as the Sirimavo-Sastri Pact, was concluded and implemented, the number of "stateless persons of Indian origin" in Ceylon would grow to 7,28,856—nearly equal to the number of applicants for Ceylonese citizenship between 1949 and 1951.[54] Outside of the official repatriation programs, the system of temporary residence permits between India and Ceylon was suspended, and the traders and merchants who crossed the Palk Strait began to look beyond, eastward to Hong Kong, westward to city-states in West Asia and the Persian Gulf, and even further westward to the Middle East, Europe, and the Americas.[55]

By 1962, the possibility of keeping up rhythms and patterns of migrant life between South and Southeast Asia appeared to fade. Although India's external affairs minister at the time, Swaran Singh, assured Indians in Burma that their interests would be protected, this was, for all intents and purposes, a hollow promise.[56] As people were repatriated or rehabilitated in India from Burma, Ceylon, and Malaya under various government schemes, returning migrants had new encounters with governments, bureaucracies, and the "law," and old patterns were repeated in new places. On the one hand, these people were labeled as "refugees," "evacuees," or "repatriates" and were subjected to extensive surveillance and documentation. Often their formal registration as Indian citizens upon arrival in India did little to better their situation. The national and local relief and rehabilitation programs for Burma refugees—and, later, refugees of the

Vietnam War and the Sri Lankan civil war in India—were extensions of programs put in place during the India-Pakistan partition, administered by the Ministry of Rehabilitation that had been established in 1948. But similarities ended there: there is a sharp contrast in the experiences of former migrants to Burma, Ceylon, and Malaya, who were able to tell their personal and familial histories of circular migration before courts and commissions and advocate for themselves, and the experiences of those migrants in later decades who, under repatriation and refugee resettlement and rehabilitation schemes, were deported, expelled, or forced back to India, where those histories barely registered.

By 1963, a Consular Manual was prepared by the Indian Foreign Service on how to register Indian citizens abroad. It noted that nationality laws had so far not been "complete." The word *nationality* was omitted because the Ministry of External Affairs thought that it would be confusing, given that the Indian Constitution and the Indian Citizenship Act did not use the language of nationality. Citizenship by registration under Article 8 of the Indian Constitution, wider in scope, as we saw earlier, was recommended only after every possibility under Article 5 was exhausted. As Deborah Sutton notes in the context of Indians in East Africa, here too the background to these choices was that of the Partition, attributing ulterior motives to those trying to acquire a certificate of citizenship in India but really being sympathetic to Pakistan.[57] Consular posts abroad, fearing a backlash from those who did not want Indians there, and prescient to the challenges that they would face in the 1970s, began to retain only partial registers in case they lost trading privileges. The term *nationality* was omitted to avoid suggesting that there was any move toward conflating nationality and race, even though the two had become synonymous over the course of two decades in Burma, Ceylon, and Malaya. The question of marriage—whether women acquired the nationality of their husbands upon marriage, and whether they were allowed to pass on nationality to their children—became especially important to prevent statelessness; clarifications on marriage and nationality were sought from Hong Kong and Rangoon just before the citizenship legislation in India was passed. Even by 1964, when the Shastri-Sirimavo Pact was signed, questions were still being raised about the proper jurisdiction of local courts like the Madras

High Court vis-à-vis that of the central government in New Delhi with respect to the determination of national status. As nationality and citizenship became central issues in conflict-of-law cases across borders, seemingly ordinary legal disputes over debt recovery or migrant remittances sank beneath the surface.

Repatriation schemes from Ceylon to India under the Sirima-Shastri Pact began in 1968 and continued until the beginning of the Sri Lankan civil war in 1983, bringing nearly four hundred thousand people. Repatriates arrived at the transit camp in Mandapam (figure 7.1), journeys for some of them coming full circle: this was the quarantine camp where, in times past, migrants had begun their journeys to Ceylon's plantations. Repatriates were handed paperwork testifying to their status and presenting the opportunity to register as Indian citizens. Some were given a small plot of land and some financial assistance. For example, the Tamil Nadu Tea Corporation (TANTEA) was a consortium of tea and coffee plantations set up to provide formal employment for repatriates. But as ethnographers Daniel Bass and Ravindran Sriramachandran show, many of these people abandoned their initial allotments to work on the tea and coffee plantations in South India, a landscape that they were often familiar with. And often, the conditions of employment were no better or worse than in Ceylon. The refugees' claims to land or welfare benefits, such as family cards or ration cards that allowed them access to public distribution systems, were often met with hostility from the local government authorities and from the dominant-caste Badaga land and plantation owners in the region, who saw the repatriates as those who only took from India rather than contributing to it. In popular and official understanding today, the claims of repatriates were—and often continue to be—incorrectly conflated with those of the refugees from the Sri Lankan civil war, although the latter only began in 1983. Repatriates were referred to as *aharthiarthal* or refugees.[58] Because of this conflation, argues Sriramachandran, repatriates—Indian nationals and often Indian citizens—were viewed as being as much outsiders as Sri Lankan Tamils, who were Sri Lankan nationals and Sri Lankan citizens.[59] Once again, the central legal claims were those of nationality and citizenship, unlike the ordinary cases involving an income tax assessment or the renewal of an immigrant permit.

FIGURE 7.1: *Signage outside Mandapam Refugee Camp, Tamil Nadu. Photograph by author.*

CITIZENS, REFUGEES, AND DEVELOPMENT

The repatriations and rehabilitations of displaced Indians from Burma were similar. In the immediate aftermath of the insurgencies in 1948, Dadachanji, a former member of the All Burma Indian Congress, Rev. Thangaraj, and John Sikka set up the Burma Indian Rehabilitation Society and represented their cause before the Indian government.[60] By 1968, according to official figures, nearly 140,000 people were part of official repatriation schemes, and many of them were resettled around the South Indian district of Vizagapatam / present-day Visakhapatanam, or sent to camps in Madras, Orissa, Bihar, West Bengal, and the Andaman and Nicobar Islands. These repatriates were primarily classed as peasants and agriculturists and occupied the same camps as post-Partition migrants from East Pakistan (present-day Bangladesh) had; indeed, arrangements for refugees from Burma and East Pakistan came up simultaneously for debate before the Andhra Pradesh Legislative Assembly.[61] Before being repatriated to India following the war, independence, and militant insurgencies in Burma, many of them had worked as rickshaw pullers, fishers, stevedores, lighthouse keepers, and petty traders, making up more than half the population of the city of Rangoon. As with the Ceylon repatriates, the acquisition of Indian citizenship proved elusive. Some did not meet the deadline mandated in the Indian Citizenship Act of 1955, which required that they must apply for naturalization after not more than six months of residence in India, and others believed that registering on a voters' roll was equivalent to acquiring citizenship.[62]

The Indian government considered the possibility of putting "able-bodied" repatriates to work on its most ambitious postindependence development projects—its dams. In Andhra Pradesh and Orissa, these included the Hirakud and Tungabhadra dams. Drawing on the expertise of Burma repatriates in the mining industry, governments considered the revival of government-owned coalfields, Singareni Collieries, which it had inherited from the princely state of Hyderabad during independence. In response to these proposals, repatriates petitioned local and national government, claiming that these employment opportunities paled in comparison to what was available to them in Burma. However, these claims, although made with the assistance of trade unionists and civil liberties groups and the support of prominent Andhra political leaders N. G. Ranga and Gouthu Latchanna, were seldom successful.[63]

The turn to employment in development projects for these repatriates was not an accident. It was, as scholars of the Partition, have shown, entirely in keeping with projects of nation building. Vazira Zamindar asks: "How was the marked refugee on the ground reconciled with the universal refugee of planning?" Looking at Karachi and Delhi as mirrored cities in the "long" partition of the Punjab, she notes that "displaced persons" in Indian government policies and laws came to stand in for "refugees."[64] Zamindar and Rotem Geva show how these rehabilitation schemes were incorporated into development projects.[65] In an eloquent discussion of rehabilitation and resettlements of refugees from East Bengal between 1948 and 1971, Uditi Sen shows how "citizen refugees" are constituted through their participation in development projects. For example, Sen points to the Dandakaranya Development Authority, which oversaw the construction of two large irrigation projects, roads and railways, and iron- and wood-working projects across present-day Chattisgarh and Odisha.[66] Sen also notes of the resettlement of Hindu East Bengali refugees on the Anda-man and Nicobar Islands that the language of development, particularly "postcolonial dreams of rapid development of 'backward' areas," was used to erase the stigma around refugee resettlement.[67] Nevertheless, as Sen's examples show, "development" is rooted in many types of displacement: the colonization schemes in the Andamans and Tripura alienated and dis-placed the indigenous communities, justified by the labeling of the orig-inal residents as "backward."[68] Just as the Burma repatriates followed in the geographic footsteps of refugees from East Pakistan, often encamped in the same places, including the Andamans, they also were funneled into some of the same strategies for incorporating refugees, including the re-settlement scheme under which the Burma repatriates, who were often Dalit, lower caste, and landless, were sent to resettle "backward" areas—a scheme that was advocated for by refugee welfare associations.[69] By 1974, the language of "development" was deeply entangled with repatriation schemes: in that year, the Planning Commission of India became officially involved in repatriation, and rehabilitation became fully commensurate with the postwar discourse of development.[70]

ORIGINS, MYTHS, AND DIASPORAS

Between 1942 and 1962, amendments to immigration, nationality, and cit-izenship legislation in South and Southeast Asia were never far removed from political organizing around race, religion, class, and language identi-ties that began before the war. In South India, as we saw in previous chap-ters, political movements leveraged diasporic communities for cultural and financial capital, which came to a head in the first decade following independence.[71] These movements challenged any easy national consensus on the question of borders, sovereignty, and self-determination. This was particularly true of South India, where a campaign centered on counter-ing Hindi imposition, derived from Dravidian nationalism, took place. But beyond the borders of India, Dravidian nationalisms, particularly the Suyamariyathai Iyakkam (Self-Respect Movement), as Darinee Alagiri-samy shows, traveled and circulated between India and Malaya, taking on distinct forms in each place.[72] These political, literary, anticaste, and language movements created a sense of political and cultural belonging that extended beyond the territorial boundaries of new states. As we saw with G. Sarangapany, the noted Tamil journalist and editor of the *Tamil Murasu* in Singapore who campaigned for Indians to register as Singaporean citizens, they were not removed from the demand for legal recognition and minority rights.[73]

Equally, linguistic nationalisms that demanded that Indian provinces be redrawn along majority language spoken also addressed diasporic communities across the oceans. We already saw in chapter 1 how the first years of independence in Burma and Ceylon were marked by measures to recognize Burmese and Sinhala languages, to the detriment of minority languages spoken by these countries' migrant communities. In Sri Lanka, the Official Language Act of 1956, installing Sinhala, and thus the majority language spoken, as the official language on the island is frequently referenced in this context. To revive interest in languages spoken by migrants, movements reached across the oceans. Rachel Leow shows that the governance of language in Malaya became central to the national imagination of postindependence Malaya; a similar project unfolded in the first decade of Indian independence.[74] Take, for example, political demands such as Aikya Keralam's demand for integration of Malayalam-speaking areas of Travancore-Cochin and Malabar in Madras state or the demand of Visalandhra, a similar movement, for the union of Telugu-speaking areas in South India. On the other shore, in the short story "Avalude Keralam," by Malayalam novelist and Communist Party of India member S. K. Pottekkat, the chief protagonist speaks of the notion of a united Kerala—Aikya Keralam—as an ideal forged in the hearts and minds of Malayalees in Malaya.[75] This fictional account reflected Pottekkat's observations from his travels in Malaya, where nascent Malayalee associational life frequently invoked and reaffirmed the demand for a United Kerala. In Ceylon, where the term *diaspora* for migrants from South India was fraught, as we saw in chapters 4 and 5, Tamil nationalisms on either side of the Palk Strait were deeply embroiled in questions of nationality and citizenship. But in people's lives, as the chapters show, these political projects likely did not feature as distinct or contradictory impulses that

were to be wholly accepted or rejected but instead installed a set of jurisdictional markers that people had to navigate to secure their legal statuses.
Aikya Keralam and Visalandhra, as political movements for legal and cultural recognition that appealed to diasporas, invoked community legends,
origin myths, and chronicles about "first" landings and arrivals in adopted
homes and places of work. As previous chapters show, access to citizenship
as legal status turned on whether minoritized communities could meet
thresholds that were tied to specific dates or years.

Scholars working with religious and literary texts or with art show how
indigeneity was articulated in local movements around decolonization.
Here language played a key role in establishing indigeneity: often only a
singular linguistic community could claim to be authentic or "original" inhabitants of the land. Harshana Rambukwella shows how the introduction
of the Sinhala Only Act in 1956 by S. W. R. D. Bandaranaike in Ceylon
mandating the use of Sinhala alone—as opposed to Tamil, Malay, or other
languages spoken by communities on the island—became the impetus for
a public discourse around *deshiya* (indigeneity) and *apewama* (our-ness).
Even those who considered themselves part of the political left, including
the celebrated author Martin Wickramasinghe, who put rural village life at
the heart of his magnum opus *Gampereliya*, made explicit the connections
between land, indigeneity, and decolonizing impulses in the first decade
following independence.[76] Similarly in Burma, Tharaphin Than analyzes
the language of Pyidawtha in the first plans for economic development,
noting the honorific *pyi* that recalls the legends and chronicles of the kings
of Ava. Even in the context of decolonization's modernizing tendencies,
an appeal to what appeared to be "ancient" and "timeless" was critical.[77] In
throwing off the shackles of colonial rule during decolonization, artists,
writers, thinkers, and scholars, particularly those who employed languages
spoken by the majority, all too quickly rushed to recover "timelessness" in
the form of ancient chronicles and origin myths.

These ideas of belonging tied to land, of affective ties to homelands
based on language, were not separate from legal determinations on citizenship. Preceding the introduction of citizenship legislation in Ceylon,
for example, D. S. Senanayake established a scheme to "return" plantation land to the Kandyan Sinhalese peasants. On August 16, 1956—the

year that Bandaranaike's government introduced the Sinhala Only Act in Ceylon, Sellappan, a plantation laborer, appeared before the commissioner at the factory office of the Kotmale Estate in Nuwara Eliya. The commissioner informed Sellappan that he had not satisfied the requirements of "permanent settlement" under the Indian and Pakistani Residents (Citizenship) Act of 1949, under which Sellappan had applied for Ceylonese citizenship. He would have to establish, by way of an authenticated paper trail, that he had lived in Ceylon uninterruptedly between January 1, 1939, and 1950. In response, as thousands of applicants had done before him, Sellappan recounted his life: how he had arrived in Ceylon in 1939, had gotten married, had had six children, and had settled down as a laborer on Kotmale estate. He recounted the births and deaths of his children and his marriage in India. He declared that he was willing to give up all his rights in India and abide by the laws in Ceylon. The inquiry then took a surprising turn. Judging from the account of questions in the inquiry report, the commissioner presumably asked him where he had been in 1939 for Thaipongal, a harvest festival celebrated in South India. Sellappan replied that he had been in India. The commissioner repeated the question thrice. Sellappan answered in the affirmative. The inquiry concluded.

From the inquiry report retained in the archives, it is unclear what prompted the commissioner's line of questioning about Thaipongal. It seems to have been a deliberate ruse: while the commissioner was aware that Thaipongal fell in January every year, the applicants may not have been aware of the legal implications of answering in the affirmative. In a brief order, the commissioner noted that since Sellappan had confessed to being in India for Thaipongal in 1939, he could not have been in Ceylon for the time required by the act. Sellappan's citizenship application was rejected. Not only did these personal and familial histories not coincide with the conditions of "permanent settlement" that the 1949 Act demanded, but the act only leveraged rhythms and patterns of migrant life to show that migrants belonged—and would always belong—only elsewhere.

In 1942 and 1962, Rangoon, city of migrants, emptied out. Twenty years elapsed between these two events. During these two decades, new nation-states in South and Southeast Asia grappled with questions of citizenship and political belonging, marking migrants and foreigners as only provisionally and liminally included. Immigration, nationality, and citizenship legislation further unraveled networks of labor, capital, trade, and finance that had been disrupted during the war. Tropes of arrival and origin dominated postwar legislation that marked minorities as perpetual migrants.

During these same two decades, the borders of South and Southeast Asia were in flux, continually being redrawn. While India grappled with the displacement of peoples across the Punjab on its western border, refugees began crossing the porous border between India and East Pakistan (later Bangladesh) in the early 1960s; the 1971 liberation war for Bangladesh pushed even more refugees across.[78] In the 1950s, Sindhi and Sikh communities displaced by the India–Pakistan partition had migrated to Malaya, Singapore, and Hong Kong. French and Portuguese settlements situated across the Indian subcontinent from Goa to Pondicherry, posed their own dilemmas of citizenship.[79] Against these narratives of return, repatriation, and resettlement, in both the 1940s and the 1960s, "evacuees" from Burma were distinguished nominally from "repatriates" from Ceylon and Malaya; the latter were granted return passage to India, along with financial compensation and compassionate appointments, while evacuees were more or less left to fend for themselves. In the 1960s, the overarching framework of relief and rehabilitation was the same as that used after the partitions of 1947–48: transit camps, welfare officers, worksites, and rehabilitation measures were undertaken with little regard to the different paths taken through the age of decolonization, as migrants grappled with a different but still amorphous understanding of the paths to legal citizenship in India.

In the late 1940s, as countries in South and Southeast Asia followed their divergent, sometimes meandering trajectories of decolonization from British, Dutch, and French rule, nation building took place within the cracks and crevices of the legal system—in disputes around paying taxes, remitting earnings to one's family members abroad, securing the "right" papers for naturalization, or writing up a will that provided for one's kin. In these banal legal encounters, migrants faced their greatest challenges. In these conflicts between migrants and emerging governments, neither political nor legal representation was able to fully compensate for postwar nation-states' deep suspicion of minoritized people who lived and worked in more than one place, in a world where familial attachments were translated as economic attachments. The new states treated these differences not as differences of cultures or customs but as markers of political loyalty. India, Ceylon, Burma, and Malaya each proceeded apace with building postindependence legal regimes around migration and citizenship and political discourse around indigeneity, authenticity, ownership, and attachment to land. These discourses all (deliberately) left migrant foreigners on the margins of these newly independent countries at a disadvantage.[80]

The postwar encounters with law and bureaucracy in South and Southeast Asia bookended by the years 1942 and 1962 should be read not merely as attempts to gain legal status but as attempts to revive the rhythms and patterns of migrant life. A focus on legislative changes to citizenship regimes offers only one glimpse into how the world of former migrants was governed and was increasingly formalized by new nation-states. As this chapter shows, forms of petitioning these states changed as rehabilitation and repatriation programs were instituted. In the midst of these changes, migrants' jurisdictional claims and counterclaims, in which they narrated their personal and familial histories, offers some possibilities to disrupt this teleological narrative of a shift from imperial subjecthood to national citizenship. Read in this fashion, the legal archive offers us a different perspective on decolonization in South and Southeast Asia, which unfolded between 1945 and 1960.[81] These encounters were at a different scale and had little to do with the global and regional diplomatic negotiations between Asian and African leaders in Colombo, Bandung, or London. But these mundane encounters over contractual obligations, remittance limits, naturalization and residence permit applications, and detention and banishment orders reveal that migrants struggled to live not only across geographic borders but also across the different legal and political temporalities that those borders produced. *Boats in a Storm* is thus an alternative history of decolonization, from the perspective of South and Southeast Asia, but with implications for the continuing struggles of diasporic communities beyond it.

AN UNEASY CALM

IN 1942, HUNDREDS OF thousands of migrants fled their adopted homes and places of work in South and Southeast Asia. These migrants could not have imagined how new nation-states, eager to perform their newly won sovereignty, would judge these displacements. In this book, I have followed a set of itineraries, escape routes, and other planned and unplanned journeys back and forth across the eastern Indian Ocean or the Bay of Bengal that followed in the wake of the Second World War. The Japanese occupation of Burma and Malaya in Southeast Asia during the war unraveled networks and assemblages of trade, labor, capital, and finance built up over a century and a half of imperial rule. After the war ended, this unraveling posed a challenge as people attempted to return to homes and places of work or attempted to begin new journeys across old routes. These journeys of displacement and return migration were forged through law, as people attempted to revive the rhythms and patterns of migrant life: carrying on trade and business, lending and borrowing money, building families, and raising children across new state borders. In legal disputes around debt recovery, enforcement of contracts, double taxation, and regulation of foreign exchange remittances, wartime displacements of migrants were rendered suspect. In military and diplomatic histories, 1942 was the year in which Japan occupied Burma and Malaya and launched attacks on India and Ceylon. But for new nation-states, 1942 became a juridical marker that indexed the political loyalty of migrants and minorities. As the chapters in this book show, former migrants narrated personal, familial, and community histories before the law. These accounts offer a new, lesser-explored perspective on decolonization, which unfolded not only as a political process but, by returning to wartime displacement and in the everyday lives of people, as a legal process. These processes generated legal temporalities that altered how decolonization was experienced in the lives of former migrants themselves.

The year 1942 became a juridical watershed in two ways. First, wartime displacements in that year and the war's disruption of trade and business prompted legal disputes, such as Seethalakshmi Achi's debt recovery case in chapter 2 and Abdul Cader's challenge to his assessment of income tax in Ceylon in chapter 5. Second, states' redesigns of taxation, immigration, and detention regimes in response to wartime displacements remained on the statute books for decades. Consider, for example, how immigration agreements between India, Burma, Ceylon, and the former Straits Settlements were recalibrated in the first two decades following their independence in 1947–48 to account for wartime absences. The continuities in litigation and in legislative and bureaucratic frameworks—particularly the provisions that linked periods of continuous residence to taxation status or the right to citizenship—linked the wartime years to the postwar years. Whether migrants fled because of wartime occupations or remained in their adopted homes and places of work during the war, their futures after the war ended depended on recollecting and remembering (and documenting) their experiences during the war: when they were in certain places, for how long, what they did there, why they came or went, whom they saw. In seemingly banal encounters with the law, issues of recollection, documentation, or narrativization swelled in importance. Unfulfilled wartime contracts affected remittances, which in turn affected immigration and citizenship prospects, which in turn placed many migrants at the risk of detention, expulsion, and permanent exile. The events of the war would be replayed and recycled in legal disputes for decades to come. As these legal disputes played out and were used as precedents for other decisions, the regimes of taxation, immigration, remittance, inheritance, detention, and expulsion that they created became interlocking legal regimes, with each producing a set of cascading legal consequences in others.

Nationality, immigration, and citizenship legislation in the former British colonies India, Ceylon, Burma, and Malaya was expected to settle questions of political belonging following the end of the war. But focusing only on questions of nationality and citizenship offers only a partial account of postwar South and Southeast Asia that privileges political negotiations and diplomatic encounters. As the chapters in this book show, from the perspective of former migrants themselves, seemingly banal encounters with the law were equally, if not more, important. Through jurisdictional claims and counterclaims—claims about *who* had the authority *where* and *when* to decide the outcome of these ordinary legal disputes—former migrants told their personal and family histories, seeking to reinstate the rhythms and patterns of migrant life. From the perspective of migrants, "law" was a set of interlinked, interlocked regimes in which the value of paperwork—documentary proof of their claims and stories—fluctuated wildly. This tangled net of jurisdictional claims and counterclaims and these stormy legal seas were what migrants had to navigate after the end of the war—there was nothing so simple as a declaration of (and confirmation of) a singular national citizenship. As this book has argued, we must attend to the complex temporalities that are generated by law when it travels; nationality, immigration, and citizenship laws must be considered not only within their historical contexts but also in their geographic and temporal contexts—which were, in this period, constantly in flux, ebbing and swelling with the circulations and migrations of people, money, and legislation. Understanding this flux is crucial if we are to rethink our ideas of citizenship and decolonization in South and Southeast Asia.

This book covers twenty years bookended by two displacements from Burma, the first during the war in 1942 and the second during the military takeover of Burma's government by Ne Win. But the chapters themselves show how these bookends are artificial, for the implicit questions raised in the context of legal disputes in the aftermath of wartime displacements over belonging and loyalty are still very much present in legal discourse as well as public memory today. The space for individual negotiations with states continued to shrink in the subsequent decades. By 1982, even the official repatriation programs from Burma to India had stopped, General Ne Win had relinquished his role has head of state, and a new citizenship law for Burma that amended the definition of "indigenous races" left hundreds of thousands of people, including the Rohingya who lived in the Rakhine state in Burma, stateless.[1] Statelessness also became a feature of lives that hung in the balance between India and China, particularly on the borderlands.[2] Beyond South and Southeast Asia, as the second wave of decolonization took place in Asia and Africa, Uganda, formerly a protectorate of the British Empire, expelled Indian nationals in 1972, under Idi Amin; officials who organized travel recalled how it mirrored displacements from Burma only a decade prior.[3] As the chapters here show, the juridical categories of "migrant," "refugee," "stateless person," "displaced person," and "asylum seeker" were not siloed off from each other but intimately bound up with each other. People navigated the spectrum from citizenship to statelessness, moving between these statuses as they navigated legal conflicts, attempted to cross geographical borders, and confronted the dissonances between temporalities generated by law and the administrative work of new nation-states.

This reframing of the political process of decolonization by way of ordinary legal processes requires us to think of partitions and of partitioning, central to how citizenship has been understood in the South Asian context. *Partition* refers to, in the first instance, the bloody territorial partition of India into India and Pakistan in 1947 that fundamentally reshaped South Asia and continues to mark the question of citizenship. The wealth of scholarship on the Partition has shown how these governmental policies resulted in ongoing violent and traumatic partitioned lives. *Partitioning*, as Sujit Sivasundaram shows in the context of nineteenth-century Ceylon, was achieved by producing knowledge—in this case, law and legalities, that marked one "territory" off from another.[4] Conceptually, both terms are at work here in understanding decolonization through the archives of law: the splitting of jurisdictions that came to a head in the postwar world—of the Straits Settlements from Bengal, of Ceylon from Madras, of Burma from India, and finally, of South Asia from Southeast Asia—was not only a matter of constructing new national borders to replace imperial ones but, through jurisdictional claims and counterclaims, a means of marking places off from each other through law. As historians have shown, the realities of people's lives did not align with new national borders drawn in Bengal, Punjab, Assam, and Kashmir during the Partition. In the partitioning of South and Southeast Asia, people pushed back against the drawing of juridical borders by narrating personal and family histories that cut across these jurisdictions, drawing on a long history of circular oceanic migrations and labor, capital, trade, and credit networks across the Bay of Bengal; in the end, that these processes were not distinct but intertwined is captured by the fact that refugees from the military coup in Burma and from East Pakistan / Bengal occupied the same transit camps along the coasts of Andhra Pradesh and Tamil Nadu and were part of similar state-led rehabilitation programs in 1962. In the space of twenty years between 1942 and 1962 that this book covers, other separations, mergers, and federations took place too—the territorial reorganization of South India based on majority languages spoken in 1956 and the federation of Malay states and the former Straits Settlements into the Federation of Malaysia in 1957 are prominent examples—that would leave a profound impact on the question of political belonging and whose borders were challenged by the realities of people's lives. These too disrupt the simple chronology of independence and decolonization as a shift from imperial to national borders in South and Southeast Asia.

Here decolonization is not only a political or diplomatic process but a legal process that ebbs and flows, stretches and convulses the experience of time for those caught in legal limbo. Consider, for example, Seethalakshmi Achi and Meyappan Chettiar waiting for the war to be over so that they could collect on debts in Burma, or Muthiah waiting for the outcome of his citizenship application for years, or Ramiah and his comrades waiting to hear if family members or political party workers would ever come to their aid while they were indefinitely detained. Moving away from the idea of citizenship as legal status, one can instead think of people navigating a spectrum of legal statuses between citizenship and statelessness, exploring the gradations of noncitizenship: sojourning, traveling, living in exile, settling, conquering, occupying. These were intimately bound up with legal processes, "stretching" the time of decolonization.

The consequences of looking at legal temporalities are not restricted to the problems of periodization within disciplinary history alone.[5] The temporalities generated within law and legal processes, invoked, and returned to wartime displacements, thrum alongside community histories and origin stories that shaped political discourse on nationality and citizenship. Consider, for example, how the histories of "ancient" Tamil migration to Southeast Asia became a central theme in the work of renowned historian K. A. Nilakanta Sastri, who was himself associated with the work of international law study group at the University of Madras in the early 1950s.[6] These myths and stories endure even now in present-day South and Southeast Asia. For example, legacies of the colonial-era debate over the identities of Muslims in Ceylon continue to mark both political discourse and scholarship on Sri Lanka today. Today, those professing Islam in the southern districts of Tamil Nadu accept the designation "Tamil Muslims" to distinguish themselves from Urdu- or Dakhani-speaking Muslims of northern Tamil Nadu; Muslims in Sri Lanka, however, reject the "Tamil Muslim" label (and the similar "Muslim Tamil" label) because of its associations with the historically marginalized and discriminated-against minority Tamil population and the fraught and fractured histories of the place of Sri Lankan Muslims vis-à-vis Sri Lankan Tamils.[7]

As new governments in South and Southeast Asia considered the place of migrants within new legislative and constitutional frameworks, as in previous iterations of the breakup of empires, detention, banishment, and expulsion ensured that these intentions were secured. Invoked as part of context of postwar counterinsurgency measures in Malaya as well as preventive/administrative detention regimes in India, the specter of a "communist" threat of disorder and violence was frequently projected onto migrant laborers, working-class leaders, and trade union leaders. Even as passport and permit regimes tightened travel, movement, and residence across the Bay and to former European metropoles, dangerous ideas, in the eyes of new states and governments, knew no territorial borders; juridical borders would have to be erected. Caught in the dragnets of detention regimes—banishment ordinances in Malaya and public order legislation in India—labor migrants often suffered because of guilt by association, and wartime affiliations of convenience or survival came back to haunt them as courts and committees adjudged accounts of their political activities.

At its most general, this book demonstrates, as Luis Eslava and Sundhya Pahuja note in their discussion of the relationship between the state, decolonization, and international law, that the historical contingencies that make international law are always ongoing; international law makes states as much as states make international law.[8] But the undercurrents of conquest and colonialism in international law did not end with the end of colonial rule. They are still evident as we write histories after empire; they are histories of the present. Displacement today, in the case of Sri Lanka, which has been scrutinized by human rights organizations, cannot be extricated from thinking about disappearances, those whose lives have been whisked away by military forces in the aftermath of the civil war on the island. Across the river Naaf on the Bangladesh-Myanmar border is Cox's Bazaar, which hosts the world's largest refugee camp, providing shelter to the Rohingya, who are stateless. Both of these contemporary "crises" show that South Asia still lives with and in the tumult and chaos produced by the transitions from colonial rule, the forms and structures of political representation put in place by colonial rule, its privileging of certain kinds of "truth." These are, as this book has shown, mired in juridical categories and legal fictions in international law. By viewing jurisdictional claims and counterclaims in legal disputes as personal stories struggling to align with official histories, by looking at the struggle to retain the rhythms and patterns of migrant life *as* decolonization, *Boats in a Storm* attempts to undo these categories and unmask these fictions.

ABBREVIATIONS USED IN NOTES

AIR	All India Reporter
BL	British Library
BLR	Burma Law Reports
Cal	Calcutta
FNR	Fortnightly Reports
IOR	India Office Records and Private Papers, British Library
Mad	Madras
MHC RR	Madras High Court Record Room
MLJ	Madras Law Journal
NAI	National Archives of India, New Delhi
NAS	National Archives of Singapore
NASL	National Archives of Sri Lanka, Colombo
NLB	National Library Board, Singapore
NLR	New Law Reports
NMML	Nehru Memorial Museum and Library, New Delhi
Rang. L.R.	Rangoon Law Reports
RMRL	Roja Muthiah Research Library, Chennai
SC	Supreme Court
TNA	The National Archives, Kew
TNSA	Tamil Nadu State Archives, Chennai
UKPC	United Kingdom Privy Council

NOTES

Introduction

1. See contributions to Luis Eslava, Michael Fakhri, and Vasuki Nesiah, eds., *Bandung, Global History, and International Law: Critical Pasts and Pending Futures* (Cambridge: Cambridge University Press, 2017); Christopher Lee, *Making a World after Empire: The Bandung Moment and Its Political Afterlives* (Athens: Ohio University Press, 2010); Carolien Stolte and Su Lin Lewis, eds., *The Lives of Cold War Afro-Asianism* (Leiden: Leiden University Press, 2022). See also Gyan Prakash, Michael Laffan, and Nikhil Menon, eds., introduction to *The Postcolonial Moment in South and Southeast Asia*, ed. Gyan Prakash, Michael Laffan, and Nikhil Menon, 1–10 (London: Bloomsbury, 2018).

2. See Sunil Amrith, *Crossing the Bay of Bengal: The Furies of Nature and the Fortunes of Migrants* (Cambridge, MA: Harvard University Press, 2013). On connected histories of South and Southeast Asia that chart circuits of commodities, penal labor, religion, and trade between the mid-nineteenth and mid-twentieth centuries, see, for example, Eric Tagliocozzo, *Secret Trades, Porous Borders: Smuggling and States along a Southeast Asian Frontier, 1865–1915* (New Haven, CT: Yale University Press, 2005); Engseng Ho, *The Graves of Tarim: Genealogy and Mobility across the Indian Ocean* (Berkeley: University of California Press, 2006); Terenjit Sevea, *Islamic Connections: Muslim Societies in South and Southeast Asia* (Singapore: Institute of Southeast Asian Studies, 2009); Ronit Ricci, *Islam Translated: Literature, Conversion, and the Arabic Cosmopolis of South and Southeast Asia* (Chicago: University of Chicago Press, 2011); Diana Kim, *Empires of Vice: The Rise of Opium Prohibition across Southeast Asia* (Princeton, NJ: Princeton University Press, 2020); and Anand Yang, *Empire of Convicts: Indian Penal Labor in Colonial Southeast Asia* (Oakland: University of California Press, 2021), as well as essays in Michael Laffan, ed., *Belonging across the Bay of Bengal: Religious Rites, Colonial Migrations, National Rights* (London: Bloomsbury, 2017).

3. Harshan Kumarasingham, "The 'Tropical Dominions': The Appeal of Dominion Status in the Decolonisation of India, Pakistan and Ceylon," *Transactions of the Royal Historical Society*, 6th ser., 23 (December 2013): 223–45.

4. Christopher Bayly and Tim Harper, *Forgotten Wars: Freedom and Revolution in Southeast Asia* (Cambridge, MA: Harvard University Press, 2007).

5. Sujit Sivasundaram, *Islanded: Britain, Sri Lanka, and the Bounds of an Indian Ocean Colony* (Chicago: University of Chicago Press, 2013).

6. Sundhya Pahuja, "Letters from Bandung: Encounters with Another International Law," in Eslava, Fakhri, and Nesiah, *Bandung, Global History*, 552–73. See also B. S. Chimni, "The International Law of Jurisdiction: A TWAIL Perspective." *Leiden Journal*

of International Law 35, no. 1 (2022): 29–54 (for a discussion on placing "territory" and "jurisdiction" within their historical and social context).

7. Glen Peterson, "Sovereignty, International Law, and the Uneven Development of the International Refugee Regime," *Modern Asian Studies* 49, no. 2 (2015): 439–68; Ria Kapoor, "Removing the International from the Refugee: India in the 1940s," *Humanity: An International Journal of Human Rights, Humanitarianism, and Development* 12, no. 1 (2021): 1–19. Much of the scholarship on refugee history, such as Gerard Daniel Cohen, *In War's Wake: Europe's Displaced Persons in the Postwar Order* (Oxford: Oxford University Press, 2011), or Pamela Ballinger, *The World Refugees Made: Decolonization and the Foundation of Postwar Italy* (Ithaca, NY: Cornell University Press, 2020), focuses on Europe, to which the international legal definition of "refugee" was initially restricted. Vazira Zamindar, *The Long Partition and the Making of Modern South Asia: Refugees, Boundaries, Histories* (New York: Columbia University Press, 2007), Haimanti Roy, *Partitioned Lives: Migrants, Refugees, Citizens in India and Pakistan, 1947–1965* (Oxford: Oxford University Press, 2012), Antara Datta, *Refugees and Borders in South Asia: The Great Exodus of 1971* (London: Routledge, 2013), Uditi Sen, *Citizen Refugee: Forging the Indian Nation after Partition* (Cambridge: Cambridge University Press, 2018), and Joya Chatterji, "From Imperial Subjects to National Citizens," in *Routledge Handbook of the South Asian Diaspora*, ed. Joya Chatterji and David Washbrook, 183–97 (London: Routledge, 2013), among others, have highlighted this exclusion in the context of South Asian history. Lauren Madokoro, *Elusive Refuge: Chinese Migrants in the Cold War* (Cambridge, MA: Harvard University Press, 2016), and Taomo Zhou, *Migration in the Time of Revolution: China, Indonesia, and the Cold War* (Ithaca, NY: Cornell University Press, 2019), also focus on how postwar refugee regimes in Asia played out against the background of escalating Cold War tensions, but with a focus on Chinese migrations in Southeast Asia.

8. On bureaucracy, citizenship, and the Partition, see Zamindar, *Long Partition*, and H. Roy, *Partitioned Lives*.

9. Renisa Mawani, "Law's Archive," *Annual Review of Law and Social Science* 8, no. 1 (2012): 337–65. See also Anjali Arondekar, *For the Record: On Sexuality and the Colonial Archive in India* (Durham, NC: Duke University Press, 2009), Bhavani Raman, *Document Raj: Writing and Scribes in Early Colonial South India* (Chicago: University of Chicago Press, 2012), Fahad Bishara, *A Sea of Debt: Law and Economic Life in the Western Indian Ocean, 1780–1950* (Cambridge: Cambridge University Press, 2017), Nandini Chatterjee, *Negotiating Mughal Law: A Family of Landlords across Three Indian Empires* (Cambridge: Cambridge University Press, 2020), and Nurfadzilah Yahaya, *Fluid Jurisdictions: Colonial Law and Arabs in Southeast Asia* (Ithaca, NY: Cornell University Press, 2020), for monographs that theorize the role of law's archive but also view the law as archive. See also Danna Agmon, "Historical Gaps and Non-existent Sources: The Case of the Chaudrie Court in French India," *Comparative Studies in Society and History* 63, no. 4 (2021): 979–1006, for reflections on the limits of law's archive.

10. Sunil Amrith, "Indians Overseas? Governing Tamil Migration to Malaya, 1870–1941," *Past and Present* 208, no. 1 (2010): 231–61.

11. Kamal Sadiq, *Paper Citizens: How Illegal Immigrants Acquire Citizenship in Developing Countries* (Oxford: Oxford University Press, 2008).

12. Yahaya, *Fluid Jurisdictions*.

13. Sundhya Pahuja, "Laws of Encounter: A Jurisdictional Account of International Law," *London Review of International Law* 1, no. 1 (2013): 63–98.

14. Antony Anghie, *Imperialism, Sovereignty, and the Making of International Law* (Cambridge: Cambridge University Press, 2005); Nurfadzilah Yahaya, "The Concept of European Jurisdiction in the Colonies," in *The Oxford Handbook of Jurisdiction in International Law*, ed. Steve Allen et al. (Oxford: Oxford University Press, 2019), 59–80.

15. Mariana Valverde, *Chronotopes of Law: Jurisdiction, Scale, and Governance* (London: Routledge, 2015).

16. Martti Koskenniemi, "Expanding Histories of International Law," *American Journal of Legal History* 56, no. 1 (2016): 104–12; Eslava, Fakhri, and Nesiah, *Bandung, Global History*.

17. Kalyani Ramnath, "Intertwined Itineraries: Debt, Decolonization and International Law in Post-WWII South Asia," *Law and History Review* 38, no. 1 (2020): 1–24.

18. Renisa Mawani and Iza Hussin, "The Travels of Law: Indian Ocean Itineraries," *Law and History Review* 32, no. 4 (2014): 733–47.

19. Julia Stephens, "An Uncertain Inheritance: The Imperial Travels of Legal Migrants, from British India to Ottoman Iraq," *Law and History Review* 32, no. 4 (2014): 749–72; Engseng Ho, "Afterword: Mobile Law and Thick Transregionalism," *Law and History Review* 32, no. 4 (2014): 883–89; Fahad Bishara, "The Sailing Scribes: Circulating Law in the Twentieth-Century Indian Ocean," prepublished August 30, 2022, 1–18, https://doi.org/10.1017/S0738248022000402.

20. On citizenship in India, see Anupama Roy, *Mapping Citizenship in India* (Oxford: Oxford University Press, 2010), and Niraja Gopal Jayal, *Citizenship and Its Discontents: An Indian History* (Cambridge, MA: Harvard University Press, 2013). For a survey of the scholarship on histories of Indian citizenship, see Kalyani Ramnath, "Histories of Indian Citizenship in the Age of Decolonisation," *Itinerario* 45, no. 1 (2021): 152–73.

21. Radhika Singha, "The Great War and a 'Proper' Passport for the Colony: Border-Crossing in British India, c. 1882–1922," *Indian Economic and Social History Review* 50, no. 3 (2013): 289–315; Radhika Mongia, *Indian Migration and Empire* (Durham, NC: Duke University Press, 2018); Renisa Mawani, *Across Oceans of Law: The Komagata Maru and Jurisdiction in the Time of Empire* (Durham, NC: Duke University Press, 2018); Neilesh Bose, ed., *South Asian Migrations in Global History: Labor, Law, and Wayward Lives* (London: Bloomsbury, 2020).

22. Sukanya Banerjee, *Becoming Imperial Citizens: Indians in the Late-Victorian Empire* (Durham, NC: Duke University Press, 2010) (focusing on the writings and speeches of civil servants and lawyers who traveled between India and South Africa). See also Mark R. Frost, "Imperial Citizenship or Else: Liberal Ideals and the India Unmaking of Empire, 1890–1919," *Journal of Imperial and Commonwealth History* 46, no. 5 (2018): 845–73.

23. Rachel Sturman, "Indian Indentured Labor and the History of International Rights Regimes," *American Historical Review* 119, no. 5 (2014): 1439–65; Mrinalini Sinha, "Premonitions of the Past," *Journal of Asian Studies* 74, no. 4 (2015): 821–41; Sana Aiyar, *Indians in Kenya: The Politics of Diaspora* (Cambridge, MA: Harvard University Press, 2015).

24. See, for example, Ramachandra Guha, *Gandhi before India* (London: Penguin,

2013) (chronicling Gandhi's career as a lawyer in South Africa before he led India's freedom struggle against the British), or Vineet Thakur, *India's First Diplomat: V. S. Srinivasa Sastri and the Making of Liberal Internationalism* (Bristol: Bristol University Press, 2021). For an exception, see Gaiutra Bahadur, *Coolie Woman: The Odyssey of Indenture* (Chicago: University of Chicago Press, 2013).

25. Alison Bashford, "Immigration Restriction: Rethinking Period and Place from Settler Colonies to Postcolonial Nations," *Journal of Global History* 9, no. 1 (2014): 26–48.

26. Jayal, *Citizenship and Its Discontents*.

27. A. Roy, *Mapping Citizenship in India*; see also Sanjib Baruah, *In the Name of the Nation: India and Its Northeast* (Stanford, CA: Stanford University Press, 2020).

28. See also Taylor Sherman, William Gould, and Sarah Ansari, eds., *From Subjects to Citizens: Society and the Everyday State in India and Pakistan, 1947–1970* (Delhi: Cambridge University Press, 2014); Clare Alexander, Joya Chatterji, and Annu Jalais, *The Bengal Diaspora: Rethinking Muslim Migration* (London: Routledge, 2015); Malini Sur, *Jungle Passports: Fences, Mobility, and Citizenship at the Northeast India-Bangladesh Border* (Philadelphia: University of Pennsylvania Press, 2021).

29. Valli Kanapathipillai, *Citizenship and Statelessness in Sri Lanka: The Case of the Tamil Estate Workers* (London: Anthem Press, 2009).

30. Jordanna Bailkinn, *The Afterlife of Empire* (Berkeley: University of California Press, 2012); Ian Sanjay Patel, *We're Here Because You Were There: Immigration and the End of Empire* (London: Verso, 2021); Sarah Ansari, "Subjects or Citizens? India, Pakistan and the 1948 British Nationality Act," *Journal of Imperial and Commonwealth History* 41, no. 2 (2013): 285–312. In the context of the end of French imperial rule, Gary Wilder terms this the "dyadic mode." Gary Wilder, *Freedom Time: Negritude, Decolonization, and the Future of the World* (Durham, NC: Duke University Press, 2015).

31. Patel, *We're Here*.

32. Bhavani Raman, "Calling the Other Shore: Tamil Studies and Decolonization," in Laffan, *Belonging across the Bay*, 161–80.

33. Frederick Cooper, *Citizenship between Empire and Nation* (Princeton, NJ: Princeton University Press, 2014); on Indian princely states and sovereignty, see Eric Beverly, "Introduction: Rethinking Sovereignty, Colonial Empires, and Nation-States in South Asia and Beyond," *Comparative Studies of South Asia, Africa and the Middle East* 40 (2020): 407–20; Sunil Purushotham, *From Raj to Republic: Sovereignty, Violence and Democracy in India* (Stanford, CA: Stanford University Press, 2021).

34. Mark Mazower, *No Enchanted Palace: The End of Empire and the Ideological Origins of the United Nations* (Princeton, NJ: Princeton University Press, 2009); Natasha Wheatley, "Spectral Legal Personality in Interwar International Law: On New Ways of Not Being a State," *Law and History Review* 35, no. 3 (2017): 753–87.

35. Mira Siegelberg, *Statelessness: A Modern History* (Cambridge, MA: Harvard University Press, 2020).

36. Eric D. Weitz, "From Vienna to the Paris System: International Politics and the Entangled Histories of Human Rights, Forced Deportations, and Civilizing Missions," *American Historical Review* 113, no. 5 (2008): 1313–43.

37. Laura Robson, *States of Separation: Transfer, Partition, and the Making of the Modern Middle East* (Oakland: University of California Press, 2017); see also compara-

tive history of partitions in South Asia and the Middle East in Arie Dubnov and Laura Robson, *Partitions: A Transnational History of Twentieth-Century Territorial Separatism* (Stanford, CA: Stanford University Press, 2019).

38. Luis Eslava and Sundhya Pahuja, "The State and International Law: A Reading from the Global South," *Humanity: An International Journal of Human Rights, Humanitarianism, and Development* 11, no. 1 (2020): 118–38; see also Priyasha Saksena, "Building the Nation: Sovereignty and International Law in the Decolonisation of South Asia," *Journal of the History of International Law* 23, no. 1 (2020): 52–79.

39. Adom Getachew, *Worldmaking after Empire: The Rise and Fall of Self-Determination* (Princeton, NJ: Princeton University Press, 2019).

40. See, for example, Usha Mahajani, *The Role of Indian Minorities in Burma and Malaya* (Westport, CT: Greenwood Press, 1960); N. R. Chakravarthi, *The Indian Minority in Burma: The Rise and Decline of an Immigrant Community* (London: Oxford University Press, 1971). See also, in this vein, Taylor Sherman and Raphaëlle Khan, "India and Overseas Indians in Ceylon and Burma, 1946–1965: Experiments in Post-imperial Sovereignty," *Modern Asian Studies* 56, no. 4 (2022): 1153–82.

41. Sugata Bose, *A Hundred Horizons: The Indian Ocean in the Age of Global Empire* (Cambridge, MA: Harvard University Press, 2006); Thomas Metcalf, *Imperial Connections: India in the Indian Ocean Arena, 1860–1920* (Berkeley: University of California Press, 2007); Aiyar, *Indians in Kenya*.

42. Susan Bayly, "Imagining Greater India: French and Indian Visions of Colonialism in the Indic Mode," *Modern Asian Studies* 38, no. 3 (2004): 703–44; Carolien Stolte and Harald Fischer-Tine, "Imagining Asia in India: Nationalism and Internationalism (ca. 1905–40)," *Comparative Studies in Society and History* 54, no. 1 (2012): 65–92.

43. Kalyani Ramnath, "Intertwined Itineraries: Debt, Decolonization and International Law in Post-WWII South Asia," *Law and History Review* 38 no. 1 (2020): 1–24.

44. Lakshmi Subramanian, "Tamils and Greater India: Some Issues of Connected Histories," *Cultural Dynamics* 24, nos. 2–3 (2012): 159–74.

45. Oliver Godsmark, *Citizenship, Community, and Democracy in India: From Bombay to Maharashtra, c. 1930–1960* (London: Routledge, 2018); Rama Mantena and Karuna Mantena, "Political Imaginaries at the End of Empire," *Ab Imperio* 2018, no. 3 (2018): 31–35; Uttara Shahani, "Language without a Land: Partition, Sindhi Refugees, and the Eighth Schedule of the Indian Constitution," *Asian Affairs* 53, no. 2 (2022): 336–62.

46. Darinee Alagirisamy, "The Self-Respect Movement and Tamil Politics of Belonging in Interwar British Malaya, 1929–1939," *Modern Asian Studies* 50, no. 5 (2016): 1547–75; see also John Solomon, "The Decline of Pan-Indian Identity and the Development of Tamil Cultural Separatism in Singapore 1856–1965," *South Asia: Journal of South Asian Studies* 35, no. 2 (2012): 257–81.

47. Kalyani Ramnath, "Other Partitions: Migrant Geographies, Disconnected Histories between India and Malaya, 1945–1965," forthcoming in *South Asia Unbound: New International Histories of the Subcontinent*, ed. Bérénice Guyot-Réchard and Elisabeth Leake (Leiden: Leiden University Press, 2023).

48. Frederick Cooper, "The Politics of Decolonization in French and British West Africa," in *Oxford Research Encyclopedia of African History*, Oxford University Press Online, January 2018, https://doi.org/10.1093/acrefore/9780190277734.013.111.

49. Pew Research Center, "Key Facts about Recent Trends in Global Migration," *Fact Tank*, December 16, 2022, pewresearch.org/fact-tank/2022/12/16/key-facts-about -recent-trends-in-global-migration.

50. According to the United Nations Department of Economic and Social Affairs data from 2020, 10.9 million out of 13.9 million international migrants from South Asia reside in the region (which includes Afghanistan, Bangladesh, Bhutan, India, Iran, Maldives, Nepal, Pakistan, and Sri Lanka); 7.1 million out of the 10.6 million migrants stay within Southeast Asia. See "Migration Data in South-Eastern Asia," Migration Data Portal, last updated February 15, 2022, www.migrationdataportal.org/regional-data-overview/ south-eastern-asia, and "Migration Data in Southern Asia," Migration Data Portal, last updated June 14, 2021, www.migrationdataportal.org/regional-data-overview/southern -asia. See also Sunil Amrith, *Migration and Diaspora in Modern Asia* (New York: Cambridge University Press, 2012), 16–17 (for reflections on the use of "Asian" migration).

51. Manav Kapur, "India's Citizenship (Amendment) Act," *Statelessness and Citizenship Review* 3, no. 1 (2021): 208–35.

52. Abirami v. Union of India, W.P. No. 12361 of 2022, Madras High Court (stating that the principles of the Citizenship (Amendment) Act may apply to Lankan Tamil refugees); see also Partha S. Ghosh, *Migrants, Refugees, and the Stateless in South Asia* (Thousand Oaks, CA: Sage Publications, 2016), 1–57.

53. Christoph Sperfeldt, "Statelessness in Southeast Asia: Causes and Responses," *Global Citizenship Observatory* (blog), March 9, 2021, globalcit.eu/statelessness-in -southeast-asia-causes-and-responses.

54. See the contributions to *Asian Affairs'* special issue on citizenship, belonging, and the Partition by Antara Datta ("Bordering Assam through Affective Closure: 1971 and the Road to the Citizenship Amendment Act of 2019") and Uttara Shahani ("Language without a Land"), and the introduction by Neeti Nair, providing a historical perspective on the amendments to the Indian Citizenship Act in 2019: Neeti Nair, "Introduction to Special Issue: Citizenship, Belonging, and the Partition of India," *Asian Affairs* 53, no. 2 (2022): 293–97. See also Anupama Roy, *Citizenship, Law, and Belonging: The CAA and the NRC* (Oxford: Oxford University Press, 2022).

Chapter 1

1. For comprehensive accounts of the Second World War in India, see Yasmin Khan, *India at War: The Subcontinent and the Second World War* (New York: Oxford University Press, 2015); Srinath Raghavan, *India's War: The Making of Modern South Asia, 1939–1945* (London: Penguin, 2016). Other useful resources include U Hla Pe, *Narrative of the Japanese Occupation of Burma*, recorded by U Khin, foreword by Hugh Tinker (Ithaca, NY: Southeast Asia Program, Dept. of Far Eastern Studies, Cornell University, 1961), and Theippan Maung Wa and U Sein Tin, *Wartime in Burma: A Diary, January to June 1942* (Athens: Ohio University Press, 2009).

2. Indivar Kamtekar, "The Shiver of 1942," *Studies in History* 18, no. 1 (2002): 187–221.

3. Bisheshwar Prasad, *Post-war Occupation Forces: Japan and South-East Asia*, vol. 7 of *Official History of the Indian Armed Forces in the Second World War*, ed. B. L. Raina (Delhi: Combined Inter-Services Historical Section, India and Pakistan, 1958) (for military-related sources on the war).

4. Christopher Bayly and Tim Harper, *Forgotten Armies: The Fall of British Asia, 1941–1945* (Cambridge, MA: Harvard University Press, 2006).

5. A. Hydari, "War and Indian Newspapers: Their Duty, Sir A. Hydari's Speech at the Editors' Conference," *Amrita Bazaar Patrika*, December 19, 1941, in *Towards Freedom: Documents on the Movement for Independence in India, 1941*, ed. Amit K. Gupta and Arjun Dev (New Delhi: Oxford University Press), 164.

6. Bérénice Guyot-Réchard, "When Legions Thunder Past: The Second World War and India's Northeastern Frontier," *War in History* 25, no. 3 (2018): 328–60.

7. Joyce Lebra, *The Indian National Army and Japan* (Singapore: Institute of Southeast Asian Studies, 2008); Sugata Bose, *His Majesty's Opponent: Subash Chandra Bose and India's Struggle against Empire* (Cambridge, MA: Harvard University Press, 2011).

8. John Solomon, *A Subaltern History of the Indian Diaspora in Singapore: The Gradual Disappearance of Untouchability, 1872–1965* (London: Routledge, 2016).

9. Ramesh Benegal, *Burma to Japan with Azad Hind: A War Memoir, 1941–1945* (Olympia Fields, IL: Lancer, 2009).

10. David Rudner, *Caste and Capitalism in Colonial India: The Nattukottai Chettiars* (Berkeley: University of California Press, 1994). For comparisons, see Sana Aiyar, *Indians in Kenya: The Politics of Diaspora* (Cambridge, MA: Harvard University Press, 2015), Fahad Bishara, *A Sea of Debt: Law and Economic Life in the Western Indian Ocean, 1780–1950* (Cambridge: Cambridge University Press (2017), and contributions to Edward A. Alpers and Chhaya Goswami, eds., *Transregional Trade and Traders: Situating Gujarat in the Indian Ocean from Early Times to 1900* (Oxford: Oxford University Press, 2019).

11. Parma Nāttukkottai Chettiārkal Cankam, *Yuthakala Parma* (Chennai, 1945), RMRL.

12. FNR, first half of February 1942, Madras Administrative Reports, TNSA.

13. Bertie Reginald Pearn, *The Indian in Burma* (Ledbury, Herefordshire: Le Play House Press, 1946), 33.

14. Yvonne Vaz Ezdani, *New Songs of the Survivors: The Exodus of Indians from Burma* (New Delhi: Speaking Tiger, 2015). Other oral history collections that contain accounts of the "long march" are hosted at the Imperial War Museum Collections, the Center for South Asian Studies at the University of Cambridge, and the BBC WW2 People's War Archive.

15. Hugh Tinker, "A Forgotten Long March: The Indian Exodus from Burma, 1942," *Journal of Southeast Asian Studies* 6, no. 1 (1975): 1–15.

16. Debendra Nath Acharya and Amit R. Baishya, *Jangam: A Forgotten Exodus in Which Thousands Died* (New Delhi: Vitasta, 2018).

17. Ketaki Pant, "Gujarat's "Rangoon Wallas," *Himal*, June 26, 2014, https://www.himalmag.com/gujarats-rangoon-wallas/; Sifra Lenin, "Bombay Burma Links Run Deep," Gateway House, October 13, 2016, https://www.gatewayhouse.in/bombay-burma-link-runs-deep; Amitav Ghosh, "Exodus from Burma, 1941," *Amitav Ghosh Blog*, June 21, 2011, http://amitavghosh.com/blog/?p=432.

18. *Indian Annual Register*, January 31, 1942, 39.

19. S. Devas, *The Future of Burma* (n.p.: n.p., 1947), RMRL.

20. A list transcribed and published by the Anglo-Burmese Library, "Evacuee List, Burma 1942: The Trek Out of Burma," 2009, is available online at http://www.anglobur

meselibrary.com/lists.html and is also available at the British Library, APAC/M/3/821. See also Michael D. Leigh, *The Evacuation of Civilians from Burma: Analysing the 1942 Colonial Disaster* (London: Bloomsbury, 2014), for a list compiled from the Evacuation Registers available at the National Archives of India, which records only about twenty-five thousand out of the estimated five hundred thousand people who escaped from Burma.

21. *Civil and Military Gazette*, February 3, 1942, Service Newspapers of World War Two Database, www.servicenewspapers.amdigital.co.uk.

22. *Indian Annual Register*, January 31, 1942, 39.

23. *Ceylon Observer*, February 22, 1942, Times Collection, NASL.

24. *Madras War Review*, April 24, 1942, 10; *Ceylon Daily News*, April 8, 1942, Times Collection, NASL.

25. "Ceylon War Council," *Press and Journal*, March 25, 1942, Service Newspapers of World War Two Database, www.servicenewspapers.amdigital.co.uk.

26. "Duty of Colombo's Citizens," *Ceylon Daily News*, April 8, 1942, Times Collection, NASL.

27. *Civil and Military Gazette*, April 7, 1942, Service Newspapers of World War Two Database, www.servicenewspapers.amdigital.co.uk.

28. Before issuing tickets to travel back to India, the government required confirmation that refugees would be able to repay the fare—an impossible burden for many who had fled Burma without any money or belongings. Leigh, *Evacuation of Civilians*, 70.

29. "Passenger Rush to India," *Ceylon Daily News*, April 7, 1942, Times Collection, NASL; "Night Mail Suspended," *Ceylon Daily News*, April 8, 1942, Times Collection, NASL; "More Trains Cancelled," *Ceylon Daily News*, April 11, 1942, Times Collection, NASL.

30. FNR, second half of April 1942, TNSA.

31. G.O. No. 4468, December 5, 1942, Proceedings of the Public Works Department, TNSA.

32. "Runaway Indians: Citizen Rights in Ceylon," *Times of Ceylon*, May 18, 1942, Times Collection, NASL.

33. Patrick Peebles, *The Plantation Tamils of Ceylon* (London: Leicester University Press, 2001).

34. *Times of Ceylon*, May 18, 1942, Times Collection, NASL.

35. Indian Legislative Assembly Debates, September 15, 1942.

36. For archival documents including testimonies in the war crimes trials, see Paul H. Kratoska, *The Thailand-Burma Railway, 1942–1946: Documents and Selected Writings* (London: Routledge, 2006).

37. Paul H. Kratoska, "Labor in the Malay Peninsula and Singapore under Japanese Occupation," in *Asian Labor in the Wartime Japanese Empire*, ed. Paul H. Kratoska (Armonk, NY: M. E. Sharpe, 2005): 242.

38. Peter Fay, *The Forgotten Army: India's Armed Struggle for Independence, 1942–1945* (Ann Arbor: University of Michigan Press, 1993).

39. See Natasha Pairaudeau, *Mobile Citizens: French Indians in Indochina, 1858–1954* (Copenhagen: NIAS Press, 2016); for overview of Indians in Indonesia, see K. S.

Sandhu and A. Mani, eds., *Indian Communities in Southeast Asia* (Singapore: Institute of Southeast Asian Studies, 2006), 46–150.

40. "Expenditure Incurred in Assam on Non-Indian Evacuees," 1947, FO 371/63422, TNA.

41. FNR, first half of June 1942; "Expenditure Incurred in Assam on Non-Indian Evacuees," FO 371/63422, TNA.

42. *Indian Annual Register*, January 26, 1942, 38.

43. *Indian Annual Register*, January 18, 1942, 36.

44. *Civil and Military Gazette*, April 26, 1942, Service Newspapers of World War Two Database, www.servicenewspapers.amdigital.co.uk.

45. Government of India, European British Evacuees Order of 1942, Section 2; Government of India, Asiatic British Evacuees (Census) Order of 1943, Section 2.

46. *Civil and Military Gazette*, June 21, 1942, Service Newspapers of World War Two Database, www.servicenewspapers.amdigital.co.uk.

47. FNR, first half of January 1944, TNSA; FNR, first half of July 1943, TNSA.

48. See Proceedings of the Public Works Department, 1943 and 1944, TNSA.

49. Anand Pandian and M. P. Mariappan, *Ayya's Accounts: A Ledger of Hope in Modern India* (Bloomington: Indiana University Press, 2014).

50. FNR, first half of June 1942, TNSA.

51. Bayly and Harper, *Forgotten Armies*.

52. Maitrii Aung-Thwin, *The Return of the Galon King: History, Law, and Rebellion in Colonial Burma* (Singapore: NUS Press, 2011).

53. Report of a Commission on Immigration into Ceylon by Sir Edward St. J. Jackson, April 1938, Ceylon Sessional Papers III of 1938, NASL.

54. James Baxter, *Report on Indian Immigration* (Rangoon: Superintendent Government Printing and Stationery, 1941).

55. On Sastri, see Vineet Thakur, *India's First Diplomat: V. S. Srinivasa Sastri and the Making of Liberal Internationalism* (Bristol: Bristol University Press, 2021).

56. For background, see Maung Maung, *Burmese Nationalist Movements, 1940–1948* (Honolulu: University of Hawai'i Press, 1989).

57. Agent of the Government of India in Ceylon to M. S. Aney, No. 9/41, January 26, 1941, M. S. Aney Papers, NMML.

58. Usha Mahajani, *The Role of Indians in Burma and Malaya* (Westport, CT: Greenwood Press, 1960), 173.

59. Jeremy Yellen, *The Greater East Asia Co-Prosperity Sphere: When Total Empire Met Total War* (Ithaca, NY: Cornell University Press, 2019).

60. Kavalam Madhava Panikkar, *The Future of India and South-East Asia* (London: Allied Publishers, 1945).

61. Harshan Kumarasingham, "The 'Tropical Dominions': The Appeal of Dominion Status in the Decolonisation of India, Pakistan, and Ceylon," *Transactions of the Royal Historical Society*, 6th ser., 23 (December 2013): 223–45

62. Christopher Bayly and Timothy Harper, *Forgotten Wars: Freedom and Revolution in Southeast Asia* (Cambridge, MA: Harvard University Press, 2007).

63. G.O. No. 1477, Proceedings of the Public Works Department (1947), TNSA.

64. G.O. No. 2319, Proceedings of the Public Works Department (1947), TNSA.

65. G.O. No. 2319, Proceedings of the Public Works Department (1947), TNSA.

66. Joint Memorandum submitted to the Government of Burma (Simla) by the Burma Muslim Evacuees Association, Calcutta (February 15, 1945), Burma-India Discussions, IOR: M/3/1411.

67. Indian Legislative Assembly Debates, 1946, Parliament of India Digital Library, https://eparlib.nic.in/handle/123456789/760007.

68. "Petition of Trader Pass," AG 1/2, Accession No. 40 (1946), National Archives of Myanmar, Yangon.

69. Copy of Special Branch Officer Report, April 7, 1948, National Archives of Myanmar.

70. Mithi Mukherjee, "The 'Right to Wage War' against Empire: Anticolonialism and the Challenge to International Law in the Indian National Army Trial of 1945," *Law and Social Inquiry* 44, no. 2 (2019): 420–43.

71. For a military history of the Indian Army in French Indochina and Netherlands East Indies, see Daniel Marston, *The Indian Army and the End of the Raj* (Cambridge: Cambridge University Press, 2014), 151–99.

72. Interrogation at the Forward Interrogation Centre and Restriction of Five Persons to Their Villages in Madras, File No. 39/54/45, Home Political (I), NAI.

73. G. V. Panicker, Repatriate from Malaya, File No. 654/46CS, Government of Travancore, Confidential Section, Kerala State Archives, Trivandrum.

74. Restriction of Bhag Singh, M. Sanmoganadan, K. L. Shanmugam, and K. G. Nambiar to Their Villages, File No. 39/69/45, Home Political (I), NAI. For a legislative history of the 1944 Ordinance, which replaced the provisions of the Defence of India Rules struck down by the Federal Court of India in 1943 and 1944, see Laxman Prasad Sharma v. United Provinces Government (1945) ILR 504 (Lucknow ser., vol. 20). See also Promulgation of the Restriction and Detention Ordinance of 1944, to replace Defence of India Rule 26, File No. 44/57/43 Political (I), NAI.

75. Kalyani Ramnath, "Other Partitions: Migrant Geographies, Disconnected Histories between India and Malaya, 1945–1965," forthcoming in *South Asia Unbound: New International Histories of the Subcontinent*, ed. Bérénice Guyot-Réchard and Elisabeth Leake (Leiden: Leiden University Press, 2023).

76. Radha Mohan, "Immigration Policy of Burma in Relation to India," *Indian Journal of Political Science* 16, no. 2 (1955), 170–71.

Chapter 2

1. Seethalakshmi Achi v. V. T. Veerappa Chettiar (1952) 1 MLJ 709.

2. Cases like *Seethalakshmi Achi* were litigated across Burma, Hong Kong, and the Philippines on the question of debts repaid in occupation currency. See, for example, Ko Maung Tin v. U Gon Man (1947) Rang. L. R. 149; U Hoke Wan v. Maung Ba San (1947) Rang. L.R. 398, *International Law Reports* (1947): 235–36 (creditor cannot be forced to accept Japanese currency notes only because the decree was passed during the occupation period); Ko Maung Tin v. U Gon Man (1947) Rang. L.R. 149 (Japanese authorities acted in excess of their powers by issuing a currency); In re Taik v. Ariff Moosagee Dooply (1948) BLR 454 (attempting to discharge a mortgage by depositing Japanese oc-

cupation currency in the City Court of Rangoon after the end of the war); Tse Chung v. Lee Yau Chu (1951) AD Case No. 200 (Hong Kong, transactions in Japanese occupation currency were illegal); but see also Haw Pia v. China Banking Corporation (80 Phil. 604, Philippines, upholding the liquidating of a debt in Japanese occupation currency).

3. "Memorial to the Governor-General from Certain Indian Chettyars in Burma Who Have Been Served with Notice of Eviction from Certain State Lands," IOR: L/PJ/7/1253.

4. Maung Maung, *Burma in the Family of Nations* (Djambatan: Institute of Pacific Relations 1981), 103. Outside of Burma, however, the kyat was worthless, and the Reserve Bank of India had been directed to stop honoring the "Burma note" except under special circumstances; see An Ordinance to Regulate the Payment in British India of the Reserve Bank of India of the Value of Burma Bank Notes (1942).

5. E Maung, "Enemy Legislation and Judgments in Burma," *Journal of Comparative Legislation and International Law* 30, nos. 3–4 (1948): 11–17.

6. Huff and Majima, "Financing Japan's World War II Occupation of Southeast Asia," *Journal of Economic History* 73, no. 4 (2013): 937–77.

7. Huff and Majima, "Financing Japan's World War II Occupation."

8. Frank Moraes, "Indian Community in Malaya: Depressing Condition of Estate Laborers," *Times of India*, December 13, 1945.

9. "Formation of Malayan Union," *Times of India*, November 26, 1945.

10. Marilyn Longmuir, *The Money Trail: Burmese Currencies in Crisis, 1937–1947* (Dekalb: Center for Southeast Asian Studies, Northern Illinois University, 2002), 6, 18.

11. Longmuir, *Money Trail*, 7–8.

12. Paul H. Kratoska, *The Japanese Occupation of Malaya: A Social and Economic History* (Honolulu: University of Hawai'i Press, 1997), 212.

13. Kratoska, *Japanese Occupation of Malaya*, 212.

14. Informal Committee Held in Calcutta to Consider the Currency Arrangements in Burma in the Event of Political Separation from India, "Currency Arrangements in Burma," report, 1933, IOR: M/3/573: 22.

15. Won Zoon Yoon, "Japan's Occupation of Burma, 1941–1945" (PhD diss., New York University, 1971), 187.

16. Longmuir, *Money Trail*, 7.

17. Parma Nattukkottai Chettiarkal Cankam, *Yuttakāla Parma* (Chennai, 1945), RMRL, 26.

18. Parma Nattukkottai Chettiarkal Cankam, *Yuttakāla Parma*. Chettiar donations are also mentioned in the *Syonan Shinbun*, the newspaper of the occupying forces. See "Chettiars to Donate $100,000 To Red Cross," April 29, 1943.

19. Sivachandralingam Sundara Raja and Umadevi Suppiah, *The Chettiar Role in Malaysia's Economic History* (Kuala Lumpur: University of Malaya Press, 2016), 119–29. See also Salma Khoo Nasution, review of Raja and Suppiah, *The Chettiar Role in Malaysia's Economic History*, by Sivachandralingam Sundara Raja and Umadevi Suppiah, *Journal of the Malaysian Branch of the Royal Asiatic Society* 91 (2018): 159–61 (highlighting the need for a legal history of Chettiar moneylending practices).

20. Kratoska, *Japanese Occupation of Malaya*, 325–26.

21. Tun Wai, *Burma's Currency and Credit* (New Delhi: Orient Longmans, 1962), 144.

22. Hugh Tinker, *The Union of Burma: A Study of the First Years of Independence* (New York: Oxford University Press, 1957).

23. "Japanese Occupation Currency in Burma," 1945, FO 371/46421, TNA.

24. Accrual of Interest (Wartime Adjustment) Act of 1947. Similar legislation was also passed in Malaya, though there a distinction was made between pre-occupation and occupation-era debt. See S. K. Das, *Japanese Occupation and Ex Post Facto Legislation in Malaya* (n.p.: Malayan Law Journal, 1960).

25. See, e.g., Ooi Phee Cheng v. Kok Yoon San, Executor of the Estate of Lee Tuck Onn (1950) *Malayan Law Reports* 118 (High Court, Federation of Malaya); Tan Khiam Wah v. Chong Fong Shen and Lee Sau Heng (1950) *Malayan Law Reports* 141 (High Court, Federation of Malaya).

26. Wai, *Burma's Currency and Credit*, 144.

27. Tinker, *Union of Burma*, 95, 245.

28. Some of the legislation includes the Moneylenders Act of 1945, the Liabilities (Wartime Adjustment) Act of 1945, the Agricultural Debts Moratorium Act of 1947, the Burma Agriculturists Debt Relief Act of 1947, and the Transfer of Immoveable Property (Restriction) Act of 1947.

29. Wai, *Burma's Currency and Credit*, 41.

30. Wai, *Burma's Currency and Credit*, 48.

31. W. S. Desai, *India and Burma: A Study* (Bombay: Orient Longmans, 1952), 35.

32. James Baxter, *Report on Indian Immigration* (Rangoon: Superintendent Government Printing and Stationery), 44.

33. "Separation Agitation in Burma: Indian Visitor's Impressions," *Times of India*, June 29, 1932.

34. "Rights of Chettiars in Separated Burma: Success of Deputation to England," *Times of India*, May 18, 1935, 15.

35. "Rajah of Chettinad Returns to India," *Times of India*, June 4, 1935, 3; "British Government Thanked: Chettiar Community Holds Conference," *Times of India*, July 6, 1935, 19.

36. Krishnaswami Nagarajan, *Dr. Rajah Sir Muthiah Chettiar: A Biography* (Annamalainagar: Annamalai University, 1989), 109.

37. S. Muthiah, *Looking Back from "Moulmein": A Biography of A. M. M. Arunachalam* (Chennai: EastWest Books, 2000).

38. But see Medha Kudaisya, "Marwari and Chettiar Merchants, c. 1850s–1950s: Comparative Trajectories," in *Chinese and Indian Business: Historical Antecedents*, ed. Medha M. Kudaisya and Chin-Keong Ng (Leiden: Brill, 2010), 85–119, 86 (arguing that following the end of the war, Chettiars, in contrast to Marwaris, "laps[ed] into economic oblivion"). But as Kudaisya herself notes, there were significant investments made in industries in South India, which remained the center of their activities. S. Muthiah also notes that after the war, Chettiars made a concerted effort to invest in education and educational institutions, which, in their understanding, would provide alternate routes to employment and would hedge risks in the case of financial disasters on the scale that the Chettiars suffered in Southeast Asia. S. Muthiah, interview by author, August 2015. This is borne out by the establishment of the Annamalai University by Raja Sir Annamalai Chettiar, as well as the many other educational institutions that bear the

Chettiar name. See Bijayeti Venkata Narayanaswami Naidu, ed., *Raja Sir Annamalai Chettiar Commemoration Volume* ([Annamalainagar?]: Annamalai University, 1941).

39. V. Swaminatha Sharma, *Pirikkapatta Parma* (n.p.: n.p., 1936), RMRL.

40. S. Devas, *The Future of Burma* (n.p.: n.p., 1947), 253, RMRL.

41. Usha Mahajani, *The Role of Indian Minorities in Burma and Malaya* (Westport, CT: Greenwood Press, 1960), 188.

42. Economic historians, including Sean Turnell and Michael Adas, in a bid to dismantle the stereotype of the "rapacious" Indian moneylender, a fixture of South Asian agrarian histories, have employed archival methods to look at whether interest rates that they charged were excessive. They conclude in the negative. Sean Turnell, *Fiery Dragons: Banks, Moneylenders and Microfinance in Burma* (Copenhagen: NIAS Press, 2009); Michael Adas, *The Burma Delta: Economic Development and Social Change on an Asian Rice Frontier, 1852–1941* (Madison: University of Wisconsin Press, 2011).

43. Indian Income Tax (Amendment) Act of 1933, Section 2.

44. Commissioner of Income Tax to G. G. Sim, member, Board of Inland Revenue, Delhi, December 12, 1922, File No. 205 (1923), Board of Inland Revenue, NAI.

45. John Leroy Christian, *Burma and the Japanese Invader* (Bombay: Thacker, 1945), 257.

46. Mahajani, *Role of Indian Minorities*, 181.

47. For details, see Tan Tai Yong, *Creating "Greater Malaysia": Decolonization and the Politics of Merger* (Singapore: Institute of Southeast Asian Studies, 2008).

48. Paul H. Kratoska, "Chettiar Moneylenders and Rural Credit in British Malaya," *Journal of the Malaysian Branch of the Royal Asiatic Society* 86, no. 1 (2013): 61–78.

49. For a comparison of Chettiar moneylending practices in Ceylon and their engagements with the law, see W. S. Weerasooria and William Tenekoon, *The Nattukottai Chettiar Merchant Bankers in Ceylon* (Dehiwala: Tisara Prakasakayo, 1973).

50. Sinnappah Arasaratnam, *Indians in Malaysia and Singapore* (London: Institute of Race Relations, 1970), 96.

51. Paul H. Kratoska, "Banana Money: Consequences of the Demonetization of Wartime Japanese Currency in British Malaya," *Journal of Southeast Asian Studies* 23, no. 2 (1992): 341.

52. Manasseh Film Co. v. Gemini Pictures Circuit (1944) 1 MLJ 58.

53. Das, *Japanese Occupation*, xc, 60.

54. Based on the model Debtor and Creditor (Occupation Period) Ordinance for Britain's Far Eastern colonies supplied to Hong Kong, Malaya, Singapore, Sarawak, North Borneo, CO 537/1375, TNA, as cited in Kratoska, "Banana Money," 322–45, 334.

55. "'Banana' Payment of Debts Valid," *Singapore Free Press*, September 2, 1948, 1, NAS; Kratoska, *Japanese Occupation of Malaya*, 333. For Hong Kong, see Debtor and Creditor (Occupation Period) Ordinance of 1948.

56. "Bananas Are 'Ripe,'" *Singapore Free Press*, August 24, 1948, 1, NAS.

57. "Postal Savings," *Malaya Tribune*, March 26, 1947, 4, NAS.

58. "The Law and You," *Straits Times*, December 16, 1951, 10, NAS.

59. Raja and Suppiah, *Chettiar Role*, 126.

60. See Mahajani, *Role of Indian Minorities*, 99–101, for a discussion of Chettiar land ownership in Malaya, which was nowhere near the scale that it was in Burma.

61. "Local Moneylending Test Case," *Morning Tribune*, January 19, 1938.

62. Memorandum of R. Ramani, January 8, 1947, Report of the Consultative Committee on the Constitutional Proposals, March 21, 1947, as cited in Arasaratnam, *Indians in Malaysia and Singapore*, 116.

63. Malaya, "Demonetisation of Japanese Military Currency, Representation from the Chettiars," File No. 75-9 / 460 S (II) / M-M (1946), NAI. Braddell and Ramani had previously represented Chettiars in Malaya in test cases to do with the Moneylending Ordinances. Suppiah also notes that Alladi Krishnaswami Aiyar, Tej Bahadur Sapru, and C. K. Dapthary, preeminent lawyers of their time in India, were also involved in attempts to salvage Chettiar wealth in Malaya. See Raja and Suppiah, *Chettiar Role*, 121.

64. Malaya, "Demonetization of Japanese Military Currency."

65. Rajah Sir Annamalai Chettiar to M. S. Aney, January 4, 1942, Correspondence, M. S. Aney Papers, NMML.

66. M. S. Aney to Rajah Sir Annamalai Chettiar, January 8, 1942, Correspondence, M. S. Aney Papers, NMML.

67. See, for example, Ajodhya Singh v. Godavari Bhai (1949) BLR (detailing how claims for remuneration for services rendered were filed by those left in charge of evacuee properties); K. E. M. Abdul Majid v. M. A. Madar (1949) BLR 577 (tenancy cannot continue after reoccupation if judgment debtors were in India during the war).

Chapter 3

1. Usha Mahajani, *The Role of Indian Minorities in Burma and Malaya* (Westport, CT: Greenwood Press, 1960), 182.

2. Yasmin Khan, *India at War: The Subcontinent and the Second World War* (New York: Oxford University Press, 2015), 80–92.

3. Janet Roitman, *Fiscal Disobedience: An Anthropology of Economic Regulation in Central Africa* (Princeton, NJ: Princeton University Press, 2005); for a legal history of the American "fiscal state," see Ajay K. Mehrotra, *Making the Modern American Fiscal State: Law, Politics, and the Rise of Progressive Taxation, 1877–1929* (Cambridge: Cambridge University Press, 2013).

4. By some accounts, in 1922, a Model Ordinance for the Administration of Income Tax was written up in London on the basis of Australian and New Zealand precedents and was used across the British Empire except for India, which was not governed by the Colonial Office. However, it was evident, in the cases that came up before various High Courts, that income tax law was influenced heavily by British practice. However, in the same year, the Indian Income Tax Act came into force, applying to British India, which included at the time both India and Burma. Several changes came in with the 1922 Act, but the most prominent changes were to the legal infrastructure that administered taxation: the setting up of the Central Board of Revenue for the administration of income tax (see Chapter II-A, Appellate Tribunal (Indian Income Tax Act of 1922).

5. See, for example, "One has to see what the course is of dealing and though the business is labelled as money lending business, if, as a matter of fact, the profits were generally got by taking lands in satisfaction of debts due and selling them for profits later on, such profits must, no doubt, be considered as derived from such business and cannot escape taxation by saying that the profits have nothing to do with the business of the

firm which was merely money lending. The finding of the Income Tax Authorities is that the profits represented the profits of the business and are not as was contended, accretions of the capital. Further this case is analogous to that of a pawn broker who lends out moneys on articles received as pledges which he sells in satisfaction of the amount due to him and realises profits. It cannot be said that the profits realised from such sales do not amount to profits derived in the course of the business." S. L. S. Chettiappa Chettiar v. Commissioner of Income Tax AIR 1930, Mad 119.

6. The Indian Income Tax Act of 1922 contained legal definitions of "income" and "residence" but did not contain the rates at which income tax was to be charged. This was to be done through annual Finance Acts.

7. Steven A. Bank, Kirk J. Stark, and Joseph J. Thorndike, *War and Taxes* (Washington, DC: Urban Institute Press, 2008).

8. Ritu Birla, *Stages of Capital: Law, Culture, and Market Governance in Late Colonial India* (Durham, NC: Duke University Press, 2008), 53–60.

9. Birla, *Stages of Capital*, 53.

10. G. L. Pophale, *A Quarter Century of Direct Taxation in India, 1939–1964* (Bombay: IMC Economic Research and Training Foundation, Sir Purshotamdas Thakurdas Research Wing, 1965), 9.

11. Indian Income Tax Act of 1918, Section 3(1). Even if one were a nonresident, a term that was not defined in the 1918 Act but was to be inferred to mean residing out of British India, a "substantial business connection" would subject a nonresident's agent or partner to income tax, as though he was himself a resident.

12. J. B. Vachha, C. W. Ayers, and S. P. Chambers, *Income Tax Enquiry Report, 1936, Submitted to the Government of India as a Result of the Investigation of the Indian Income-Tax System* (Delhi: Government of India, 1937), 57–64. See BIR File No. 73 of 1923, Board of Inland Revenue, NAI (for a discussion of attempts to divide up the income tax assessments of Nattukottai Chettiars trading in Pegu and Burma).

13. David Rudner, *Caste and Capitalism in Colonial India: The Nattukottai Chettiars* (Berkeley: University of California Press, 1994), 89–103.

14. "Novel Income Tax Case: Insurance Company Assessed by Indian State," *Times of India*, May 28, 1935.

15. S. Muthiah et al., *The Chettiar Heritage* (Chennai: Chettiar Heritage, 2002).

16. "Question of Nattukottai Chettiars Trading in Pegu and Madras," BIR File No. 73 of 1923, Board of Inland Revenue, NAI.

17. S. L. S. Chettiappa Chettiar v. Commissioner of Income Tax AIR 1930 Mad 119.

18. Copy of the reference to the Registrar, High Court of Judicature, Madras No. ITA 316 and STA 64/21–22, dated October 16, 1922; Case under IT Act of 1918 by the Secretary, Board of Revenue, Land Revenue and Settlement (IT); File No. 205 (1923), Board of Inland Revenue, NAI.

19. Marina Martin, "Hundi/Hawala: The Problem of Definition," *Modern Asian Studies* 43, no. 4 (2009): 909–37. See also Fahad Bishara and Hollian Wint, "Into the Bazaar: Indian Ocean Vernaculars in the Age of Global Capitalism," *Journal of Global History* 16, no. 1 (2021): 44–64.

20. Rudner, *Caste and Capitalism*, 92–94.

21. *Madras Provincial Banking Enquiry Committee Reports* (1930), oral evidence, 4:247,

https://southasiacommons.net/artifacts/2340738/the-madras-provincial-banking-en quiry-committee/3125350/.

22. Testimony of T. A. R. C. T. Arunachalam Chettiar, January 28, 1930, *Madras Provincial Banking Enquiry Committee Reports*, 4:260.

23. Oral evidence of A. Savarinatha Pillai, January 31, 1930, *Madras Provincial Banking Enquiry Committee Reports*, 4:337.

24. Hizkiel Pershad, *Indian Taxation during and after World War II* (Bombay: Allied Publishers, 1964), 13.

25. This was a break from the English Act, where the source of income was the basis of income taxation. Pophale, *Quarter Century of Direct Taxation*, 52.

26. "The Burma Indian Delegation," *Times of India*, November 17, 1938, 13.

27. Pophale, *Quarter Century of Direct Taxation*, 52.

28. For an exception, see W. S. Weerasooria and William Tenekoon, *The Nattukottai Chettiar Merchant Bankers in Ceylon* (Dehiwala: Tisara Prakasakayo, 1973).

29. Fahad Bishara, *A Sea of Debt: Law and Economic Life in the Western Indian Ocean, 1780–1950* (Cambridge: Cambridge University Press, 2017).

30. See also Johan Mathew, "On Principals and Agency: Reassembling Trust in Indian Ocean Commerce," *Comparative Studies in Society and History* 61, no. 2 (2019): 242–68 (showing that law is not constitutive but one of many factors that support the assemblage of long-distance trade).

31. Mitra Sharafi, *Law and Identity in Colonial South Asia: Parsi Legal Culture, 1772–1947* (Cambridge: Cambridge University Press, 2014).

32. Mawani and Hussin, "The Travels of Law: Indian Ocean Itineraries," *Law and History Review* 32, no. 4 (November 2014): 733–47.

33. Birla, *Stages of Capital*, 199–231.

34. Rachel Sturman, *The Government of Social Life in Colonial India: Liberalism, Religious Law, and Women's Rights* (Cambridge: Cambridge University Press, 2012).

35. Eleanor Newbigin, *The Hindu Family and the Emergence of Modern India: Law, Citizenship and Community* (Cambridge: Cambridge University Press, 2013).

36. By 1929–30, there was only one private bank—the Bank of Chettinad—promoted by Raja Annamalai Chettiar, which was incorporated as a limited company. *Madras Provincial Banking Enquiry Committee Reports*, 1930, 1:30. Other Chettiar firms constituted themselves as Hindu Undivided Families (HUF) to claim tax benefits, which also posed a problem in terms of legally determining "residence." An HUF consisted of a *karta* (manager) and their kin and descendants that shared a home and a common income and was a common legal arrangement among trading communities like Chettiars. Only the HUF could be taxed, and not the individual members. Although the unregistered firm was also taxed as an entity, the difference was that the profits accruing to each partner of the unregistered firm were included in their total income for determining the tax rate for the other income. So although both an HUF and an unregistered firm were treated as separate legal entities for the purposes of income tax, there were benefits to being constituted as an HUF or as a registered firm. M. Subbaraya Aiyar, "Hindu Undivided Family," *Lawyer* 1, no. 4 (July 1956): 41.

37. Birla, *Stages of Capital*.

38. Indian Income Tax Act of 1922, Section 26.

39. Indian Income Tax Act of 1918, Section 34. For a definition of a collector, see Indian Income Tax Act of 1918, Section 2(5). The principal place of business would be declared by the government. Indian Income Tax Act of 1918, Section 47.

40. V. Rajagopala Aiyar, *The Indian Income Tax Act, 1922*, 2nd ed. (Mylapore: Madras Law Journal, 1935), 630–31 (for a discussion of the initial legal position on Hindu Undivided Family and income tax); Ramesh Sharma, ed., *Tax Circulars and Press Notes, Containing Circulars and Press Notes Issued by the Central Board of Revenue and the Ministry of Finance on Income Tax* (Delhi: Practical Tax Publishers, 1960), 19–20 (including the circular issued by the Central Board of Revenue in 1951, following the decision in Commissioner of Income Tax v. Erin Estate (1951) 2 MLJ 577, noting the tax residence of a Hindu Undivided Family C. No. 54 (6) [IT/50], February 20, 1951).

41. Pierre-Yves Trouillet, "Overseas Temples and Tamil Migratory Space," *South Asia Multidisciplinary Academic Journal* (2012): 6.

42. In re S. Rm. Ar. Ramanathan Chettiar, Case Referred No. 4 of 1919 (Madras High Court Record Room).

43. K. Bashyam, "S. Srinivasa Ayyangar as I Knew Him," *Lawyer* (1955): 71.

44. Suresh Balakrishnan, *Famous Judges and Lawyers of Madras* (Chennai: C. Sitaraman, 2012), 373.

45. Balakrishnan, *Famous Judges and Lawyers*, 375.

46. Pophale, *Quarter Century of Direct Taxation*, 30, for distinctions between the popular and judicial understanding of "income."

47. "Rehabilitation of Burma: Government's Financial Difficulties," *Times of India*, November 21, 1945.

48. Anandagopal Banerjee, *Income-Tax Law and Practice in India* (Calcutta: India International, 1946), 122.

49. Mahajani, *Role of Indian Minorities*, 175.

50. J. Andrus Russell, introduction to *An Introduction to the Political Economy of Burma*, by J. S. Furnivall (Rangoon: Peoples' Literature Committee, 1957), 2.

51. S. Sridevi, "Local Banking and Material Culture amongst the Nattukottai Chettiars of Tamil Nadu" (PhD diss., Jawaharlal Nehru University, 2004).

52. "Subsidy for Every Extra Acre of Paddy," *New Times of Burma*, n.d., Burma Currency Arrangements, IOR: M/3/573.

53. "Tax on Incomes in the Far East: Agreement Reached," *Times of India*, March 24, 1942; "Income Tax Relief for Refugees: Concessions Announced," *Times of India*, March 28, 1942.

54. Bertie Reginald Pearn, *The Indian in Burma* (Ledbury, Herefordshire: Le Play House Press, 1946), 36.

55. "Burma India Discussions," IOR: M/3/1411.

56. File 45 (44) 17 / 46, Central Board of Revenue, NAI.

57. Commissioner of Income Tax v. Shanmugham Rubber Estate Kuala Lumpur AIR 1945 Mad 366; (1945) 2 MLJ 93.

58. Commissioner of Income Tax v. V. V. R. N. M. Subbiah Chettiar (1947) 2 MLJ 474.

59. Commissioner of Income Tax v. Erin Estate, Galah, Ceylon (1951) 2 MLJ 577; Erin Estate, Galah, Ceylon v. Commissioner of Income Tax, Madras AIR 1958 SC 779.

60. "1942–'47 Income Tax Assessments Held Up: Malaya and Burma Indians," *Indian Daily Mail*, January 4, 1947, NLB.

61. "How Can We Pay, Asks Chettiar?," *Malaya Tribune*, August 22, 1947, NAS.

62. "Taxation of Hindu Merchants in Malaya," *Indian Daily Mail*, March 16, 1950, NLB.

63. "Objects to New Tax Proposal," *Singapore Standard*, September 27, 1950, NAS.

64. *Indian Daily Mail*, January 31, 1947, NLB.

65. B/E 345/46, Reconstruction: Agricultural Credit, IOR/M/4/453.

66. G. R. Seton, Imperial Bank of India (Rangoon), to Mr. Morehouse, Imperial Bank of India (Calcutta), February 27, 1946, Burma Currency Arrangements, IOR: M/3/573.

67. Nattukottai Chettiarkal Cankam, Burma, *Irupaththi Ondram Andu Arikai* (Rangoon: Nattukottai Chettiarkal Cankam, 1951–52), 16 (University of Wisconsin-Madison Library).

68. *Report of the Income Tax Investigation Commission* (New Delhi: Government of India, 1949), 16.

69. "1942–47 Income Tax Assessment Held Up: Malaya and Burma Indians," *Indian Daily Mail*, January 4, 1947, NLB.

70. Pophale, *Quarter Century of Direct Taxation*, 65–66.

71. "Money to Return from Abroad," *Times of India*, November 15, 1949.

72. K. V. Al. M. Ramanathan Chettiar v. Commissioner of Income-Tax (1969) AIR 1973 SC 2172.The Indian Bank was an intervener in this case. Cases involving war damage lasted well into the 1970s, when the Supreme Court of India noted that damages to the stock in trade of a moneylending business in Malaya during were to be treated as incidental to business.

73. Michael D. Leigh, *The Evacuation of Civilians from Burma: Analysing the 1942 Colonial Disaster* (London: Bloomsbury, 2014), 74.

74. Minutes of the Twelfth Meeting, Burma India Discussions (February 17, 1944), IOR: M/3/1411.

75. "Exodus of Indian Capital from Malaya?," *Indian Daily Mail*, July 16, 1951, NLB.

76. Pershad, *Indian Taxation*; Paul H. Kratoska, "Chettiar Moneylenders and Rural Credit in British Malaya," *Journal of the Malaysian Branch of the Royal Asiatic Society* 86, no. 1 (2013): 61–78.

77. Kumar Jagdish Chandra Sinha v. Commissioner of Income Tax AIR 1956 Cal 48; M. Ct. M. Chidambaram Chettiar v. Commissioner of Income Tax AIR 1966 SC 1453.

Chapter 4

1. The details of Muthiah's life are drawn from his citizenship application to the commissioner for the registration for Indian and Pakistani residents and from the papers relating to his Supreme Court of Ceylon appeal from the decision of the commissioner. Application No. N-1946, Files of the Department of Emigration and Immigration, NASL.

2. See, for example, Robert N. Kearney, "The Partisan Involvement of Trade Unions in Ceylon," *Asian Survey* 8 (1968): 576–88.

3. Report of Commissioner for Indian and Pakistani Residents, *Ceylon Administration Reports* (1952).

4. There are rare instances where the investigating officers and deputy commissioners admit this. For example, in twenty-eight-year-old Ramaswamy Periannanan's application, the investigating officer wrote to the deputy commissioner, in a candid admission: "The application referred to could not be traced in time as all applications were in a disorganized state. This was [?] due to the pressure of work I could not afford to devote much time in tracing out this particular application among 3000 applications, and it was overlooked. Under the circumstances, pp [word unclear] could not be submitted in time. Delay is very much regretted." Periannan's inquiry was finally held in May 1957, six years after he first filed the application. During this time, he had married and had children (this also probably entailed much more paperwork, for amending the application). And even after the commission acknowledged its delays and oversights, Periannan's application was rejected. Application No. K-7312, K/267, Department of Emigration and Immigration, NASL.

5. Sujit Sivasundaram, *Islanded: Britain, Sri Lanka, and the Bounds of an Indian Ocean Colony* (Chicago: University of Chicago Press, 2013); Sujit Sivasundaram, "Ethnicity, Indigeneity, and Migration in the Advent of British Rule to Sri Lanka," *American Historical Review* 115, no. 2 (2010): 428–52.

6. Some scholars claim that toward the end of the century, coffee was replaced by tea, and the latter demanded more care and attention. Many of the laborers who had gone back and forth began to "settle" on the island on a semipermanent basis. Peebles disputes this understanding, saying that a plantation economy could not in any case be created without a settled population. Patrick Peebles, *The Plantation Tamils of Ceylon* (London: Leicester University Press, 2001), 82.

7. Peebles suggests that there was every reason to believe that the kangany system produced a "new kind of slave." Peebles, *Plantation Tamils*, 53. Even as late as 1937, newspapers reported that kanganies kept the laborers in a cycle of debt so as to keep them on the estates, detaining family members and withholding discharge tickets until they repaid loans. "Indian Labour in Ceylon: Scope Restricted," *Times of India*, October 21, 1937.

8. Eric Meyer, "Aspects of the Sinhalese-Tamil Relations in the Plantation Areas of Sri Lanka under the British Raj," *Indian Economic and Social History Review* 27, no. 2 (1990): 165–88; Roland Wenzlhuemer, "The Sinhalese Contribution to Estate Labour in Ceylon, 1881–1891," *Journal of the Economic and Social History of the Orient* 48, no. 3 (2005): 442–58.

9. Report of a Commission on Immigration into Ceylon, Sessional Paper III of 1938, NASL.

10. Citizenship by registration was common across the British Empire, from Singapore to the Gold Coast.

11. "Malaya-Born Ceylonese Also Up against It! Difficulty in Acquiring Ceylonese Citizenship," *Indian Daily Mail*, July 30, 1951, NLB.

12. Indian and Pakistani Residents (Citizenship) Act of 1949, Section 3(2).

13. Indian and Pakistani Residents (Citizenship) Act of 1949, Section 6.

14. Valli Kanapathipillai, *Citizenship and Statelessness in Sri Lanka: The Case of the Tamil Estate Workers* (London: Anthem Press, 2009). For a discussion of the *jus sanguinis* principle as employed in the colonies, see Christopher Lee, "*Jus Soli* and *Jus Sanguinis* in

the Colonies: The Interwar Politics of Race, Culture, and Multiracial Legal Status in British Africa," *Law and History Review* 29, no. 2 (2011): 497–522. Lee's argument—that British African colonies moved away from the *jus sanguinis* rule with a view to obscuring the racial origins of their nationality laws—gains more traction when considered in the Sri Lankan case. The Senanayake government, unlike in the British African case, seems to have not been concerned about obscuring these origins.

15. Constitution of India, 1950, Article 5–11.

16. Deborah Sutton, "Imagined Sovereignty and the Indian Subject: Partition and Politics beyond the Nation, 1948–1960," *Contemporary South Asia* 19, no. 4 (2011): 409–25.

17. Annual Report for 1976 from Kandy, Ministry of External Affairs, NAI.

18. Nira Wickramasinghe, *Sri Lanka in the Modern Age: A History of Contested Identities* (Honolulu: University of Hawai'i Press, 2006), 47–53, 163–83.

19. A. G. Ranasinha, *Census of Ceylon, 1946* (Colombo: Ceylon Government Press, 1950), 157.

20. Despite the consequences of these racial designations, plantation workers (who were often equated with "Indian Tamil") were insufficiently represented by the Tamil political leadership in Colombo, who were preoccupied with securing minority rights for themselves under the postwar Soulbury Commission's constitution. A. Jeyaratnam Wilson, "The Colombo Man, the Jaffna Man and the Batticaloa Man: Regional Identities and the Rise of the Federal Party," in *The Sri Lankan Tamils: Ethnicity and Identity*, ed. Chelvadurai Manogaran and Bryan Pfaffenberger (Boulder, CO: Westview Press, 1994), 126–42.

21. Under an order issued under the IPRA, plantation laborers like Muthiah did not need a passport. They did, however, need an immigration certificate issued under the Estate Labor (Indian) Ordinance. Both estate laborers and their children could go back and forth. They had to meet two conditions. First, they had to be "genuine" unskilled workers who were registered and were guaranteed re-employment on return. Second, the immigration certificate would have to note that they had been unskilled laborers for at least five years prior to November 1, 1949. Third, they had to return within twelve months. The second condition was waived for children under twelve years and for newly married wives. Exemptions were granted to get around the third condition as well, nearly 502 out of 730 cases that were submitted. Report of the Controller of Labor, *Ceylon Administration Reports* (1950).

22. Govindan Sellappah Nayar Kodakan Pillai v Punchi Banda Mundanayake (1953) UKPC 13.

23. In 1950, an ordinary "visa" for Ceylon cost two rupees and a transit visa was one rupee. Report of the Controller of Labour, *Ceylon Administration Reports* (1946).

24. C. Kondapi, *Indians Overseas, 1838–1949* (New Delhi: Indian Council of World Affairs, 1975): 188–89.

25. "Midnight Raid on Fishermen's Huts," *Times of Ceylon*, September 9, 1953, Times Collection, NASL.

26. "Mandapam Camp 'Shocks,'" *Ceylon Daily News*, May 4, 1953, Times Collection, NASL.

27. Report of the Controller of Immigration and Emigration, *Ceylon Administration Reports* (1951).

28. *Ceylon Daily News*, May 13, 1953, Times Collection, NASL. See also Mae Ngai, *Impossible Subjects: Illegal Aliens and the Making of Modern America* (Princeton, NJ: Princeton University Press, 2004); S. Deborah Kang, *The INS on the Line: Making Immigration Law on the US Mexico Border, 1917–1954* (Oxford: Oxford University Press, 2017), and Julian Lim, *Porous Borders: Multiracial Migrations and the Law in the U.S.-Mexico Borderlands* (Chapel Hill: University of North Carolina Press, 2017), for comparison with borders and borderlands in the United States.

29. Report of the Controller of Immigration and Emigration, *Ceylon Administration Reports* (1952).

30. Labor leader A. E. Goonesinha's speeches were frequently reprinted in leftist newspapers like the *Colombo City News*.

31. "Indians Get a Rude Letter," clipping, newspaper unknown, July 17, 1953, Times Collection, NASL. On the significance of Dutugemunu to Sinhala Buddhist nationalism, see Steven Kemper, *The Presence of the Past: Chronicles, Politics, and Culture in Sinhala Life* (Ithaca, NY: Cornell University Press, 1991), 12.

32. Nira Wickramasinghe, "Citizens, Aryans, and Indians in Colonial Lanka: Discourses on Belonging in the 1920s-1930s," in *Belonging across the Bay of Bengal: Religious Rites, Colonial Migrations, National Rights*, ed. Michael Laffan (London: Bloomsbury, 2017), 139–60.

33. Ranasinha, *Census of Ceylon, 1946*, 96.

34. Report of the Deputy Commissioner, November 7, 1955, on Application No. N-1946, M/267, Department of Immigration and Emigration, NASL.

35. David Dery, "'Papereality' and Learning in Bureaucratic Organizations," *Administration and Society* 29, no. 6 (1998): 677–89; see also Bhavani Raman, *Document Raj: Writing and Scribes in Early Colonial South India* (Chicago: University of Chicago Press, 2012).

36. Report of the Commissioner for the Registration of Indian and Pakistani Residents, *Ceylon Administration Reports* (1950).

37. Report of the Commissioner for the Registration of Indian and Pakistani Residents, *Ceylon Administration Reports* (1950). Some never filed at all. In the first year of the act (i.e., 1950), many of the applications from the plantation laborers were stalled because of a ban called for by the Ceylon Indian Congress on potential applications. Between 1951 and 1952, 824,430 people of Indian origin claimed citizenship, and 134,188 were admitted.

38. Cited in A. P. Kanapathypillai, *The Epic of Tea: Politics in the Plantations of Sri Lanka* (Colombo: Social Scientists' Association, 2011), 84.

39. Report of the Controller of Immigration and Emigration, *Ceylon Administration Reports* (1951).

40. Report of the Controller of Immigration and Emigration, *Ceylon Administration Reports* (1952).

41. Report of the Commissioner for Indian and Pakistani Residents, *Ceylon Administration Reports* (1952).

42. Palaniyandi v. Commissioner for the Registration of Indian and Pakistani Residents (1955) 56 NLR 374.

43. Sockalingam Chettiar v. Commissioner for the Registration of Indian and Paki-

stani Residents (1957) 58 NLR 283; Easiah v. Commissioner for Registration of Indian and Pakistani Residents (1953) 58 NLR 37. But see *contra* Sivan Pillai v. Commissioner for the Registration of Indian and Pakistani Residents (1953) 54 NLR 310.

44. Soosey Fernando v. Commissioner for the Registration of Indian and Pakistani Residents (1955) 57 NLR 67 (this also goes to principles of natural justice); K. P. P. Pillai v. Commissioner for the Registration of Indian and Pakistani Residents (1956) 60 NLR 64.

45. Karuppan Muniandy v. Commissioner for the Registration of Indian and Pakistani Residents (1958) 60 NLR 403.

46. Application No. M-6061, M/267, Department of Immigration and Emigration, NASL.

47. Application No. M-6059, M/267, Department of Immigration and Emigration, NASL.

48. Charles A. Gunawardena, *Encyclopedia of Sri Lanka*, 2nd, rev. ed. (New Delhi: New Dawn Press, 2005), 14.

49. S. Thondaman, *Tea and Politics—An Autobiography*, vol. 2, *My Life and Times* (New Delhi: Navrang, 1994), 137–38.

50. Extracts from the *Congress News*, Case Papers of Govindan Sellapah Nadar Kodakan Pillai, Govindan Sellappah Nayar Kodakan Pillai Papers, Mss Eur E322, BL. To the best of my knowledge, these are the only copies of *Congress News* available.

51. S. P. Amarasingam, "Jaffna May Turn Out to Be a Political Volcano If Its Problems Are Not Solved," *Indian Daily Mail*, June 3, 1950, NLB.

52. Kodakan Pillai Papers, Mss Eur E322.

53. C. C. Desai, high commissioner for India, to K. Ramunni Menon, chief secretary to Government of Madras, October 29, 1953, G.O. No. 512, March 1, 1954, Proceedings of the Industries, Labor and Cooperation Department, TNSA.

54. G.O. No. 512, Proceedings of the Industries, Labor and Cooperation Department (1954), TNSA.

55. G.O. No. 3948, Proceedings of the Development Department (1946), TNSA.

56. "Passports in a Tin of Tea Leaves," clipping, newspaper unknown, October 29, 1953, Times Collection, NASL.

57. G.O. No. 512, Proceedings of the Industries, Labor, and Cooperation Department (1954), TNSA.

58. Although the language of "illicit" immigration was employed beginning only in 1950, the monitoring of migrants in Mannar began in the 1920s, possibly after the passage of the Indian Emigration Act. See "Illegal Landings," 20/2059, Delft Administration Records, NASL.

59. This was also the gist of a letter written to the editor of the *Ceylon Daily News* by a Mr. Victor Corea on December 4, 1941, which caught attention of the representative on the Indian Viceroy's Executive Council, lawyer-politician M. S. Aney: "This story of the Ceylon Government inviting Indian laborers to this Island is all a myth. The real truth is that in the days of the East India Company a class of touts had come into being whose business was to induce indigent Indians to emigrate from the Company's territories for the purpose of being employed as laborers in foreign countries." M. S. Aney Papers, NMML.

60. "The Indian Exodus to Ceylon," clipping, newspaper unknown, August 6, 1952, Times Collection, NASL.

61. *Ceylon Daily News*, July 31, 1952, Times Collection, NASL.

62. *Ceylon Observer*, August 1, 1952, Times Collection, NASL.

63. *Times of Ceylon*, July 31, 1952, Times Collection, NASL.

64. "Illegal Immigrants Find," *Indian Daily Mail*, December 17, 1950, NLB.

65. Report of the Controller of Emigration and Immigration, *Ceylon Administration Reports* (1953).

66. Ranasinha, *Census of Ceylon, 1946*, 219.

67. Ranasinha, *Census of Ceylon 1946*, 219. Per the definitions in the census, Ceylon Tamils were those who traced their origin to the Tamil districts in Ceylon (so, northern and eastern provinces) and Indian Tamils were those who did not. The census was already using the rule of *jus sanguinis*, so even if a Tamil was born in Jaffna but had migrated from Tuticorin, they would be classified as Indian Tamil. Those Moors who were "permanently settled" in Ceylon were classified as Ceylon Moors, and those who "intended" to return to India were classified as Indian Moors. However, we have no record of the way in which these questions were posed to those being surveyed, even though permanent settlement was at the heart of the legal disputes regarding the 1949 Act.

68. Ranasinha, *Census of Ceylon, 1946*, 221.

69. Application No. G-1669, Department of Immigration and Emigration, NASL.

70. Report of the Controller of Emigration and Immigration, *Ceylon Administration Reports* (1950); Report of the Controller of Emigration and Immigration, *Ceylon Administration Reports* (1953).

71. On the plight of Sri Lanka's Muslims during and after the civil war, see Sharika Thiranagama, *In My Mother's House: Civil War in Sri Lanka* (Philadelphia: University of Pennsylvania Press, 2011).

72. Report of the Controller of Emigration and Immigration, *Ceylon Administration Reports* (1954).

73. "Many Got Citizenship by Bribing Officials," *Times of India*, August 6, 1955.

74. Kanapathipillai, *Citizenship and Statelessness*.

75. Section 15 allowed appeals to the Supreme Court from the orders of the commissioner. Annamalai v. Commissioner for Registration of Indian and Pakistani Residents (1957) 58 NLR 354 (noting that the procedure in Section 9 of the act must be followed before taking recourse to Section 13 and affirming the decision in the case of Solamuthu v. Commissioner for Registration of Indian and Pakistani Residents [1956] 58 NLR 157); Murugiah v. Commissioner for Registration of Indian and Pakistani Residents (1957) 58 NLR 391 (ruling that the deputy commissioner cannot hold an inquiry wherein he deals with only one issue and not with the others, by saying that he is convinced that the remaining issues do not need to be dealt with because of his ruling in the first issue). In Caruppiah v. Commissioner for Registration of Indian and Pakistani Residents (1960) 62 NLR 17, Justice Sinnetamby held that the deputy commissioner cannot bring up the question of an improperly signed form at the 9(3) inquiry.

76. A deputy commissioner asked "wide-ranging" questions at a 9(3) inquiry and eventually refused an application. Once again, Justice Sinnetamby, speaking for the court,

said: "To pounce upon a remark made by a witness under such circumstances in regard to a matter which does not form the subject matter of the inquiry and utilise it to reject his application is neither fair nor consistent with principles of natural justice." Marianthony v. Commissioner for Registration of Indian and Pakistani Residents (1957) 58 NLR 431.

77. Solamuthu v. Commissioner for Registration of Indian and Pakistani Residents (1956) 58 NLR 157 (citing *obiter* in Paramasivam v. Commissioner for Registration of Indian and Pakistani Residents [1955] 56 NLR 514 with approval, distinguishing Pitchamuthu v. Commissioner for Registration of Indian and Pakistani Residents [1955] 57 NLR 184, which had held that the powers of the Supreme Court with respect to the procedure under the IPRA were restricted to the four corners of the statute).

78. Raj Retty v. Commissioner for Indian and Pakistani Residents (1955) 57 NLR 402.

79. "Local Ration Books Sold in India," *The Guardian*, May 5, 1955.

80. Report of the Controller of Emigration and Immigration, *Ceylon Administration Reports* (1952).

81. Union Government of Burma v. Quah Chun Bee (1950) BLR 14.

82. Ko Mya Din v. Ko Bin Nga (1952) BLR 240; Ko Aung v. Abdul Latiff (1958) BLR 216.

83. S. R. M. C. T. Annamalai Chettyar v. Gor Kyin Sein (1953) BLR 95.

84. "Indians in Burma: A Difficult Choice," *Times of India*, August 9, 1958. For Malayan-born Ceylon Tamils, G. G. Ponnambalam in Singapore announced that there was no question of dual citizenship and everyone would have to choose between Ceylon or Malaya. If they did later want to take up citizenship in Ceylon, then they had to renounce the other citizenship. The deadline given was December 31, 1952. As Darren Wan's forthcoming work shows, citizenship by registration in Malaya also afflicted South Indian and South Chinese laborers on mines and plantation in similar ways, with applications being rejected on the grounds of insufficient moral character. Darren Wan, "Phony Citizens: Bureaucratic Encounters and Migrant Claims-Making in Malaya, 1957 to 1963," paper presented at the Annual Meeting of the Association for Asian Studies, 2022.

85. Kamal Sadiq, *Paper Citizens: How Illegal Immigrants Acquire Citizenship in Developing Countries* (Oxford: Oxford University Press, 2008).

86. Kalpana, "A Ballad of Satyagrahis," *Congress News*, September 8, 1952, Kodakan Pillai Papers, Mss Eur E322, BL.

87. For a contemporary account of *malaiyaha* Tamil identity and politics, see Daniel Bass, *Everyday Ethnicity in Sri Lanka: Up-Country Tamil Identity Politics* (London: Routledge, 2013); Mythri Jegathesan, *Tea and Solidarity: Tamil Women and Work in Postwar Sri Lanka* (Seattle: University of Washington Press, 2019).

88. Kanapathipillai, *Citizenship and Statelessness*, 3. See also *Engengum Anniamakkapattavargal: A Study of the Conditions of the Sri Lankan Tamils of Indian Origin and the Sri Lanka Repatriates in India* (Kodaikanal: Ceylon Repatriate Association, 1984).

Chapter 5

1. "Coast Moor" is a colonial-era label used to identify Muslims who were involved in trade between India and Sri Lanka. The term "Moor" is often used derogatorily against Muslims in Europe.

2. Application No. G-1669, Department of Immigration and Emigration, NASL.

3. Veena Das, "The Figure of the Abducted Woman: The Citizen as Sexed," in *Life and Words: Violence and the Descent into the Ordinary* (Berkeley: University of California Press, 2007), 18–37.

4. Farhana Ibrahim, "Cross-Border Intimacies: Marriage, Migration and Citizenship in Western India," *Modern Asian Studies* 52, no. 5 (2018): 1664–91.

5. Mytheli Sreenivas, *Wives, Widows, and Concubines: The Conjugal Family Ideal in Colonial India* (Bloomington: Indiana University Press, 2008).

6. Kalpana Hiralal, "'What Is the Meaning of the Word "Wife"?' The Impact of the Immigration Laws on the Wives of Resident Indians in South Africa, 1897–1930," *Contemporary South Asia* 26, no. 2 (2018): 206–20.

7. Victoria Degtyareva, "Defining Family in Immigration Law: Accounting for Nontraditional Families in Citizenship by Descent," *Yale Law Journal* 120, no. 4 (2011): 862–908.

8. Parliamentary Debates, House of Representatives, August 19, 1948 (Dr. N. M. Perera).

9. Parliamentary Debates, House of Representatives, August 19, 1948 (Colvin de Silva).

10. Dennis B. McGilvray, *Crucible of Conflict: Tamil and Muslim Society on the East Coast of Sri Lanka* (Durham, NC: Duke University Press, 2008).

11. Polygamy was permitted for Muslims in Sri Lanka, but by 1951 it was rarely recorded. M. A. M. Shukri, *Muslims of Sri Lanka: Avenues to Antiquity* (Beruwala, Sri Lanka: Jamiah Naleemia Institute, 1986).

12. Parliamentary Debates, House of Representatives, August 19, 1948 (J. R. Jayawardena).

13. Daniel Bass, *Everyday Ethnicity in Sri Lanka: Up-Country Tamil Identity Politics* (London: Routledge, 2013); Ravindran Sriramachandran, "Life Is Where We Are Not: Making and Managing the Plantation Tamil" (PhD diss., Columbia University, 2010).

14. Kumari Jayawardena, *Nobodies to Somebodies: The Rise of the Colonial Bourgeoisie in Sri Lanka* (New York: Zed Books, 2000); Shukri, *Muslims of Sri Lanka*, 23.

15. Shukri, *Muslims of Sri Lanka*, 20. For an account of the early modern Muslim trading diasporas, see Kenneth R. Hall, "Ports-of-Trade, Maritime Diasporas, and Networks of Trade and Cultural Integration in the Bay of Bengal Region of the Indian Ocean: C. 1300–1500," *Journal of the Economic and Social History of the Orient* 53, nos. 1–2 (2010): 109–45; Markus Vink, *Encounters on the Opposite Coast: The Dutch East India Company and the Nayaka State of Madurai in the Seventeenth Century* (Brill: Leiden, 2015). See also Sinnappah Arasaratnam, *Indians in Malaysia and Singapore* (London: Institute of Race Relations, 1970), 8–9, for a similar account for Malaya.

16. Shukri, *Muslims of Sri Lanka*, 22.

17. Anoma Pieris, *Architecture and Nationalism in Sri Lanka: The Trouser under the Cloth* (Abingdon, Oxon: Routledge, 2013), 40.

18. Nihal Perera, "Indigenizing the Colonial City: The Ceylonese Transformation of Nineteenth Century Colombo," in *People's Spaces: Coping, Familiarizing, Creating* (New York: Routledge, 2015), 31.

19. Llyn Smith, "The Constitution of Islamic Community in Sri Lanka: Sufi Net-

works, Saints' Shrines and Ritual Practice," in *Journeys and Dwellings: Indian Ocean Themes in South Asia*, ed. Helene Basu (Hyderabad: Orient Longman, 2008), 147–73, 152.

20. Cyrus Abeyakoon, "The Ceylon Moors Can Be Proud of Their History," in *Glimpses from the Past of the Moors of Sri Lanka*, ed. A. H. Macam Markar, A. L. M. Lafir, and A. I. L. Marikar (Colombo: Moors' Islamic Cultural Home, 1976), 93.

21. E. B. Denham, *Census of Ceylon, 1911* (Colombo: H. C. Cottle, Government Printer, 1911). For Moors in the Kandyan kingdom and their trade relations with South India, see Sivasundaram, "Ethnicity, Indigeneity, and Migration in the Advent of British Rule to Sri Lanka," *American Historical Review* 115, no. 2 (2010): 439.

22. Ronit Ricci, "Jawa, Melayu, Malay or Otherwise? The Shifting Nomenclature of the Sri Lankan Malays," *Indonesia and the Malay World* 44, no. 130 (2016): 409–23.

23. Dennis McGilvray and Mirak Raheem, "Origins of the Sri Lankan Muslims and Varieties of the Muslim Identity," in *The Sri Lanka Reader: History, Culture, Politics*, ed. John Holt (Durham, NC: Duke University Press, 2011): 410–19, 410.

24. There are multiple explanations for how the term *sonakar* came about. In one explanation, the Arab settlers on the Coromandel Coast were given land by the Pandya Raja of the time. Since he had given the land by word of mouth (*sonna*), they became *sonnavar/sonahar*. Note that this explanation ties the Ceylon Moors back to India, another instance of an "origin" myth that sustains political categories. Tayka Shu⬛ayb, ⬛*Ālim, Arabic, Arwi, and Persian in Sarandib and Tamil Nadu: A Study of the Contributions of Sri Lanka and Tamil Nadu to Arabic, Arwi, Persian, and Urdu Languages, Literature, and Education* (Colombo: Imāmul ⬛Arūs Trust for the Ministry of State for Muslim Religious and Cultural Affairs, 1993).

25. M. M. Thawfeeq, *Muslim Mosaics* (Colombo: Al Eslam and the Moors' Islamic Cultural Home, 1972).

26. A. G. Ranasinha, *Census of Ceylon, 1946* (Colombo: Ceylon Government Press).

27. M. A. Nuhman, *Sri Lankan Muslims: Ethnic Identity within Cultural Diversity* (Colombo: International Centre for Ethnic Studies, 2007), 31.

28. Gyanendra Pandey, "Can a Muslim Be an Indian?," *Comparative Studies in Society and History* 41, no. 4 (1999): 608–29.

29. Deborah Sutton, "Imagined Sovereignty and the Indian Subject: Partition and Politics beyond the Nation, 1948–1960," *Contemporary South Asia* 19, no. 4 (December 1, 2011): 409–25.

30. Nira Wickramasinghe, *Sri Lanka in the Modern Age: A History of Contested Identities* (Honolulu: University of Hawai'i Press, 2006), 161–62.

31. John Rogers, "Post-Orientalism and the Interpretation of Premodern and Modern Political Identities: The Case of Sri Lanka," *Journal of Asian Studies* 53, no. 1 (1994): 10–23, 19.

32. Tschacher compares the ways in which Marakkayars of Tamil Nadu and those of Pondicherry make a claim to Arab origins to differentiate themselves from Urdu-speaking Muslims. At the same time, in Ceylon, the Ceylon Moors claimed Arab origins to distinguish themselves from "Tamils" and "Sinhalese." These opposite dynamics show the limits of colonial records in establishing community identities. Torsten Tschacher, "The Challenges of Diversity: 'Casting' Muslim Communities in South India," in *Being Muslim in South Asia: Diversity and Daily Life*, ed. Robin Jeffrey and Ronojoy Sen (New Delhi: Oxford University Press, 2014), 64–86, 75.

33. I. L. M. Abdul Azeez, "A Criticism of Mr. Ramanathan's 'Ethnology of the Moors of Ceylon,'" in Holt, *Sri Lanka Reader*, 424–28, 426.

34. Azeez, "Criticism," 427.

35. Nuhman, *Sri Lankan Muslims*.

36. McGilvray and Raheem, "Origins," 425.

37. See Tschacher, "Challenges of Diversity," 72.

38. Nira Wickramasinghe, "Citizens, Aryans and Indians in Colonial Lanka: Discourses on Belonging in the 1920s and 1930s," in *Belonging across the Bay of Bengal: Religious Rites, Colonial Migrations, National Rights*, ed. Michael Laffan, 139–60 (London: Bloomsbury, 2017), 139–60.

39. Great Britain Parliament, House of Commons, *Papers by Command*, vol. 10 (London: HMSO, 1916), 35.

40. Great Britain Parliament, House of Commons, *Papers by Command*, 10:35; Stanley J. Tambiah, *Leveling Crowds: Ethnonationalist Conflicts and Collective Violence in South Asia* (Berkeley: University of California Press, 1997), 58; Robert N. Kearney, "Introduction: The 1915 Riots in Ceylon," *Journal of Asian Studies* 29, no. 2 (1970): 219–22.

41. Edward W. Perera, *Memorandum upon on Recent Disturbances in Ceylon* (London: Edward Hughes, 1915).

42. McGilvray and Raheem, "Origins," 417.

43. Ponnambalam Ramanathan, "The Ethnology of the 'Moors' of Ceylon," in Holt, *Sri Lanka Reader*, 420–23, 422.

44. Shamara Wettimuny, "A Brief History of Anti-Muslim Violence in Sri Lanka," *History Workshop Online*, July 22, 2019, https://www.historyworkshop.org.uk/a-brief -history-of-anti-muslim-violence-in-sri-lanka/.

45. Nuhman, *Sri Lankan Muslims*, 25.

46. A. M. M. Sayed Abdul Cader v. Commissioner of Income Tax AIR 1950 Mad 715; (1950) 1 MLJ 715.

47. On "attachments," which connote "relationships of obligation, affect, dependence, inheritance, loyalty, debt and the like," see Rachel Sturman, "Property and Attachments: Defining Autonomy and the Claims of Family in Nineteenth-Century Western India," *Comparative Studies in Society and History* 47, no. 3 (2005): 611–37, 613.

48. S. M. Zackariah Sahib v. Commissioner of Income Tax (1952) 2 MLJ 877.

49. The Report of the Controller of Labor noted in 1952 that remittances increased from Rs. 2,516,700 to Rs. 5,392,060 in 1952. Report of the Controller of Labour, *Ceylon Administration Reports* (1952).

50. Shahul Hameed v. Commissioner for the Registration of Indian and Pakistani Residents (1954) 56 NLR 152.

51. Report of the Controller of Labour, *Ceylon Administration Reports* (1950).

52. Report of the Controller of Emigration and Immigration, *Ceylon Administration Reports* (1950).

53. By 1953, 90 percent of all temporary residence permits issued by the Ceylon government had been issued to "Indian nationals." Report of the Controller of Emigration and Immigration, *Ceylon Administration Reports* (1953).

54. Chie Ikeya, "Colonial Intimacies in Comparative Perspective: Intermarriage, Law and Cultural Difference in British Burma," *Journal of Colonialism and Colonial*

History 14, no. 1 (2013), http://doi.org/10.1353/cch.2013.0014; Rajashree Mazumder, "'I Do Not Envy You': Mixed Marriages and Immigration Debates in the 1920s and 1930s Rangoon, Burma," *Indian Economic and Social History Review* 51, no. 4 (2014): 497–527.

55. Mazumder, "'I Do Not Envy You.'"

56. Mazumder, "'I Do Not Envy You.'"

57. "Soulbury Commission on Constitutional Reform; Criticisms of the Tamil Proposals," FCO 141/2324, TNA.

58. Caroline B. Brettell, *Men Who Migrate, Women Who Wait: Population and History in a Portuguese Parish* (Princeton, NJ: Princeton University Press, 2014).

59. Gary Oikhiro claims that women who "waited" were not passive but labored and formed communities of their own. Gary Y. Okihiro, *Margins and Mainstreams: Asians in American History and Culture* (Seattle:. University of Washington Press, 1994), 74. In response, Yen Le Espiritu claims that the question is not merely the absence of women (as it is here in Umbichi's case) but the ways in which a gendered workforce is perceived, and the possibilities that those who stayed on in Canton or Hong Kong benefited—even materially. Yen Le Espiritu, *Asian American Women and Men: Labor, Laws, and Love* (Lanham, MD: Rowman and Littlefield, 2008), 16.

60. Arunima Datta, *Fleeting Agencies: A Social History of Indian Coolie Women in British Malaya* (Cambridge: Cambridge University Press, 2021), 125–50.

61. Veettil Puthu Parambil Muhammad Koya and Others v. Ponmanichandakath Katheessa Bi (1944) 2 MLJ 365; AIR 1945 Mad 81.

62. Aleena Sebastian, "Matrilineal Practices along the Coasts of Malabar," *Sociological Bulletin* 65, no. 1 (2016): 89–106.

63. The question of what law applied to the *tharavad* and self-acquired property of Mappilla Muslims was the subject of cases before the Madras High Court in the late nineteenth century. *Marumakkathayam* was seen as the exception, and "Mohammedan law" as the rule. Eventually, this contradictory legal position was resolved by the Mappilla Succession Act (I of 1918), where the self-acquired sole property of a Mappilla otherwise governed by *marumakkathayam* law would descend to heirs via "Mohammedan law." See Puthucode Rama Sundara Aiyar and B. Sitarama Rao, *A Treatise on Malabar and Aliyasanthana Law* (Mylapore: Madras Law Journal Office, 1922), 233–36.

64. For examples of nationality, commerce, and conflict of law through a microhistorical lens, see Fahad Bishara, "No Country but the Ocean: Reading International Law from the Deck of an Indian Ocean Dhow, ca. 1900," *Comparative Studies in Society and History* 60, no. 2 (2018): 338–66; Jessica Marglin, *The Shamama Case: Contesting Citizenship across the Modern Mediterranean* (Princeton, NJ: Princeton University Press, 2022).

65. Ravinder Kaur, "Distinctive Citizenship: Refugees, Subjects and the Postcolonial State in India's Partition," *Cultural and Social History* 6, no. 4 (2009): 429–46, 430 (making a distinction between the self-rehabilitating and self-reliant refugees).

66. Muthiah's appeal was argued by the same C. Shanmuganayagam who had represented Zackariah Sahib in his appeal to the Supreme Court in Colombo. Commissioner for the Registration of Indian and Pakistani Residents v. Mohideen Abdul Cader Badrudeen (1952) UKPC 29.

Chapter 6

1. For details about the SS *Vasna* and its routes, see "Merchant Shipping Movement Cards, Vasna," BT 389/31/48, TNA.

2. The Bihar Maintenance of Public Order Act, the East Punjab Public Safety Act of 1949, and the CP & Berar Maintenance of Public Order Act are other examples. For a report of the working of these laws, see *The Indian Civil Liberties Conference: Report of Proceedings* (Madras: Madras Civil Liberties' Union, 1949). For an account of the Punjab Public Safety Act, see Rotem Geva, *Delhi Reborn: Partition and Nation Building in India's Capital* (Stanford, CA: Stanford University Press, 2022).

3. G.O. No. 2128, July 12, 1947, Proceedings of the Home Department, TNSA.

4. C. S. Subramanyam, *Our Party's Growth in Tamil Nadu* (Communist Party of India, n.d.), 36.

5. Madras Maintenance of Public Order Bill and Ordinance of 1947, G.O. No. 66, June 4, 1947, Proceedings of the Legal Department, TNSA.

6. Madras Legislative Assembly Debates, February 3, 1947, TNSA.

7. Madras Legislative Assembly Debates, February 3, 1947, TNSA.

8. FNR, second half of September 1948, Government of Madras, TNSA.

9. Madras Maintenance of Public Order Act High Court judgments, USSF 77/49, October 19, 1949, TNSA.

10. *Indian Civil Liberties Conference*, Part II, 14.

11. D. Veeraraghavan, *The Making of the Madras Working Class* (New Delhi: LeftWord Books, 2013).

12. On M. N. Roy as one among a global network of revolutionaries from Asia against empire, see Tim Harper, *Underground Asia: Global Revolutionaries and the Assault on Empire* (Cambridge, MA: Harvard University Press, 2021).

13. Achin Vanaik, "The Indian Left," *New Left Review*, no. 159 (1986): 49–70.

14. Sanjoy Bhattacharya, "The Colonial State and the Communist Party of India, 1942–45: A Reappraisal," *South Asia Research* 15, no. 1 (1995): 48–77.

15. Bhattacharya, "Colonial State," 62.

16. Government of India, Ministry of Home Affairs, *Communist Violence in India* (New Delhi: Ministry of Home Affairs, 1949), 1.

17. See, for comparison, Kamran Asdar Ali, "The Enemy Within: Communism and the New Pakistani State," in *The Postcolonial Moment in South and Southeast Asia*, ed. Gyan Prakash, Michael Laffan, and Nikhil Menon (London: Bloomsbury, 2018), 31–48.

18. Taylor C. Sherman, "Migration, Citizenship and Belonging in Hyderabad (Deccan), 1946–1956," *Modern Asian Studies* 45, no. 1 (2011): 81–107.

19. K. C. George, *Immortal Punnapra-Vayalar* (New Delhi: Communist Party of India, 1975).

20. G.O. No. 187, January 22, 1949, Proceedings of the Public Department, TNSA.

21. Jessica Namakkal, *Unsettling Utopia: The Making and Unmaking of French India* (New York: Columbia University Press, 2021).

22. A. K. Gopalan, *Ente Jeevitha Katha*, 12th ed. (Thiruvanathapuram: Chinta, 2015), 132–47. Sources for the communist movement in Kerala were consulted at the A. K. Gopalan Center at Thiruvananthapuram and the P. C. Joshi Archives at Jawaharlal Nehru University in New Delhi.

23. Charles Wesley Ervin, *Tomorrow Is Ours: The Trotskyist Movement in India and Ceylon, 1935–48* (Colombo: Social Scientists' Association, 2006).

24. Low Choo Chin, "Immigration Control during the Malayan Emergency: Borders, Belonging and Citizenship, 1948–1960," *Journal of the Malaysian Branch of the Royal Asiatic Society* 89, no. 1 (2016): 35–60.

25. See Madras Maintenance of Public Order Act of 1947, Preamble.

26. Christopher Baker, "Colonial Rule and the Internal Economy in Twentieth-Century Madras," *Modern Asian Studies* 15, no. 3 (1981): 575–602.

27. *In re R. Ramanathan* (1948) 2 MLJ 634.

28. FNR, first half of May 1948, TNSA.

29. Kernial Singh Sandhu, *Indians in Malaya: Some Aspects of Their Immigration and Settlement (1786–1957)* (Cambridge: Cambridge University Press, 1969), 17.

30. "The Emergency in Singapore," May 1, 1949, FCO 141/14593, TNA.

31. Usha Mahajani, *The Role of Indian Minorities in Burma and Malaya* (Westport, CT: Greenwood Press, 1960), 203.

32. Cited in Mahajani, *Role of Indian Minorities,* 194n5.

33. Sunil Amrith, "Mobile City and the Coromandel Coast: Tamil Journeys to Singapore, 1920–1960," *Mobilities* 5, no. 2 (2010): 237–55.

34. Amrith, "Mobile City."

35. Amrith, "Mobile City."

36. G.O. No. 2921, August 31, 1949, Proceedings of the Public Department, TNSA.

37. Parmer, *Colonial Labor Policy and Administration: A History of Labor in the Rubber Plantation Industry in Malaya, c. 1910–1941* (Locust Valley, NY: J. J. Augustin, 1960), 51.

38. Parmer, *Colonial Labor Policy,* 7–8.

39. W. G. Huff, "The Development of the Rubber Market in Pre-World War II Singapore," *Journal of Southeast Asian Studies* 24, no. 2 (1993): 285–306.

40. Paul H. Kratoska, *Asian Labor in the Wartime Japanese Empire* (New York: M. E. Sharpe, 2005), 240.

41. John Solomon, "The Decline of Pan-Indian Identity and the Development of Tamil Cultural Separatism in Singapore, 1856–1965," *South Asia: Journal of South Asian Studies* 35, no. 2 (2012): 257–81.

42. K. Nadarajah, "The Thondar Padai Movement in Kedah" (1981), cited in Parameswari Krishnan, "Anti-toddy Movement in Malaya, 1900–1957," *Journal of Indian Culture and Civilization* 1 (2014): 1–22. See also the Central Indian Association of Malaya response to the Sastri report, admonishing it for not taking a stronger stance on closing toddy shops on estates. See also "Comments on the Reports Submitted to the Government of India by the Delegation Led by V. S. Srinivasa Sastri on the Conditions of Indian Labor in Malaya," 1937, CO 1073/247, TNA.

43. Carl Vadivella Belle, *Tragic Orphans: Indians in Malaysia* (Singapore: Institute of Southeast Asian Studies, 2014), 244.

44. Gareth Curless, "The Triumph of the State: Singapore's Dockworkers and the Limits of Global History c. 1920–1965," *Historical Journal* 60 (December 2017): 1–27.

45. Rajeswary Ampalavanar, *The Indian Minority and Political Change in Malaya, 1945–1957* (Oxford: Oxford University Press, 1981), 18.

46. Judgment in Criminal Miscellaneous Petitions (Crl. M. P.), Nos. 442–47 of 1949, Madras High Court. The judgment is reported as P. Ramiah v. Chief Secretary to the Government of Madras AIR 1950 Mad 100.

47. In re G. Narayanaswami Naidu (1949) 1 MLJ 1 had earlier ruled that courts could strike down detention orders that were vague or imprecise in their articulation of the grounds for detention.

48. (1949) 2 MLJ 61, 64.

49. K. S. Subramanian, "Intelligence Bureau, Home Ministry and Indian Politics," *Economic and Political Weekly* 40, no. 21 (2005): 2147–50, 2148.

50. Nasser Hussain, *The Jurisprudence of Emergency: Colonialism and the Rule of Law* (Ann Arbor: University of Michigan Press, 2003). Habeas corpus, often referred to as "the great writ" and "the palladium of liberty," evolved through judicial practice in England and elsewhere in the empire. It literally translates into "produce the body," suggesting that the individual who is under confinement must be physically produced in the law court that had issued the writ. As Hussain (*Jurisprudence of Emergency*) and Paul Delaney Halliday (*Habeas Corpus: From England to Empire* [Cambridge, MA: Harvard University Press, 2010]) both point out in their studies of the working of the habeas corpus writ, it was originally intended not to protect the individual from the sovereign (as the MMPOA cases suggest) but to allow the sovereign to take account of his or her subjects by bringing them before the court. However, from the seventeenth century onwards, prisoners in England began using the writ to question their detention and invoke protection against arbitrary judges. After 1858, when the British monarch assumed direct rule over India and criminal procedures were codified, detainees invoked Section 491 of the Code of Criminal Procedure of 1898 (which codified the habeas corpus remedy) in order to secure their release from police custody.

51. P. Kesavan Nair v. District Magistrate, Coimbatore Crl. M. P. No. 1682 of 1949, MHC RR.

52. P. G. Natarajan v. District Magistrate, North Arcot Crl. M. P. No. 1664 of 1949, MHC RR.

53. Pappala Appa Rao v. District Magistrate, West Godavari Crl. M. P. No. 1703 of 1949, MHC RR.

54. R. Madhava Rao v. District Magistrate, Visakhapatanam Crl. M. P. No. 1707 of 1949, MHC RR.

55. P. Kesavan Nair v. District Magistrate, Coimbatore Crl. M. P. No. 1682 of 1949, MHC RR.

56. G.O. S/889–6/48, March 19, 1948, TNSA.

57. (1949) 2 MLJ 634, 636.

58. Minute by the governor and high commissioner, T. Shenton Thomas, May 17, 1941, FCO 141/16270.

59. *Straits Times*, May 24, 1941, NAS.

60. Deportation Order under Regulation 22 of the Emergency Regulations of 1939. Note that the deportation order contains the word *banish*, which would later prove to be a bone of contention in cases like Ramiah's. For details about the Klang strikes and the involvement of Nathan as well as the CIAM, see "Strikes by Tamil Labourers in

Klang District," FCO 141 /16270 and FCO 141/16271, TNA. These files contain a wealth of information about how the Malayan government dealt with the strikes, as well as the dynamics between the CIAM and other working-class movements.

61. I am grateful to Arun Senkuttavan for these details about Ramanathan and his brothers. In British Malaya during the 1940s, Ramiah and Ramanathan would have been seen as belonging to very different spheres of political action, although they were both of Indian origin. Ramiah was born in Singapore to Indian parents and received only a fifth-grade education; he came of age during the Japanese occupation of Malaya and reportedly joined Subhas Chandra Bose's Indian National Army to wage war against the British Indian government from outside its borders. He emblematized the violent external threat posed by communism. In contrast, Ramanathan was part of the literate elite; any threat he posed to British India was an abstract and epistemological one, not a literal physical one. Paradoxically, journalists like Ramanathan were *more* invested in an idea of a Greater India—an India that went beyond its subcontinental borders—than the labor leaders who were seen as the face of the violent communist threat. Indeed, Indian trade union leaders in Malaya worked against the idea of Greater India; they wanted to close down the circulation of labor between the two countries by curbing further emigration of laborers from India.

62. (1949) 2 MLJ 634, 636–637.

63. Ivor Jennings, "Politics in Ceylon since 1952," *Pacific Affairs* 27, no. 4 (1954): 338–52.

64. I am grateful to retired justice K. Chandru, Madras High Court, for alerting me to this aspect during an interview. Before being elevated to the Madras High Court, Chandru worked at the offices of Row and Reddy. Personal interview, Chennai, September 13, 2015.

65. Affidavit of the Petitioner, Pericharla China Somaraju v. District Magistrate, West Godavari, Crl. M.P. No. 1699 of 1949, MHC RR.

66. Bangariah v. District Magistrate, Visakhapatanam, Crl. M. P. No. 1700 of 1949, MHC RR.

67. *Indian Express*, May 4, 1949.

68. G.O. No. 2921, August 31, 1949, Proceedings of the Public Department, TNSA.

69. FNR, second half of December 1948, TNSA.

70. F. E. Mitchin, superintendent, Vellore Jail, to the chief secretary, Fort St. George, G.O. No. 2921, August 31, 1949, Proceedings of the Public Department, TNSA. See also "Indian Communists from Malaya," USSF 95/48, date unrecorded, TNSA.

71. Sambasivam v. Public Prosecutor, Privy Council No. 32 of 1949; (1950) UKPC 7. See also Case of Mr. Sambasivam, CO 537/4770; CO 537/4771, TNA.

72. Letter to John D. Higham, July 21, 1949, CO 537/4768, TNA.

73. "Case of Mr. S. A. Ganapathy," CO 537/4769, TNA; Mr. S. A. Ganapathy, Public Reactions, CO 717/179/1. See also "Death Sentences for S. A. Ganapathy and Sambasivam," D.O. 142/405; High Commissioner of India who sought reprieve for Ganapathy and Sambasivam, PREM 8/967, TNA.

74. Michael R. Stenson, *Class, Race and Colonialism in West Malaysia: The Indian Case* (Vancouver: University of British Columbia Press, 1980); Sunil Amrith, "Reconstructing the 'Plural Society': Asian Migration between Empire and Nation, 1940–1948," *Past and Present* 210, no. 6 (2011): 237–57.

75. Tim Harper, *The End of Empire and the Making of Malaya* (Cambridge: Cambridge University Press, 2001), 133.

76. (1949) 2 MLJ 310.

77. G.O. No. 446, January 28, 1950, Proceedings of the Public Department, TNSA.

78. G.O. No. 446, January 28, 1950.

79. G.O. No. 378, January 24, 1950, Proceedings of the Public Department, TNSA.

80. G.O. No. 378, January 24, 1950.

81. G.O. No. 2921, August 31, 1949, Proceedings of the Public Department, TNSA.

82. Ampalavanar, *Indian Minority*, 47.

83. G.O. No. 2921, August 31, 1949.

84. G.O. No. 1795, June 13, 1949, Proceedings of the Public Department, TNSA.

85. G.O. No. 1795, June 13, 1949.

86. "Deportation of British Subjects in the Federation of Malaya," March 26, 1953, CO 1022/137, TNA.

87. "Chettiars Will Not Pay Protection Money," *Indian Daily Mail*, February 27, 1949, NLB.

88. "Indians in Malaya: Banishment," D.O. 142/404, TNA.

89. In re M. Subramaniam AIR 1950 Mad 405.

90. Vanaik, "Indian Left."

91. Vanaik, "Indian Left."

92. Hussain, *Jurisprudence of Emergency.*

93. Kalyani Ramnath, "ADM Jabalpur's Antecedents: Political Emergencies, Civil Liberties, and Arguments from Colonial Continuities in India," *American University International Law Review* 31 (2016): 209.

94. Colonial Office to Commissioner General, South East Asia, June 8, 1948, "Indians in Malaya: Banishment," DO 142/404, TNA.

95. See Karl Hack, "The Origins of the Asian Cold War: Malaya 1948," *Journal of Southeast Asian Studies* 40, no. 3 (2009): 471–96, Karl Hack, *The Malayan Emergency: Revolution and Counterinsurgency at the End of Empire* (Cambridge: Cambridge University Press, 2022).

96. Colonial Office to Commissioner General, South East Asia, June 8, 1948, "Indians in Malaya: Banishment."

Chapter 7

1. Hugh Tinker, *The Union of Burma: A Study of the First Years of Independence* (New York: Oxford University Press, 1957).

2. Valli Kanapathipillai, *Citizenship and Statelessness in Sri Lanka: The Case of the Tamil Estate Workers* (London: Anthem Press, 2009).

3. Andrew Harding, *The Constitution of Malaysia: A Contextual Analysis* (London: Bloomsbury, 2022); Thaatchaayini Kananatu, *Minorities, Rights, and the Law in Malaysia* (London: Routledge, 2020).

4. Sana Aiyar, *Indians in Kenya: The Politics of Diaspora* (Cambridge, MA: Harvard University Press, 2015); for a memoir of Ugandan Asians resettled in Britain after 1972, Mahmood Mamdani, *From Citizen to Refugee: Ugandan Asians Come to Britain*, 2nd ed. (Cape Town: Pambazuka Press, 2011); Ned Bertz, *Diaspora and Nation in the Indian*

Ocean: Transnational Histories of Race and Urban Space in Tanzania (Honolulu: University of Hawai'i Press, 2015); Savita Nair, "Despite Dislocations: Uganda's Indians Remaking Home," *Africa* 88, no. 3 (2018): 492–517.

5. Compare with the discussion in Claire Eldridge, Christoph Kalter, and Becky Taylor, "Migrations of Decolonization, Welfare, and the Unevenness of Citizenship in the UK, France and Portugal," *Past and Present*, prepublished online, November 2022, https://doi.org/10.1093/pastj/gtac005, which distinguishes between resident-citizens and returnee citizens from former colonies in Asia and Africa.

6. Cindy Ewing, "The Colombo Powers: Crafting Diplomacy in the Third World and Launching Afro-Asia at Bandung," *Cold War History* 19, no. 1 (2019): 1–19; Lydia Walker, "Decolonization in the 1960s: On Legitimate and Illegitimate Nationalist Claims-Making," *Past and Present* 242, no. 1 (2019): 227–64.

7. Sunil Amrith, "Struggles for Citizenship around the Bay of Bengal," in *The Postcolonial Moment in South and Southeast Asia*, ed. Gyan Prakash, Michael Laffan, and Nikhil Menon (London: Bloomsbury, 2018), 107–20.

8. Niraja Gopal Jayal, *Citizenship and Its Discontents: An Indian History* (Cambridge, MA: Harvard University Press, 2013), 51–81 (discussing the context for including Article 8 in the Constitution of India that allowed for this registration); see also File No. T/4150/2/63, NAI.

9. Amrith, "Struggles for Citizenship."

10. Patrick Peebles, *The Plantation Tamils of Ceylon* (London: Leicester University Press, 2001).

11. Joint Memorandum submitted to the Government of Burma (Simla) by the Burma Muslim Evacuees Association, Calcutta (February 15, 1945), Burma-India Discussions, IOR: M/3/1411.

12. Frederick Cooper, "Federation, Confederation, Territorial State: Debating a Postimperial Future in French West Africa, 1945–1960," in *Forms of Pluralism and Democratic Constitutionalism*, ed. Andrew Arato, Jean Cohen, and Astrid von Busekist (New York: Columbia University Press, 2018), 33–51.

13. Raphaëlle Khan, "Sovereignty after the Empire and the Search for a New Order: India's Attempt to Negotiate a Common Citizenship in the Commonwealth (1947–1949)," *Journal of Imperial and Commonwealth History* 49, no. 6 (2021): 1141–74; Kalathmika Natarajan, "Entangled Citizens: The Afterlives of Empire in the Indian Citizenship Act, 1947–1955," in *The Break-Up of Greater Britain*, ed. Christian D. Pedersen and Stuart Ward (Manchester: Manchester University Press, 2021), 63–83.

14. "Registration of Persons as Indian Citizens: Whether the Mission Can Register Persons of Indian Origin under Article 8 of the Constitution Instead of Section 5(1)(b) of the Citizenship Act, 1955," File No.20/93/58-IC, NAI.

15. Citizenship (Registration at Indian Consulates) Rules, 1956.

16. "Alleged Harassment of Indians in Malaya," *Times of India*, September 30, 1949.

17. Kernial Singh Sandhu, *Indians in Malaya: Some Aspects of Their Immigration and Settlement (1786–1957)* (Cambridge: Cambridge University Press, 1969), 150. Sunil Amrith, "Indians Overseas? Governing Tamil Migration to Malaya 1870–1941," *Past and Present* 208, no. 1 (2010): 231–61.

18. Kalyani Ramnath, "Other Partitions: Migrant Geographies and Disconnected

Histories between India and Malaya, 1945–1965," forthcoming in *South Asia Unbound: New International Histories of the Subcontinent*, ed. Bérénice Guyot-Réchard and Elisabeth Leake (Leiden: Leiden University Press, 2023)

19. Sarah Ansari, "Subjects or Citizens? India, Pakistan and the 1948 British Nationality Act," *Journal of Imperial and Commonwealth History* 41, no. 2 (2013): 285–312.

20. Frederick Cooper, *Citizenship between Empire and Nation: Remaking France and French Africa, 1945–1960* (Princeton, NJ: Princeton University Press, 2014); Todd Shepard, *The Invention of Decolonization: The Algerian War and the Remaking of France* (Ithaca, NY: Cornell University Press, 2006).

21. Jessica Namakkal, *Unsettling Utopia: The Making and Unmaking of French India* (New York: Columbia University Press, 2021).

22. Pamila Gupta, *Portuguese Decolonization in the Indian Ocean World* (London: Bloomsbury, 2018) (emphasizing materiality, migration, and decolonization around the western Indian Ocean); see also Jason Keith Fernandes, *Citizenship in a Caste Polity: Religion, Language, and Belonging in Goa* (Hyderabad: Orient Black Swan, 2020) (focusing on the role of religion and caste in the making of citizenship in Goa).

23. Kalathmika Natarajan, "The Privilege of the Indian Passport (1947–1967): Caste, Class, and the Afterlives of Indenture in Indian Diplomacy," *Modern Asian Studies*, pre-published online July 11, 2022, 1–30, https://doi.org/10.1017/S0026749X22000063.

24. Alison Bashford, "Immigration Restriction: Rethinking Period and Place from Settler Colonies to Postcolonial Nations," *Journal of Global History* 9, no. 1 (2014): 26–48 (describing how postwar immigration laws and the category of "British subject" blurred the boundaries between allegiance and ethnicity).

25. Here, the example of what Maria Kaladeen and David Dabydeen call "the other Windrush" that brought former British subjects from the Caribbean to Britain between 1948 and 1971, including the descendants of indentured laborers who had traveled there from India during the nineteenth century, is most pertinent. See Maria del Pilar Kaladeen and David Dabydeen, eds., *The Other Windrush: Legacies of Indenture in Britain's Caribbean Empire* (London: Pluto Press, 2021).

26. Su Lin Lewis and Carolien Stolte, "Other Bandungs: Afro-Asian Internationalisms in the Early Cold War," *Journal of World History* 30, no. 1 (2019): 1–19.

27. Su Lin Lewis, "Asian Socialism and the Forgotten Architects of Post-colonial Freedom, 1952–1956," *Journal of World History* 30, no. 1 (2019): 55–88.

28. Cindy Ewing, "The 'Fate of Minorities' in the Early Afro-Asian Struggle for Decolonization," *Comparative Studies of South Asia, Africa and the Middle East* 41, no. 3 (2021): 340–46.

29. In 1956 there were three cases concerning the Immigration (Emergency Provisions) Act of 1947 that the Supreme Court in Rangoon heard together: Karam Singh v. Controller of Immigration, John Chew v. Controller of Immigration, and Tan Choon Chaung v. Controller of Immigration (1956) BLR 6. In all three cases, the order of deportation was quashed because the court ruled that there was no grounds on which people who were born in Burma—even those who had evacuated during the war years—could come within the ambit of the 1947 Act.

30. Kanapathipillai, *Citizenship and Statelessness*, 1–7.

31. Renaud Egreteau, "The Idealization of a Lost Paradise: Narratives of Nostal-

gia and Traumatic Return Migration among Indian Repatriates from Burma since the 1960s," *Journal of Burma Studies* 18, no. 1 (2014): 137–80.

32. Thant Myint-U, *The River of Lost Footsteps: A Personal History of Burma* (New York: Farrar, Straus, and Giroux, 2007).

33. The Union Citizenship Act of 1948. In Hasan Ali v. Secretary, Ministry of Immigration and National Registration and Meher Ali v. Secretary, Ministry of Immigration and National Registration (1959) BLR 67, the Supreme Court ruled that just because a person did not "look" Burmese or speak Burmese or Arakanese did not mean that they were not statutory citizens under the Union Citizenship Act. They could not be deported as aliens.

34. Usha Mahajani, *The Role of Indian Minorities in Burma and Malaya* (Westport, CT: Greenwood Press, 1960), 180.

35. W. S. Desai, *India and Burma: A Study* (Bombay: Orient Longmans, 1952).

36. Mahajani, *Role of Indian Minorities*, 185.

37. Annual Reports, Rangoon, Ministry of External Affairs, 1963, NAI.

38. Regarding confiscation of properties of Indian nationals in Pakistan, Burma, and Ceylon, Progs. Nos. 125 (8) GA (1966), NAI. See also Rohit De, "Evacuee Property and the Management of Economic Life in Postcolonial India," in Prakash, Laffan, and Menon, *Postcolonial Moment*, 87–106.

39. Mahajani, *Role of Indian Minorities*, 179.

40. "Miserable Plight of Indians in Burma: Local Harassments and an Unhelpful Embassy," *Times of India*, May 11, 1964.

41. Natarajan, "Privilege of the Indian Passport."

42. Mahajani, *Role of Indian Minorities*, 179.

43. Annual Reports from Rangoon, 1964.

44. "To Burma, for Our Properties," *Business Standard*, June 3, 2014; "Sepia-Tinted Memories: Tamil Nadu's Enduring Links with Burma," *The Hindu*, February 24, 2021.

45. See, for example, Commissioner of Income Tax, Madras v. V. Mr. P. Firm and Ors. AIR (1965) SC 1216, see also S. L. N. Sathappa Chettiar v. Commissioner of Income Tax (1959) 35 ITR 641 Mad; M. L. M. Muthiah Chettiar v. Commissioner of Income-Tax (1959) 2 MLJ 196.

46. A. M. K. M. K. v. M. R. M. Periyanan Chettiar (1955) UKPC 1.

47. G1693, Citizenship Application of Nallan Ramaswamy, NASL.

48. Govindan Sellappah Nayar Kodakan Pillai v. Punchi Banda Mundanayake (1953) UKPC 13.

49. Kodakan Pillai v. Mundanayake.

50. Report of the Controller of Immigration, Ceylon Administration Reports, 1963–1964, NASL.

51. Kanapathipillai, *Citizenship and Statelessness*, 1–7.

52. "Repatriation of Indian Tamils," FCO 37/345, TNA.

53. HI/1011/7/77, Annual Report for 1976 from Kandy, Ministry of External Affairs (Historic Division, Research, and Intelligence), NAI.

54. Kanapathipillai, *Citizenship and Statelessness*.

55. Nethra Samarawickrema, "Speculating Sapphires: Mining, Trading, and Dreams That Move Gems across the Indian Ocean" (PhD diss., Stanford University, 2020).

56. "Indian Interests in Burma Safe, Says Ne Win," *Times of India*, September 6, 1964.

57. Deborah Sutton, "Imagined Sovereignty and the Indian Subject: Partition and Politics beyond the Nation, 1948–1960," *Contemporary South Asia* 19, no. 4 (December 1, 2011): 409–25.

58. "Revisiting Our Estate Repatriates," *The Island*, December 19, 2000.

59. Ravindran Sriramachandran, "Life Is Where We Are Not: Making and Managing the Plantation Tamil" (PhD diss., Columbia University, 2010).

60. Mahajani, *Role of Indian Minorities*, 189.

61. In 1968, the camps for Burma repatriates were as follows: Madras (Gummidipoondi and Sholavaram), Andhra Pradesh (Hanumantavaka and Kancharapalem), Orissa (Berhampore and Sunabeda), West Bengal (Hasnabad), and Bihar (Maranga). In Maranga and Sunabeda, the camps were initially set up for migrants from East Pakistan. By July 1968, the Government of India estimated that nearly 86,674 repatriates had arrived in India by air and sea in Madras and 24,509 in Andhra Pradesh, while 38,146 left for unknown destinations. Out of these numbers, by June 1968, 36,619 stayed in camps in Madras, and 18,753 stayed in camps in Andhra Pradesh. See "Camps in India for Repatriates from Burma," File No. SI/411/8/68, Ministry of External Affairs, NAI; "Burma Repatriates," Andhra Pradesh Legislative Assembly Debates, March 30, 1965.

62. "Repatriates from Burma," File No. SI/411/8/68, Ministry of External Affairs, NAI.

63. "Question of Granting Citizenship Passports to the Returnees of Indian Origin from Burma," File No. 1/2/66, Ministry of Home Affairs, NAI.

64. Vazira Fazila-Yacoobali Zamindar, *Long Partition and the Making of Modern South Asia: Refugees, Boundaries, Histories* (Ithaca, NY: Columbia University Press, 2007).

65. Zamindar, *Long Partition*; Rotem Geva, *Delhi Reborn: Partition and Nation Building in India's Capital* (Stanford, CA: Stanford University Press, 2022).

66. Uditi Sen, *Citizen Refugee: Forging the Indian Nation after Partition* (Cambridge: Cambridge University Press, 2018), 94.

67. Sen, *Citizen Refugee*, 109.

68. Sen, *Citizen Refugee*, 109.

69. Emma Meyer, "Resettling Burma's Displaced: Labor, Rehabilitation, and Citizenship in Visakhapatnam, India, 1937–1979" (PhD diss., Emory University, 2020).

70. Gyanesh Kudaisya and Tan Tai Yong, "From Displacement to Development: East Punjab Countryside after Partition," in *The Aftermath of Partition in South Asia* (New York: Routledge, 2000), 125–40; Ria Kapoor, *Making Refugees in India* (New York: Oxford University Press, 2022). Similar initiatives of incorporating refugees into the nation-state took place through expulsions as in the case of Malaysia and Singapore.

71. Lakshmi Subramanian, "Tamils and Greater India: Some Issues of Connected Histories," *Cultural Dynamics* 24, nos. 2–3 (2012): 159–74.

72. Darinee Alagirisamy, "The Self-Respect Movement and Tamil Politics of Belonging in Interwar British Malaya, 1929–1939," *Modern Asian Studies* 50, no. 5 (2016): 1547–75.

73. National Heritage Board, "G. Sarangapany: Publisher and Reformist," Roots, accessed November 8, 2022, https://www.roots.gov.sg/stories-landing/stories/g-sarangapany/story.

74. Rachel Leow, *Taming Babel: Language in the Making of Malaysia* (Cambridge: Cambridge University Press, 2016).

75. S. K. Pottekkat, "Avalude Keralam," in *Antharvahini* (Kozhikode: Mathrubhumi Books, 2020).

76. Harshana Rambukwella, "What Got 'Left' Behind: The Limits of Leftist Engagements with Art and Culture in Postcolonial Sri Lanka," in *Forms of the Left in Postcolonial South Asia: Aesthetics, Networks and Connected Histories*, ed. Sanjukta Sunderason et al. (London: Bloomsbury, 2021).

77. Tharaphi Than, "The Languages of Pyidawtha and the Burmese Approach to National Development," *South East Asia Research* 21, no. 4 (2013): 639–54.

78. Antara Datta, *Refugees and Borders in South Asia: The Great Exodus of 1971* (London: Routledge, 2013).

79. Namakkal, *Unsettling Utopia*.

80. Kara Moskowitz, *Seeing Like a Citizen: Decolonization, Development, and the Making of Kenya, 1945–1980* (Athens: Ohio University Press, 2019).

81. On African decolonization in historical perspective, see Jean Allman, "The Fate of All of Us: African Counterrevolutions and the Ends of 1968," *American Historical Review* 123, no. 3 (2018): 728–32.

Conclusion

1. Nick Cheesman, "How in Myanmar 'National Races' Came to Surpass Citizenship and Exclude Rohingya," *Journal of Contemporary Asia* 47, no. 3 (2017): 461–83; Nyi Nyi Kaw, "Citizenship Stripping in Myanmar as Lawfar," *Statelessness and Citizenship Review* 4, no. 2 (2022): 280–85.

2. "Note on Indian and Stateless Indian Nationals in West Asia, South Asia, and Stateless Persons of Indian Descent in Burma, Sri Lanka Malaysia and Singapore," FIII/102/16/81, NAI.

3. Niranjan Desai, "Revisiting the 1972 Expulsion of Asians from Uganda," *Indian Foreign Affairs Journal* 7, no. 4 (2012): 446–58.

4. Sujit Sivasundaram, *Islanded: Britain, Sri Lanka, and the Bounds of an Indian Ocean Colony* (Chicago: University of Chicago Press, 2013).

5. Sugata Bose, "Space and Time on the Indian Ocean Rim," in *A Hundred Horizons: The Indian Ocean in the Age of Global Empire* (Cambridge, MA: Harvard University Press, 2006).

6. Kalyani Ramnath, "Intertwined Itineraries: Debt, Decolonization and International Law in Post-WWII South Asia," *Law and History Review* 38 no. 1 (2020): 1–24.

7. Dennis B. McGilvray, *Crucible of Conflict: Tamil and Muslim Society on the East Coast of Sri Lanka* (Durham, NC: Duke University Press, 2008); Torsten Tschacher, "The Challenges of Diversity: 'Casting' Muslim Communities in South India," in *Being Muslim in South Asia: Diversity and Daily Life*, ed. Robin Jeffrey and Ronojoy Sen (New Delhi: Oxford University Press, 2014), 64–86.

8. Luis Eslava and Sundhya Pahuja. "The State and International Law: A Reading from the Global South," *Humanity: An International Journal of Human Rights, Humanitarianism, and Development* 11, no. 1 (2020): 118–38.

SELECTED BIBLIOGRAPHY

Archives
India Office Records and Private Papers, British Library
Burma Office Records
Privy Council Papers, Case Papers of Govindan Sellapah Nadar Kodakan Pillai (1952)
Public and Judicial Department
Reports from Indian Newspapers published in Burma (1938–42)

The National Archives, Kew
Colonial Office Records
Dominion Office Records
Foreign and Commonwealth Office Records
War Office Records

National Archives of India, New Delhi
Board of Inland Revenue
Central Board of Revenue
Commonwealth Relations Department
Indians Overseas Department
Ministry of External Affairs

Nehru Memorial Museum and Library, New Delhi
M. S. Aney Papers
S. A. S. Tyabji Papers
V. S. Srinivasa Sastri Papers

Tamil Nadu State Archives, Chennai
Fortnightly Reports
Native Newspaper Reports
Proceedings of the Food Department
Proceedings of the Home Department
Proceedings of the Industries, Labour, and Cooperation Department
Proceedings of the Public Works Department
Undersecretary's Safe Secret Files

Madras High Court Record Room
Civil Appeals

Criminal Miscellaneous Petitions
Referred Cases

Kerala State Archives, Trivandrum
Confidential Section Files

National Archives of Sri Lanka, Colombo
Department of Immigration and Emigration
Ceylon Administration Reports

The Notes cite additional archival sources consulted at the National Archives of Myanmar, the National Archives of Singapore, the A. K. Gopalan Research Center in Trivandrum, and the Roja Muthiah Research Library in Chennai, among others.

Law Reports
All India Reporter
Burma Law Reports
International Law Reports
Madras Law Journal
Malayan Law Reports
New Law Reports
Rangoon Law Reports

Secondary Sources
Abraham, Itty. *How India Became Territorial: Foreign Policy, Diaspora, Geopolitics.* Stanford, CA: Stanford University Press, 2014.
Adas, Michael. *The Burma Delta: Economic Development and Social Change on an Asian Rice Frontier, 1852–1941.* Madison: University of Wisconsin Press, 2011.
Aiyar, Sana. *Indians in Kenya: The Politics of Diaspora.* Cambridge, MA: Harvard University Press, 2015.
Alagirisamy, Darinee. "The Self-Respect Movement and Tamil Politics of Belonging in Interwar British Malaya, 1929–1939." *Modern Asian Studies* 50, no. 5 (2016): 1547–75.
Ali, Kamran Asdar. "The Enemy Within: Communism and the New Pakistani State." In Prakash, Laffan, and Menon, *Postcolonial Moment*, 31–48.
Alpers, Edward A., and Chhaya Goswami, eds. *Transregional Trade and Traders: Situating Gujarat in the Indian Ocean from Early Times to 1900.* Oxford: Oxford University Press, 2019.
Alwis, Malathi De. "'Disappearance' and 'Displacement' in Sri Lanka." *Journal of Refugee Studies* 22, no. 3 (2009): 378–91.
Ampalavanar, Rajeswary. *The Indian Minority and Political Change in Malaya, 1945–1957.* Oxford: Oxford University Press, 1981.
Amrith, Sunil. *Crossing the Bay of Bengal: The Furies of Nature and the Fortunes of Migrants.* Cambridge, MA: Harvard University Press, 2013.
———. "Indians Overseas? Governing Tamil Migration to Malaya, 1870–1941." *Past and Present* 208, no. 1 (2010): 231–61.

———. "Mobile City and the Coromandel Coast: Tamil Journeys to Singapore, 1920–1960." *Mobilities* 5, no. 2 (2010): 237–55.

———. "Reconstructing the 'Plural Society': Asian Migration between Empire and Nation, 1940–1948." *Past and Present* 210, no. 6 (2011): 237–57.

———. "Struggles for Citizenship around the Bay of Bengal." In Prakash, Laffan, and Menon, *Postcolonial Moment*, 107–20.

———. "Tamil Diasporas across the Bay of Bengal." *American Historical Review* 114, no. 3 (2009): 547–72.

Ansari, Sarah. "Subjects or Citizens? India, Pakistan and the 1948 British Nationality Act." *Journal of Imperial and Commonwealth History* 41, no. 2 (2013): 285–312.

Arasaratnam, Sinnappah. *Indians in Malaysia and Singapore*. London: Institute of Race Relations, 1970.

———. "Indian Society of Malaysia and Its Leaders: Trends in Leadership and Ideology among Malaysian Indians, 1945–60." *Journal of Southeast Asian Studies* 13, no. 2 (1982): 236–51.

Aung-Thwin, Maitrii. *The Return of the Galon King: History, Law, and Rebellion in Colonial Burma*. Singapore: NUS Press, 2011.

Azeez, I. L. M. Abdul. "A Criticism of Mr. Ramanathan's 'Ethnology of the Moors of Ceylon.'" In *The Sri Lanka Reader: History, Culture, Politics*, edited by John Holt, 424–28. Durham, NC: Duke University Press, 2011.

Bailkin, Jordanna. *The Afterlife of Empire*. Berkeley: University of California Press, 2012.

Baker, Christopher. "Colonial Rule and the Internal Economy in Twentieth-Century Madras." *Modern Asian Studies* 15, no. 3 (1981): 575–602.

Ballantyne, Tony, and Antoinette M. Burton. *Moving Subjects: Gender, Mobility, and Intimacy in an Age of Global Empire*. Urbana: University of Illinois Press, 2009.

Banerjee, Anandagopal. *Income-Tax Law and Practice in India*. Calcutta: India International, 1946.

Banerjee, Sukanya. *Becoming Imperial Citizens: Indians in the Late-Victorian Empire*. Durham, NC: Duke University Press, 2010.

Bashford, Alison. "Immigration Restriction: Rethinking Period and Place from Settler Colonies to Postcolonial Nations." *Journal of Global History* 9, no. 1 (2014): 26–48.

Bass, Daniel. *Everyday Ethnicity in Sri Lanka: Up-Country Tamil Identity Politics*. London: Routledge, 2013.

Bayly, Christopher, and Timothy Harper. *Forgotten Armies: The Fall of British Asia, 1941–1945*. Cambridge, MA: Harvard University Press, 2006.

———. *Forgotten Wars: Freedom and Revolution in Southeast Asia*. Cambridge, MA: Harvard University Press, 2007.

Benton, Lauren. *Law and Colonial Cultures: Legal Regimes in World History, 1400–1900*. Cambridge: Cambridge University Press, 2002.

———. *A Search for Sovereignty: Law and Geography in European Empires, 1400–1900*. Cambridge: Cambridge University Press, 2009.

Bhattacharya, Sanjoy. "The Colonial State and the Communist Party of India, 1942–45: A Reappraisal." *South Asia Research* 15, no. 1 (1995): 48–77.

Birla, Ritu. "Law as Economy: Convention, Corporation, Currency." *UC Irvine Law Review* 1 (2011): 1015.

———. *Stages of Capital: Law, Culture, and Market Governance in Late Colonial India.* Durham, NC: Duke University Press, 2008.

Bishara, Fahad Ahmad. "The Sailing Scribes: Circulating Law in the Twentieth-Century Indian Ocean." *Law and History Review*, prepublished online, August 30, 2022, 1–18. https://doi.org/10.1017/S0738248022000402.

———. *A Sea of Debt: Law and Economic Life in the Western Indian Ocean, 1780–1950.* Cambridge: Cambridge University Press, 2017.

Bishara, Fahad, and Hollian Wint. "Into the Bazaar: Indian Ocean Vernaculars in the Age of Global Capitalism." *Journal of Global History* 16, no. 1 (2021): 44–64.

Bose, Neilesh. "New Settler Colonial Histories at the Edges of Empire: 'Asiatics,' Settlers, and Law in Colonial South Africa." *Journal of Colonialism and Colonial History* 15, no. 1 (2014). https://doi.org/10.1353/cch.2014.0017.

Bose, Sugata. *His Majesty's Opponent: Subash Chandra Bose and India's Struggle against Empire.* Cambridge, MA: Harvard University Press, 2011.

———. *A Hundred Horizons: The Indian Ocean in the Age of Global Empire.* Cambridge, MA: Harvard University Press, 2006.

Chandra, Bipan Visalakshi Menon, and Salil Misra, eds. *Towards Freedom: Documents on the Movement for Independence in India, 1942: Part I.* New Delhi: Oxford University Press, 2016.

Chatterjee, Indrani. *Unfamiliar Relations: Family and History in South Asia.* New Brunswick, NJ: Rutgers University Press, 2004.

Chatterji, Joya. "From Imperial Subjects to National Citizens: South Asians and the International Migration Regime since 1947." In *Routledge Handbook of the South Asian Diaspora*, edited by Joya Chatterji and David Washbrook, 183–97. London: Routledge, 2013.

———. "South Asian Histories of Citizenship, 1946–1970." *Historical Journal* 55, no. 4 (December 1, 2012): 1049–71.

Cheah, Boon Kheng. *Red Star over Malaya: Resistance and Social Conflict during and after the Japanese Occupation of Malaya, 1941–1946.* Singapore: Singapore University Press, National University of Singapore, 2003.

Cheesman, Nick. "How in Myanmar 'National Races' Came to Surpass Citizenship and Exclude Rohingya." *Journal of Contemporary Asia* 47, no. 3 (2017): 461–83.

Cheng, Siok-Hwa. *The Rice Industry of Burma, 1852–1940.* Kuala Lumpur: University of Malaya Press, 1968.

Chimni, B. S. "The International Law of Jurisdiction: A TWAIL Perspective." *Leiden Journal of International Law* 35, no. 1 (2022): 29–54.

Chin, Low Choo. "Immigration Control during the Malayan Emergency: Borders, Belonging and Citizenship, 1948–1960." *Journal of the Malaysian Branch of the Royal Asiatic Society* 89, no. 1 (2016): 35–60.

Cohen, Gerard Daniel. *In War's Wake: Europe's Displaced Persons in the Postwar Order.* Oxford: Oxford University Press, 2011.

Cohn, Bernard S. *Colonialism and Its Forms of Knowledge: The British in India.* Princeton, NJ: Princeton University Press, 1996.

Cons, Jason, and Romola Sanyal. "Geographies at the Margins: Borders in South Asia—an Introduction." *Political Geography* 35 (2013): 5–13.

Constable, Marianne. "Afterword: Conflicts as a Law of Laws?" *Law and Contemporary Problems* 71, no. 3 (2008): 343–49.

Cooper, Frederick. *Citizenship between Empire and Nation: Remaking France and French Africa, 1945–1960.* Princeton, NJ: Princeton University Press, 2014.

Curless, Gareth. "The Triumph of the State: Singapore's Dockworkers and the Limits of Global History c. 1920–1965." *Historical Journal* 60 (December 2017): 1–27.

Das, Sudhir Kumar. *Japanese Occupation and Ex Post Facto Legislation in Malaya.* N.p.: Malayan Law Journal, 1960.

Das, Veena. ""The Figure of the Abducted Woman: The Citizen as Sexed." In *Life and Words: Violence and the Descent into the Ordinary,* 18–37. Berkeley: University of California Press, 2007.

Datta, Antara. *Refugees and Borders in South Asia: The Great Exodus of 1971.* London: Routledge, 2013.

Datta, Arunima. *Fleeting Agencies: A Social History of Indian Coolie Women in British Malaya.* Cambridge: Cambridge University Press, 2021.

———. "'Immorality,' Nationalism and the Colonial State in British Malaya: Indian 'Coolie' Women's Intimate Lives as Ideological Battleground." *Women's History Review* 25, no. 4 (2016): 584–601.

De, Rohit. "'Commodities Must Be Controlled': Economic Crimes and Market Discipline in India (1939–1955)." *International Journal of Law in Context* 10, no. 3 (September 2014): 277–94.

———. "Evacuee Property and the Management of Economic Life in Postcolonial India." In Prakash, Laffan, and Menon, *Postcolonial Moment,* 87–106.

Devas, S. *The Future of Burma.* N.p.: n.p., 1947.

Dubnov, Arie, and Laura Robson. *Partitions: A Transnational History of Twentieth-Century Territorial Separatism.* Stanford, CA: Stanford University Press, 2019.

Egreteau, Renaud. "The Idealization of a Lost Paradise: Narratives of Nostalgia and Traumatic Return Migration among Indian Repatriates from Burma since the 1960s." *Journal of Burma Studies* 18, no. 1 (2014): 137–80.

Ervin, Charles Wesley. *Tomorrow Is Ours: The Trotskyist Movement in India and Ceylon, 1935–48.* Colombo: Social Scientists' Association, 2006.

Eslava, Luis, Michael Fakhri, and Vasuki Nesiah, eds. *Bandung, Global History, and International Law: Critical Pasts and Pending Futures.* Cambridge: Cambridge University Press, 2017.

Eslava, Luis, and Sundhya Pahuja. "The State and International Law: A Reading from the Global South." *Humanity: An International Journal of Human Rights, Humanitarianism, and Development* 11, no. 1 (2020): 118–38.

Ewing, Cindy. "The Colombo Powers: Crafting Diplomacy in the Third World and Launching Afro-Asia at Bandung." *Cold War History* 19, no. 1 (2019): 1–19.

———. "The 'Fate of Minorities' in the Early Afro-Asian Struggle for Decolonization." *Comparative Studies of South Asia, Africa and the Middle East* 41, no. 3 (2021): 340–46.

Getachew, Adom. *Worldmaking after Empire: The Rise and Fall of Self-Determination.* Princeton, NJ: Princeton University Press, 2019.

Geva, Rotem. *Delhi Reborn: Partition and Nation Building in India's Capital.* Stanford, CA: Stanford University Press, 2022.

Ghosh, Durba. *Sex and the Family in Colonial India: The Making of Empire*. Cambridge: Cambridge University Press, 2006.

Godsmark, Oliver. *Citizenship, Community, and Democracy in India: From Bombay to Maharashtra, c. 1930–1960*. London: Routledge, 2018.

Gopalan, A. K. *Ente Jeevitha Katha*. 12th ed. Thiruvanathapuram: Chinta, 2015.

Gopalratnam, V. C. *A Century Completed: A History of the Madras High Court, 1862–1962*. Madras: Madras Law Journal Office, 1962.

Goswami, Manu. "Imaginary Futures and Colonial Internationalisms." *American Historical Review* 117, no. 5 (2012): 1461–85.

———. *Producing India: From Colonial Economy to National Space*. Chicago: University of Chicago Press, 2010.

Gross, Ariela Julie. *What Blood Won't Tell*. Cambridge, MA: Harvard University Press, 2009.

Gupta, Amit Kumar, and Arjun Dev. *Towards Freedom: Documents on the Movement for Independence in India, 1941*. Oxford: Oxford University Press, 2010.

Gupta, D. N. *Communism and Nationalism in Colonial India, 1939–45*. New Delhi: Sage Publications India, 2008.

Guyot-Réchard, Bérénice. "When Legions Thunder Past: The Second World War and India's Northeastern Frontier." *War in History* 25, no. 3 (2018): 328–60.

Hack, Karl. *Defence and Decolonisation in Southeast Asia: Britain, Malaya and Singapore, 1941–1968*. Richmond: Curzon, 2001.

———. "'Iron Claws on Malaya': The Historiography of the Malayan Emergency." *Journal of Southeast Asian Studies* 30, no. 1 (1999): 99–125.

———. "The Origins of the Asian Cold War: Malaya 1948." *Journal of Southeast Asian Studies* 40, no. 3 (October 2009): 471–96.

Hall, Kenneth R. "Ports-of-Trade, Maritime Diasporas, and Networks of Trade and Cultural Integration in the Bay of Bengal Region of the Indian Ocean: C. 1300–1500." *Journal of the Economic and Social History of the Orient* 53, nos. 1–2 (2010): 109–45.

Halliday, Paul Delaney. *Habeas Corpus: From England to Empire*. Cambridge, MA: Harvard University Press, 2010.

Hanley, Will. *Identifying with Nationality: Europeans, Ottomans, and Egyptians in Alexandria*. New York: Columbia University Press, 2017.

Hansen, Thomas Blom, and Finn Stepputat. *Sovereign Bodies: Citizens, Migrants, and States in the Postcolonial World*. Princeton, NJ: Princeton University Press, 2009.

Harding, Andrew. *The Constitution of Malaysia: A Contextual Analysis*. London: Bloomsbury, 2022.

Harper, Timothy. *The End of Empire and the Making of Malaya*. Cambridge: Cambridge University Press, 2001.

———. *Underground Asia: Global Revolutionaries and the Assault on Empire*. Cambridge, MA: Harvard University Press, 2021.

Hartog, Hendrik. *Man and Wife in America: A History*. Cambridge, MA: Harvard University Press, 2000.

———. *The Trouble with Minna: A Case of Slavery and Emancipation in the Antebellum North*. Chapel Hill: University of North Carolina Press, 2018.

Hassan, M. C. A. *Sir Razik Fareed: The Political and Personal Life of Sir Razik Fareed, O.B.E., M.P., J.P.U.M., the Ceylon Moor Leader, with a Biographical Sketch of His Father and Grandfather.* [Colombo?]: Sir Razik Fareed Foundation, 1968.

Hiralal, Kalpana. "'What Is the Meaning of the Word "Wife?"' The Impact of the Immigration Laws on the Wives of Resident Indians in South Africa, 1897–1930." *Contemporary South Asia* 26, no. 2 (2018): 206–20.

Ho, Engseng. "Afterword: Mobile Law and Thick Transregionalism." *Law and History Review* 32, no. 4 (November 2014): 883–89.

———. *The Graves of Tarim: Genealogy and Mobility across the Indian Ocean.* Berkeley: University of California Press, 2006.

Holt, John, ed. *Buddhist Extremists and Muslim Minorities: Religious Conflict in Contemporary Sri Lanka.* Oxford: Oxford University Press, 2016.

Huff, Gregg, and Shinobu Majima. "Financing Japan's World War II Occupation of Southeast Asia." *Journal of Economic History* 73, no. 4 (2013): 937–77.

Huff, W. G. "The Development of the Rubber Market in Pre-World War II Singapore." *Journal of Southeast Asian Studies* 24, no. 2 (1993): 285–306.

Hussain, Nasser. *The Jurisprudence of Emergency: Colonialism and the Rule of Law.* Ann Arbor: University of Michigan Press, 2003.

Ibrahim, Farhana. "Cross-Border Intimacies: Marriage, Migration and Citizenship in Western India." *Modern Asian Studies* 52, no. 5 (2018): 1664–91.

Ibrahim, Farhana, and Tanuja Kothiyal. "Beyond Territorial and Jurisdictional Confines." *Economic and Political Weekly* 52, no. 15 (2015): 7–8.

Ikeya, Chie. "Colonial Intimacies in Comparative Perspective: Intermarriage, Law and Cultural Difference in British Burma." *Journal of Colonialism and Colonial History,* 14, no. 1 (2013). http://doi.org/10.1353/cch.2013.0014.

Jayal, Niraja Gopal. *Citizenship and Its Discontents: An Indian History.* Cambridge, MA: Harvard University Press, 2013.

Jayawardena, Kumari, and Rachel Kurian. *Class, Patriarchy and Ethnicity on Sri Lankan Plantations: Two Centuries of Power and Protest.* Hyderabad: Orient Black Swan, 2015.

Jegathesan, Mythri. *Tea and Solidarity: Tamil Women and Work in Postwar Sri Lanka.* Seattle: University of Washington Press, 2019.

Kamtekar, Indivar. "A Different War Dance: State and Class in India, 1939–1945." *Past and Present,* no. 176 (2002): 187–221.

———. "The Shiver of 1942." *Studies in History* 18, no. 1 (2002): 81–102.

Kananatu, Thaatchaayini. *Minorities, Rights and the Law in Malaysia.* London: Routledge, 2020.

Kanapathipillai, Valli. *Citizenship and Statelessness in Sri Lanka: The Case of the Tamil Estate Workers.* London: Anthem Press, 2009.

Kanapathypillai, A. P. *The Epic of Tea: Politics in the Plantations of Sri Lanka.* Colombo: Social Scientists' Association, 2011.

Kapoor, Ria. "Removing the International from the Refugee: India in the 1940s." *Humanity: An International Journal of Human Rights, Humanitarianism, and Development* 12, no. 1 (2021): 1–19.

Kaur, Amarjit. "Indian Labour, Labour Standards, and Workers' Health in Burma and Malaya, 1900–1940." *Modern Asian Studies* 40, no. 2 (May 2006): 425–75.

Kaur, Ravinder. "Distinctive Citizenship: Refugees, Subjects and the Postcolonial State in India's Partition." *Cultural and Social History* 6, no. 4 (2009): 429–46.

Kearney, Robert N. "Introduction: The 1915 Riots in Ceylon." *Journal of Asian Studies* 29, no. 2 (1970): 219–22.

Kesby, Alison. *The Right to Have Rights: Citizenship, Humanity, and International Law.* Oxford: Oxford University Press, 2012.

Khan, Raphaëlle. "Sovereignty after the Empire and the Search for a New Order: India's Attempt to Negotiate a Common Citizenship in the Commonwealth (1947–1949)." *Journal of Imperial and Commonwealth History* 49, no. 6 (2021): 1141–74.

Khan, Yasmin. *India at War: The Subcontinent and the Second World War.* New York: Oxford University Press, 2015.

Kim, Diana, *Empires of Vice: The Rise of Opium Prohibition across Southeast Asia.* Princeton, NJ: Princeton University Press, 2020.

Kim, Sophie-Jung H., Alastair McClure, and Joseph McQuade. "Making and Unmaking the Nation in World History: Introduction." *History Compass* 15, no. 2 (2017). https://doi.org/10.1111/hic3.12321.

Knop, Karen, Ralf Michaels, and Annelise Riles. "From Multiculturalism to Technique: Feminism, Culture, and the Conflict of Laws Style." *Stanford Law Review* 64, no. 3 (2012): 589–656.

Kondapi, C. *Indians Overseas, 1838–1949.* New Delhi: Indian Council of World Affairs, 1951.

Koskenniemi, Martii. "Expanding Histories of International Law." *American Journal of Legal History* 56, no. 1 (2016): 104–12.

Kratoska, Paul. *Asian Labor in the Wartime Japanese Empire.* New York: M. E. Sharpe, 2005.

———. "Banana Money: Consequences of the Demonetization of Wartime Japanese Currency in British Malaya." *Journal of Southeast Asian Studies* 23, no. 2 (1992): 322–45.

———. "Chettiar Moneylenders and Rural Credit in British Malaya." *Journal of the Malaysian Branch of the Royal Asiatic Society* 86, no. 1 (2013): 61–78.

———. *The Japanese Occupation of Malaya: A Social and Economic History.* Honolulu: University of Hawai'i Press, 1997.

Kudaisya, Medha. "Marwari and Chettiar Merchants, c. 1850s–1950s: Comparative Trajectories." In *Chinese and Indian Business: Historical Antecedents*, edited by Medha M. Kudaisya and Chin-Keong Ng, 85–119. Leiden: Brill, 2010.

Kumarasingham, Harshan. *Constitution-Making in Asia: Decolonisation and State-Building in the Aftermath of the British Empire.* London: Routledge, 2016.

———. "The 'Tropical Dominions': The Appeal of Dominion Status in the Decolonisation of India, Pakistan, and Ceylon." *Transactions of the Royal Historical Society*, 6th ser., 23 (December 2013): 223–45.

Laffan, Michael, ed. *Belonging across the Bay of Bengal: Religious Rites, Colonial Migrations, National Rights.* London: Bloomsbury, 2017.

Lee, Christopher J. "Jus Soli and Jus Sanguinis in the Colonies: The Interwar Politics of Race, Culture, and Multiracial Legal Status in British Africa." *Law and History Review* 29, no. 2 (2011): 497–522.

Leigh, Michael D. *The Evacuation of Civilians from Burma: Analysing the 1942 Colonial Disaster.* London: Bloomsbury, 2014.

Leow, Rachel. *Taming Babel: Language in the Making of Malaysia*. Cambridge: Cambridge University Press, 2016.

Lewis, Su Lin. "Asian Socialism and the Forgotten Architects of Post-colonial Freedom, 1952–1956." *Journal of World History* 30, no. 1 (2019): 55–88.

Lewis, Su Lin, and Carolien Stolte. "Other Bandungs: Afro-Asian Internationalisms in the Early Cold War." *Journal of World History* 30, no. 1 (2019): 1–19.

Longmuir, Marilyn V. *The Money Trail: Burmese Currencies in Crisis, 1937–1947*. Dekalb: Center for Southeast Asian Studies, Northern Illinois University, 2002.

Ludden, David. "Spectres of Agrarian Territory in Southern India." *Indian Economic and Social History Review* 39, nos. 2–3 (September 1, 2002): 233–57.

Maclean, Kama, and J. David Elam. *Revolutionary Lives in South Asia: Acts and Afterlives of Anticolonial Political Action*. London: Routledge, 2016.

Madokoro, Lauren. *Elusive Refuge: Chinese Migrants in the Cold War*. Cambridge, MA: Harvard University Press, 2016.

Mahajani, Usha. *The Role of Indian Minorities in Burma and Malaya*. Westport, CT: Greenwood Press, 1960.

Mantena, Karuna, and Rama Sundari Mantena. "Introduction: Political Imaginaries at the End of Empire." *Ab Imperio* 2018, no. 3 (2018): 31–35.

Markovits, Claude. *The Global World of Indian Merchants, 1750–1947: Traders of Sind from Bukhara to Panama*. Cambridge: Cambridge University Press, 2000.

———. "Indian Merchant Networks outside India in the Nineteenth and Twentieth Centuries: A Preliminary Survey." *Modern Asian Studies* 33, no. 4 (October 1, 1999): 883–911.

Martin, Marina. "Hundi/Hawala: The Problem of Definition." *Modern Asian Studies* 43, no. 4 (2009): 909–37.

Mathew, Johan. "On Principals and Agency: Reassembling Trust in Indian Ocean Commerce." *Comparative Studies in Society and History* 61, no. 2 (2019): 242–68.

Mathur, Nayanika. *Paper Tiger: Law, Bureaucracy and the Developmental State in Himalayan India*. Cambridge: Cambridge University Press, 2015.

Maunaguru, Sidharthan. "Brides as Bridges? Tamilness through Movements, Documents and Anticipations." In *Pathways of Dissent: Tamil Nationalism in Sri Lanka*, edited by Dr. R. Cheran. New Delhi: Sage Publications, 2010.

Maung, E. "Enemy Legislation and Judgments in Burma." *Journal of Comparative Legislation and International Law* 30, nos. 3–4 (1948): 11–17.

Maung Maung. *Burma in the Family of Nations*. Djambatan: Institute of Pacific Relations, 1981.

———. *Burmese Nationalist Movements, 1940–1948*. Honolulu: University of Hawai'i Press, 1990.

Mawani, Renisa. "Law's Archive." *Annual Review of Law and Social Science* 8, no. 1 (2012): 337–65.

———. "The Times of Law." *Law and Social Inquiry* 40, no. 1 (2015): 253–63.

Mawani, Renisa, and Iza Hussin. "The Travels of Law: Indian Ocean Itineraries." *Law and History Review* 32, no. 4 (2014): 733–47.

Mazower, Mark. "Minorities and the League of Nations in Interwar Europe." *Daedalus* 126, no. 2 (1997): 47–63.

—. *No Enchanted Palace: The End of Empire and the Ideological Origins of the United Nations*. Princeton, NJ: Princeton University Press, 2009.

Mazumder, Rajashree. "Constructing the Indian Immigrant to Colonial Burma, 1885–1948." PhD diss., Duke University, 2013.

—. "'I Do Not Envy You': Mixed Marriages and Immigration Debates in the 1920s and 1930s Rangoon, Burma." *Indian Economic and Social History Review* 51, no. 4 (2014): 497–527.

McCoy, Alfred W. *Southeast Asia under Japanese Occupation*. New Haven, CT: Yale University, Southeast Asia Studies, 1985.

McGilvray, Dennis B. *Crucible of Conflict: Tamil and Muslim Society on the East Coast of Sri Lanka*. Durham, NC: Duke University Press, 2008.

—. "Rethinking Muslim Identity in Sri Lanka." In *Buddhist Extremists and Muslim Minorities: Religious Conflict in Contemporary Sri Lanka*, edited by John Holt, 54–77. Oxford: Oxford University Press, 2016.

McGilvray, Dennis B., and Mirak Raheem. "Origins of the Sri Lankan Muslims and Varieties of Muslim Identity." In *The Sri Lanka Reader: History, Culture, Politics*, edited by John Holt, 410–23. Durham, NC: Duke University Press, 2011.

Mckeown, Adam. "Global Migration, 1846–1940." *Journal of World History* 15, no. 2 (July 16, 2004): 155–89.

Metcalf, Thomas R. *Imperial Connections: India in the Indian Ocean Arena, 1860–1920*. Berkeley: University of California Press, 2007.

Meyer, Emma. "Resettling Burma's Displaced: Labor, Rehabilitation, and Citizenship in Visakhapatnam, India, 1937–1979." PhD diss., Emory University, 2020.

Mohammed, J Raja. *Maritime History of the Coromandel Muslims: A Socio-Historical Study on the Tamil Muslims 1750–1900*. Chennai: Director of Museums, Government Museum, 2004.

Mongia, Radhika. *Indian Migration and Empire: A Colonial Genealogy of the Modern State*. Durham, NC: Duke University Press, 2018.

More, J. B. Prashant. *The Political Evolution of Muslims in Tamilnadu and Madras, 1930–1947*. New Delhi: Orient Blackswan, 1997.

Moskowitz, Kara. *Seeing Like a Citizen: Decolonization, Development, and the Making of Kenya, 1945–1980*. Athens: Ohio University Press, 2019.

Mukherjee, Mithi. "The 'Right to Wage War' against Empire: Anticolonialism and the Challenge to International Law in the Indian National Army Trial of 1945." *Law and Social Inquiry* 44, no. 2 (2019): 420–43.

Muthiah, S. *Looking Back from "Moulmein": A Biography of A. M. M. Arunachalam*. Chennai: EastWest Books, 2000.

Muthiah, S., Meenakshi Meyappan, Visalakshi Ramaswamy, and V. Muthuraman. *The Chettiar Heritage*. Chennai: Chettiar Heritage, 2002.

Myint-U, Thant. *The River of Lost Footsteps: Histories of Burma*. New York: Farrar, Straus, and Giroux, 2007.

Nagarajan, Krishnaswami. *Dr. Rajah Sir Muthiah Chettiar: A Biography*. Annamalainagar: Annamalai University, 1989.

Nair, Neeti. "Introduction to Special Issue: Citizenship, Belonging, and the Partition of India." *Asian Affairs* 53, no. 2 (2022): 293–97.

Namakkal, Jessica. *Unsettling Utopia: The Making and Unmaking of French India*. New York: Columbia University Press, 2021.

Narayanaswami Naidu, Bijayeti Venkata, ed. *Raja Sir Annamalai Chettiar Commemoration Volume*. [Annamalainagar?]: Annamalai University, 1941.

Natarajan, Kalathmika. "Entangled Citizens: The Afterlives of Empire in the Indian Citizenship Act, 1947–1955." In *The Break-Up of Greater Britain*, edited by Christian D. Pedersen and Stuart Ward, 63–83. Manchester: Manchester University Press, 2021.

———. "The Privilege of the Indian Passport (1947–1967): Caste, Class, and the Afterlives of Indenture in Indian Diplomacy." *Modern Asian Studies*, prepublished online July 11, 2022, 1–30. https://doi.org/10.1017/S0026749X22000063.

Newbigin, Eleanor. *The Hindu Family and the Emergence of Modern India: Law, Citizenship and Community*. Cambridge: Cambridge University Press, 2013.

Nuhman, M. A. *Sri Lankan Muslims: Ethnic Identity within Cultural Diversity*. Colombo: International Centre for Ethnic Studies, 2007.

Pahuja, Sundhya. "Laws of Encounter: A Jurisdictional Account of International Law." *London Review of International Law* 1, no. 1 (2013): 63–98.

———. "Letters from Bandung: Encounters with Another International Law." In *Bandung, Global History, and International Law: Critical Pasts and Pending Futures*, edited by Luis Eslava, Michael Fakhri, and Vasuki Nesiah, 552–73. Cambridge: Cambridge University Press, 2017.

Pandey, Gyanendra. "Can a Muslim Be an Indian?" *Comparative Studies in Society and History* 41, no. 4 (1999): 608–29.

Panikkar, Kavalam Madhava. *The Future of India and South-East Asia*. London: Allied Publishers, 1945.

Parma Nāttukkottai Chettiārkal Cankam. *Yuttakāla Parma*. Chennai, 1945.

Patel, Ian Sanjay. *We're Here Because You Were There: Immigration and the End of Empire*. London: Verso, 2021.

Peebles, Patrick. *The Plantation Tamils of Ceylon*. London: Leicester University Press, 2001.

Pershad, Hizkiel. *Indian Taxation during and after World War II*. Bombay: Allied Publishers, 1964.

Peterson, Glen. "Sovereignty, International Law, and the Uneven Development of the International Refugee Regime." *Modern Asian Studies* 49, no. 2 (2015): 439–68.

Pillai, Anitha Devi, and Puva Arumugam. *From Kerala to Singapore: Voices from the Singapore Malayalee Community*. Singapore: Marshall Cavendish Editions, 2017.

Prakash, Gyan. "Introduction: After Colonialism." In *After Colonialism: Imperial Histories and Postcolonial Displacements*, edited by Gyan Prakash. Princeton, NJ: Princeton University Press, 1994.

Prakash, Gyan, Michael Laffan, and Nikhil Menon. Introduction to Prakash, Laffan, and Menon, *Postcolonial Moment*, 1–10.

———, eds. *The Postcolonial Moment in South and Southeast Asia*. London: Bloomsbury, 2018.

Purushotham, Sunil. *From Raj to Republic: Sovereignty, Violence and Democracy in India*. Stanford, CA: Stanford University Press, 2021.

Raghavan, Srinath. *India's War: The Making of Modern South Asia, 1939–1945*. London: Penguin, 2016.

Raja, Sivachandralingam Sundara, and Ummadevi Suppiah. *The Chettiar Role in Malaysia's Economic History*. Kuala Lumpur: University of Malaya Press, 2016.

Rajah, Jothie. *Authoritarian Rule of Law: Legislation, Discourse and Legitimacy in Singapore*. Cambridge: Cambridge University Press, 2012.

Rajah, N. L. *The Madras High Court: A 150-Year Journey from a Crown Court to a People's Court*. Chennai: Veena Rajah, 2012.

Raman, Bhavani. "Calling the Other Shore: Tamil Studies and Decolonization." In Laffan, *Belonging across the Bay*, 161–80.

———. *Document Raj: Writing and Scribes in Early Colonial South India*. Chicago: University of Chicago Press, 2012.

———. "Genealogies of Return: Postwar, Tamil Culture and the Bay of Bengal." In Prakash, Laffan, and Menon, *Postcolonial Moment*, 121–40.

Ramanathan, Ponnambalam. "The Ethnology of the 'Moors' of Ceylon." In *The Sri Lanka Reader: History, Culture, Politics*, edited by John Holt, 420–23. Durham, NC: Duke University Press, 2011.

Ramaswamy, Sumathi. *The Lost Land of Lemuria: Fabulous Geographies, Catastrophic Histories*. Berkeley: University of California Press, 2004.

Rambukwella, Harshana, "What Got 'Left' Behind: The Limits of Leftist Engagements with Art and Culture in Postcolonial Sri Lanka." In *Forms of the Left in Postcolonial South Asia: Aesthetics, Networks and Connected Histories*, edited by Sanjukta Sunderason, Janaki Nair, Lotte Hoek, Mrinalini Sinha, and Shabnum Tejani. London: Bloomsbury, 2022.

Ramnath, Kalyani. "ADM Jabalpur's Antecedents: Political Emergencies, Civil Liberties, and Arguments from Colonial Continuities in India." *American University International Law Review* 31 (2016): 209.

———. "Histories of Indian Citizenship in the Age of Decolonisation." *Itinerario* 45, no. 1 (2021): 152–73.

———. "Intertwined Itineraries: Debt, Decolonization and International Law in Post-WWII South Asia." *Law and History Review* 38, no. 1 (2020): 1–24.

Ricci, Ronit. *Islam Translated: Literature, Conversion, and the Arabic Cosmopolis of South and Southeast Asia*. Chicago: University of Chicago Press, 2011.

———. "Jawa, Melayu, Malay or Otherwise? The Shifting Nomenclature of the Sri Lankan Malays." *Indonesia and the Malay World* 44, no. 130 (2016): 409–23.

Robson, Laura. *States of Separation: Transfer, Partition, and the Making of the Modern Middle East*. Oakland: University of California Press, 2017.

Rogers, John D. "Post-Orientalism and the Interpretation of Premodern and Modern Political Identities: The Case of Sri Lanka." *Journal of Asian Studies* 53, no. 1 (1994): 10–23.

Roy, Anupama. *Citizenship, Law, and Belonging: The CAA and the NRC*. Oxford: Oxford University Press, 2022.

———. *Mapping Citizenship in India*. Oxford: Oxford University Press, 2010.

Roy, Haimanti. *Partitioned Lives: Migrants, Refugees, Citizens in India and Pakistan, 1947–65*. Oxford: Oxford University Press, 2012.

Roy, Tirthankar. *A Business History of India: Enterprise and the Emergence of Capitalism from 1700*. Cambridge: Cambridge University Press, 2018.

Rudner, David. *Caste and Capitalism in Colonial India: The Nattukottai Chettiars*. Berkeley: University of California Press, 1994.

Sadiq, Kamal. *Paper Citizens: How Illegal Immigrants Acquire Citizenship in Developing Countries*. Oxford: Oxford University Press, 2008.

Saksena, Priyasha. "Building the Nation: Sovereignty and International Law in the Decolonisation of South Asia." *Journal of the History of International Law* 23, no. 1 (2020): 52–79.

Samarawickrema, Nethra. "Speculating Sapphires: Mining, Trading, and Dreams That Move Gems across the Indian Ocean." PhD diss., Stanford University, 2020.

Sandhu, Kernial Singh. *Indians in Malaya: Some Aspects of Their Immigration and Settlement (1786–1957)*. Cambridge: Cambridge University Press, 1969.

Sandhu, Kernial Singh, and A. Mani, eds. *Indian Communities in Southeast Asia*. Singapore: Institute of Southeast Asian Studies, 2006.

Schendel, Willem van. *The Bengal Borderland: Beyond State and Nation in South Asia*. London: Anthem Press, 2005.

Sebastian, Aleena. "Matrilineal Practices along the Coasts of Malabar." *Sociological Bulletin* 65, no. 1 (2016): 89–106.

Sen, Uditi. *Citizen Refugee: Forging the Indian Nation after Partition*. Cambridge: Cambridge University Press, 2018.

Sevea, Terenjit. *Islamic Connections: Muslim Societies in South and Southeast Asia*. Singapore: Institute of Southeast Asian Studies, 2009.

Shahani, Uttara. "Language without a Land: Partition, Sindhi Refugees, and the Eighth Schedule of the Indian Constitution." *Asian Affairs* 53, no. 2 (2022): 336–62.

Sharafi, Mitra. *Law and Identity in Colonial South Asia: Parsi Legal Culture, 1772–1947*. Cambridge: Cambridge University Press, 2014.

Sherman, Taylor C. "Migration, Citizenship and Belonging in Hyderabad (Deccan), 1946–1956." *Modern Asian Studies* 45, no. 1 (2011): 81–107.

Sherman, Taylor C., William Gould, and Sarah Ansari. "From Subjects to Citizens: Society and the Everyday State in India and Pakistan, 1947–1970." *Modern Asian Studies* 45, no. 1 (2011): 1–6.

Shukri, M. A. M. *Muslims of Sri Lanka: Avenues to Antiquity*. Beruwala, Sri Lanka: Jamiah Naleemia Institute, 1986.

Siegelberg, Mira. *Statelessness: A Modern History*. Cambridge, MA: Harvard University Press, 2020.

Singha, Radhika. "The Great War and a 'Proper' Passport for the Colony: Border-Crossing in British India, c.1882–1922." *Indian Economic and Social History Review* 50, no. 3 (2013): 289–315.

Sinha, Mrinalini. "Premonitions of the Past." *Journal of Asian Studies* 74, no. 4 (2015): 821–41.

Sivasundaram, Sujit. "Ethnicity, Indigeneity, and Migration in the Advent of British Rule to Sri Lanka." *American Historical Review* 115, no. 2 (2010): 428–52.

———. *Islanded: Britain, Sri Lanka, and the Bounds of an Indian Ocean Colony*. Chicago: University of Chicago Press, 2013.

Solomon, John. "The Decline of Pan-Indian Identity and the Development of Tamil Cultural Separatism in Singapore, 1856–1965." *South Asia: Journal of South Asian Studies* 35, no. 2 (2012): 257–81.

Sreenivas, Mytheli. *Wives, Widows, and Concubines: The Conjugal Family Ideal in Colonial India*. Bloomington: Indiana University Press, 2008.

Sridevi, S. "Local Banking and Material Culture amongst the Nattukkottai Chettiars of Tamil Nadu." PhD diss., Jawaharlal Nehru University, 2004.

Sriramachandran, Ravindran. "Life Is Where We Are Not: Making and Managing the Plantation Tamil." PhD diss., Columbia University, 2010.

Stenson, Michael R. *Class, Race and Colonialism in West Malaysia the Indian Case*. Vancouver: University of British Columbia Press, 1980.

Stolte, Carolien, and Harald Fischer-Tiné. "Imagining Asia in India: Nationalism and Internationalism (ca. 1905–1940)." *Comparative Studies in Society and History* 54, no. 1 (January 2012): 65–92.

Stolte, Carolien, and Su Lin Lewis. *The Lives of Cold War Afro-Asianism*. Leiden: Leiden University Press, 2022.

Sturman, Rachel. *The Government of Social Life in Colonial India: Liberalism, Religious Law, and Women's Rights*. Cambridge: Cambridge University Press, 2012.

———. "Indian Indentured Labor and the History of International Rights Regimes." *American Historical Review* 119, no. 5 (2014): 1439–65.

———. "Property and Attachments: Defining Autonomy and the Claims of Family in Nineteenth-Century Western India." *Comparative Studies in Society and History* 47, no. 3 (2005): 611–37.

Subramanian, Ajantha. *Shorelines: Space and Rights in South India*. Stanford, CA: Stanford University Press, 2009.

Subramanian, K. S. "Intelligence Bureau, Home Ministry and Indian Politics." *Economic and Political Weekly* 40, no. 21 (2005): 2147–50.

Subramanian, Lakshmi. "Tamils and Greater India: Some Issues of Connected Histories." *Cultural Dynamics* 24, nos. 2–3 (July 1, 2012): 159–74.

Subramanyam, C. S. *Our Party's Growth in Tamil Nadu*. N.p.: Communist Party of India, n.d.

Sur, Malini. *Jungle Passports: Fences, Mobility, and Citizenship at the Northeast India-Bangladesh Border*. Philadelphia: University of Pennsylvania Press, 2021.

Sutton, Deborah. "Imagined Sovereignty and the Indian Subject: Partition and Politics beyond the Nation, 1948–1960." *Contemporary South Asia* 19, no. 4 (December 1, 2011): 409–25.

Swaminatha Sharma, V. *Pirikkapatta Parma*. N.p.: n.p., 1936.

Tagliocozzo, Eric. *Secret Trades, Porous Borders: Smuggling and States along a Southeast Asian Frontier, 1865–1915*. New Haven, CT: Yale University Press, 2005.

Tan, Tai Yong. *Creating "Greater Malaysia": Decolonization and the Politics of Merger*. Singapore: Institute of Southeast Asian Studies, 2008.

Than, Tharaphi. "The Languages of Pyidawtha and the Burmese Approach to National Development." *South East Asia Research* 21, no. 4 (2013): 639–54.

Thawfeeq, M. M. *Muslim Mosaics*. Colombo: Al Eslam and the Moors' Islamic Cultural Home, 1972.

Thiranagama, Sharika. *In My Mother's House: Civil War in Sri Lanka*. Philadelphia: University of Pennsylvania Press, 2011.

Tinker, Hugh. "A Forgotten Long March: The Indian Exodus from Burma, 1942." *Journal of Southeast Asian Studies* 6, no. 1 (1975): 1–15.

———. *The Union of Burma: A Study of the First Years of Independence*. New York: Oxford University Press, 1957.

Torpey, John. *The Invention of the Passport: Surveillance, Citizenship and the State*. Cambridge: Cambridge University Press, 2000.

Toxey, Walter W. "Restrictive Citizenship Policies within the Commonwealth." *McGill Law Journal* 13 (1967): 494–502.

Trager, Frank N. *Burma: Japanese Military Administration, Selected Documents, 1941–1945*. Philadelphia: University of Pennsylvania Press, 1971.

Tschacher, Torsten. "The Challenges of Diversity: 'Casting' Muslim Communities in South India." In *Being Muslim in South Asia: Diversity and Daily Life*, edited by Robin Jeffrey and Ronojoy Sen, 64–86. New Delhi: Oxford University Press, 2014.

———. "'Moneymaking Is Their Prime Concern': Markets, Mobility and Marriage among South Indian Muslims." In Laffan, *Belonging across the Bay*, 99–116.

Turnell, Sean. *Fiery Dragons: Banks, Moneylenders and Microfinance in Burma*. Copenhagen: NIAS Press, 2009.

Vachha, J. B., C. W. Ayers, and S. P. Chambers. *Income Tax Enquiry Report, 1936, Submitted to the Government of India as a Result of the Investigation of the Indian Income-Tax System*. Delhi: Manager of Publications, 1937.

Valverde, Mariana. *Chronotopes of Law: Jurisdiction, Scale and Governance*. London: Routledge, 2015.

———. "Jurisdiction and Scale: Legal 'Technicalities' as Resources for Theory." *Social and Legal Studies* 18, no. 2 (June 1, 2009): 139–57.

Veeraraghavan, D. *The Making of the Madras Working Class*. New Delhi: LeftWord Books, 2013.

Wai, Tun. *Burma's Currency and Credit*. New Delhi: Orient Longmans, 1962.

Walker, Lydia. "Decolonization in the 1960s: On Legitimate and Illegitimate Nationalist Claims-Making." *Past and Present* 242, no. 1 (2019): 227–64.

Weerasooria, W. S., and William Tenekoon. *The Nattukottai Chettiar Merchant Bankers in Ceylon*. Dehiwala: Tisara Prakasakayo, 1973.

Weitz, Eric D. "From the Vienna to the Paris System: International Politics and the Entangled Histories of Human Rights, Forced Deportations, and Civilizing Missions." *American Historical Review* 113, no. 5 (2008): 1313–43.

Wettimuny, Shamara. "A Brief History of Anti-Muslim Violence in Sri Lanka." *History Workshop Online*, July 22, 2019. https://www.historyworkshop.org.uk/a-brief-history-of-anti-muslim-violence-in-sri-lanka/.

Wheatley, Natasha. "Spectral Legal Personality in Interwar International Law: On New Ways of Not Being a State." *Law and History Review* 35, no. 3 (2017): 753–87.

Welke, Barbara Young. *Law and the Borders of Belonging in the Long Nineteenth Century United States*. Cambridge: Cambridge University Press, 2010.

Welke, Barbara Young, and Hendrik Hartog. "'Glimmers of Life': A Conversation with Hendrik Hartog." *Law and History Review* 27, no. 3 (2009): 629–55.

Wickramasinghe, Nira. "Citizens, Aryans and Indians in Colonial Lanka: Discourses on Belonging in the 1920s and 1930s." In Laffan, *Belonging across the Bay*, 139–60.

———. *Sri Lanka in the Modern Age: A History*. Oxford: Oxford University Press, 2015.

Wilder, Gary. *Freedom Time: Negritude, Decolonization, and the Future of the World*. Durham, NC: Duke University Press, 2014.

———. *The French Imperial Nation-State: Negritude and Colonial Humanism between the Two World Wars*. Chicago: University of Chicago Press, 2005.

Wilson, A. Jeyaratnam. "The Colombo Man, the Jaffna Man and the Batticaloa Man: Regional Identities and the Rise of the Federal Party." In *The Sri Lankan Tamils: Ethnicity and Identity*, edited by Chelvadurai Manogaran and Bryan Pfaffenberger, 126–42. Boulder, CO: Westview Press, 1994.

Yahaya, Nurfadzilah. *Fluid Jurisdictions: Colonial Law and Arabs in Southeast Asia*. Ithaca, NY: Cornell University Press, 2020.

Yang, Anand. *Empire of Convicts: Indian Penal Labor in Colonial Southeast Asia*. Oakland: University of California Press, 2021.

Yellen, Jeremy. *The Greater East Asia Co-Prosperity Sphere: When Total Empire Met Total War*. Ithaca, NY: Cornell University Press, 2019.

Zamindar, Vazira Fazila-Yacoobali. *The Long Partition and the Making of Modern South Asia: Refugees, Boundaries, Histories*. Ithaca, NY: Columbia University Press, 2007.

INDEX

Communist Party (Singapore), 170
Consular Manual, 200
Cooper, Frederick, 15, 189
Corea, Victor, 240n59
Cox's Bazaar, 216
currency. *See* banana money

Dadachanji, 202
Dapthary, C. K., 232n63
Das, Veena, 132
Datta, Arunima, 149
Debtor and Creditor (Occupation) Ordinance (1948), 74
debt recovery, and demonetization of
    banana money litigation, 54–55, 56,
    73–77, 83
decolonization
    administrative, 4
    as bound up with migration and citizenship, 14–15, 53
    citizenship during, 46–48
    events marking, 3
    family as central to mythmaking of
        nation-states during, 132–33
    as fluid legal process, 214
    indigeneity and local movements
        around, 206
    as intercolonial, 15
    law as archive for reconstructing histories of, 6–11
    and scholarship on diasporic South
        Asian citizenship, 13–14
    second wave of, 187–88, 213
Democratic Workers' Congress, 117
Department of Indians Overseas, 39, 42
deportation, 162, 166–69, 171–72, 181–83,
    187, 213
Desai, C. C., 119
detention without trial, 167–69, 171–72,
    174–78, 180–84, 214. *See also* anticommunist fears and strategies
Devas, S., 35, 68
development projects, and repatriation
    schemes, 203–4
Dhillon, Gurbaksh Singh, 51

displaced people. *See* refugees; transit
    camps
Dorman-Smith, Reginald, 33
Dravidian nationalisms, 204–5
dual nationality, 47, 189, 242n84
Duraiswamy (detainee), 177, 182
Dutugemunu Secret Society, 112

East Africa, 187, 213
economic reconstruction, postwar, 55–56,
    62–65
Ediriwara, G. W., 113–14, 116–17, 118–19
Egreteau, Renaud, 193
"Emergency, the," 161
Eslava, Luis, 16, 216
evacuee identification cards, 125
evacuees. *See* refugees; transit camps

family
    as central to mythmaking of nation-states during decolonization, 132–33
    in citizenship and immigration, 133–35,
        155–56
    as legal fiction with political and social
        consequences, 141–46, 147–49,
        156–57
    presumptions about, in immigration
        regimes, 133–34, 148–51
    and suspicion of loyalty in immigration
        cases, 130–31
    in taxation and immigration legislations, 131–32
    and women who wait, 148–55, 246n59
Federation of Malaya. *See also* Malaya
    creation of, 3, 71
    and decolonization, 4
    deportation from, 181–83
    postwar citizenship in, 52
    restricted entry into, 190–91
Finance Bill (1939), 67
food control, under MMPOA, 167
"forum shopping," 154
France, postwar citizenship for former
    imperial possessions of, 191

For a complete listing of titles in this series, visit the
Stanford University Press website, www.sup.org.

CPSIA information can be obtained
at www.ICGtesting.com
Printed in the USA
JSHW080715210623
43522JS00003B/4